CHICAGO IN 1818.

FROM THE COURT HOUSE, LOOKING SOUTH AND SOUTH-EAST.

THE GREAT CONFLAGRATION.

CHICAGO:

ITS PAST, PRESENT AND FUTURE.

EMBRACING A DETAILED NARRATIVE OF THE GREAT CONFLAGRATION IN THE NORTH, SOUTH, AND WEST DIVISIONS:

ORIGIN, PROGRESS AND RESULTS OF THE FIRE.

PROMINENT BUILDINGS BURNED, CHARACTER OF BUILDINGS, LOSSES AND INSURANCE, GRAPHIC DESCRIPTION OF THE FLAMES, SCENES AND INCIDENTS, LOSS OF LIFE, THE FLIGHT OF THE PEOPLE.

ALSO,

A CONDENSED HISTORY OF CHICAGO, ITS POPULATION, GROWTH AND GREAT PUBLIC WORKS.

AND

A STATEMENT OF ALL THE GREAT FIRES OF THE WORLD.

BY JAMES W. SHEAHAN AND GEORGE P. UPTON,
ASSOCIATE EDITORS OF THE CHICAGO DAILY TRIBUNE.

WITH NUMEROUS ILLUSTRATIONS.

UNION PUBLISHING CO.:
165 TWENTY-SECOND STREET, CHICAGO, ILL.
26 SOUTH SEVENTH ST., PHILADELPHIA, PA.
176 WEST FOURTH STREET, CINCINNATI, OHIO.
1872.

PREFACE.

THIS volume is devoted to a connected account of the great Chicago conflagration, with an incidental narrative of the destruction caused by the terrible forest fires in Wisconsin and Michigan, and a necessarily brief statement of the great fires of the world, which may serve for purposes of comparison. It is the account of witnesses of, and actors in the terrible scenes that closed with the destruction of a great city. No person saw the whole, or even any considerable part of the fire field. It was too mighty and vast. We have sought to comprehend in our account all that is vital to an intelligent conception of the origin and progress of the fire, and the condition of the city, both before and afterwards; and in so doing to make the work valuable as a book of reference. With this end in view, it is compiled as a condensed statement of the commercial and industrial resources of the city, its private enterprises and great public improvements, and the record of its marvellous growth. The work opens with the very beginning of the fire and follows it, street by street, along its terrible path of devastation; describes the prominent buildings consumed; the thrilling, heroic and even humorous scenes in the streets, during the fire, and gives careful estimates of the losses, somewhat in detail, and a statement of insurance from official sources. The operations of the Relief Society are touched upon sufficiently to give the reader a general idea of the manner, in which charity has been disbursed. The losses in churches, schools, and institutions of music, art and amusement, as well as the public libraries, are also dwelt upon somewhat at length. In order to arrive at official reports as far as possible, the pages of the book have been held open to the latest possible moment, and thus much valuable matter has been secured. Liberal space has also been given to the narrative of the Northwestern fires, the great fires of the world, and the work of rebuilding the city. With this preliminary statement the authors give their work to the public.

CHICAGO, *December 1, 1871.*

ILLUSTRATIONS
BY
BAKER & Co
CHICAGO

CONTENTS.

THE GREAT CONFLAGRATION.

INCIDENTS.

RELIEF MEASURES.

RELIEF INCIDENTS.

NEW CHICAGO.

EMINENT CITIZENS OF CHICAGO.

POEMS.

NORTHWESTERN FIRES.

THE GREAT FIRES OF THE WORLD.

APPENDIX.

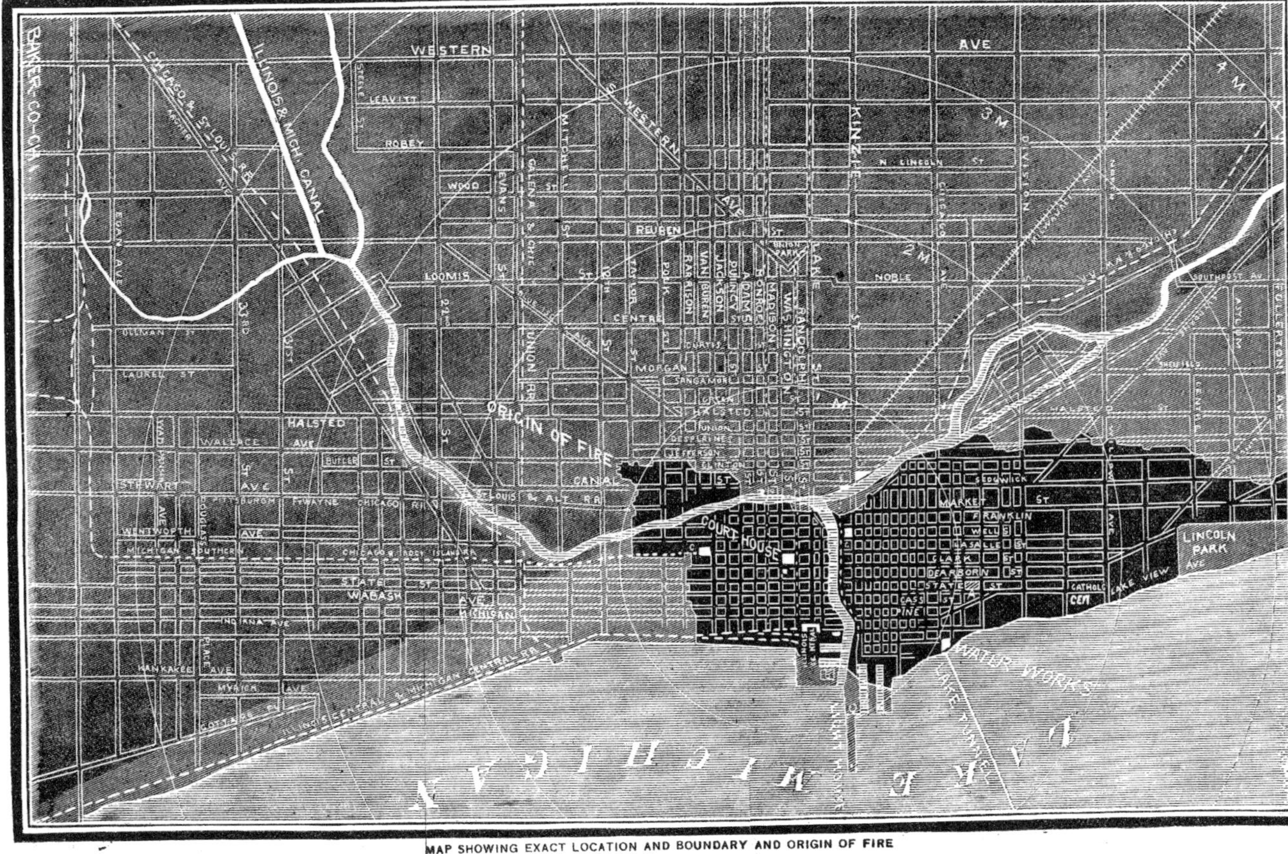

MAP SHOWING EXACT LOCATION AND BOUNDARY AND ORIGIN OF FIRE

CHICAGO AS IT WAS.

Richard Cobden, it is said, once remarked that no man ought to die without visiting America to see Niagara and Chicago. The City of Chicago has been regarded as one of the marvels of the age. Her rapid growth and her stately magnificence have been the astonishment of the world. Her early history, when contrasted with her wealth and grandeur on the 7th of October, 1871, becomes of peculiar interest, even to those whose particular concern for Chicago dates with the recent calamity.

Chicago is situated near the head of Lake Michigan; has an elevation of five hundred and ninety-one feet above the sea. It is situated upon both sides of the Chicago river, a slow stream, which at a point little over half a mile from the mouth, is formed by the junction of two streams, or branches, one flowing from the northwest, and the other from the southwest. The river and branches divide the city into three natural parts, legally known as the South, North and West Divisions. The South Division included all the territory east of the south branch, and south of the main river. The North Division included the area east of the north branch, and north of the river; while the West Division included all that part of the city west of the two branches. From 1681 to 1795, during the time of the French possession, and after its cession to England, very little is known of Chicago or the surrounding country. After the declaration of peace, between the Colonists and the English, the latter, by intrigue, stirred up the border Indian warfare, which became general in the Western States, and continued until 1795, at which period, having been effectually chastised by General Wayne, the chiefs of the several tribes of Indians, by his invitation, assembled at Greenville, Ohio, and there effected a treaty of peace, which closed the War of the West. Among the numerous small tracts of land where forts and trading posts had been established, then ceded by the Indians to the United States, was one described as follows: One piece of land, six miles square, at the mouth of the Chikajo River, emptying into the southwest end of Lake Michigan, where a fort formerly stood.

Here we have an account of the *first land trade* of Chicago—the first transaction in that line of business which has at times distinguished Chicago above every other city of the nation—the first link in the chain of title to thousands upon thousands of transfers that have been made of the soil thus parted with by the Indians.

When the first settlers of Chicago began to congregate and erect their cabins, with the view of forming the nucleus of a town, the point selected as the most available for village purposes, was the tract on the west side, at the junction of the north and south branches, and at first called Wolf's Point. In addition to the few buildings that were standing in 1818, we have only to mention this group at Wolf's Point, two or three buildings on the south side, between the point and the fort, and the Miller House, on the north side.

The Miller House stood on the point of land between the north branch and the main channel. It was a log structure partly sided, and was erected by Mr. Samuel Miller, who resided here with his family and a brother by the name of John Miller. This house was used as a tavern. A little above its mouth on the north branch, was a log bridge, which gave access from that quarter to the business of the agency, and the little trade which may have continued up to this time on the north branch.

But the centre of attraction was at Wolf's Point, opposite the Miller House. Here, too, was another tavern, the public house, par excellence, of Chicago —the school house and church, as well as the store. On the south side, the most prominent object of interest was the tavern kept by Mr. Elijah Wentworth, a man familiarly known as "Old Geese," not as a burlesque on the worthy landlord, but as a compliment to his distinctive and original character. This building was partly log and partly frame, and was situated on the ground north of Lake Street Bridge, now occupied as a lumber yard. North of this tavern was an oblong building which had been erected by Father Walker, a missionary of the Methodist Episcopal Church, for a place of worship, and for a school house. Mr. Walker had at times ministered to the spiritual wants of the settlement, from this rude temple. Mr. W. had a residence in the country known as Walker's, which distinguished the locality at that time, which is now Plainfield, Will Co. This log tabernacle was the meeting house of the town. Mr. See, who, it seems, was the local preacher or exhorter, and who resided at the Point, was the supply which was most generally afforded. Preaching was upon a par with other callings and employments of the place. Mr. Wentworth's tavern was the best one kept in Chicago. It was the place where men of character who visited the town always stopped. It was the headquarters of Gen. Scott, when he came to Chicago with the troops for the Black Hawk War, in 1832. The distinctive name of this celebrated tavern, as familiarly used by all the settlers, was "Rat Castle," in contrast with its rival in distinction on the north side, "Cobweb Castle," and in commemoration of a large class of regular boarders that infested its premises, as well as every other cabin on the river shore. Next south of Wentworth's tavern was the residence of James Kinzie. Next to these were log cabins, in which resided Alexander Robinson, and here occasionally, resided Billy Caldwell, whose wife was the wild daughter of an Indian Chief, and her presence did not always hallow his wigwam with the sanctity of peace. Still further south of these was the store-house of Mr. Robert A. Kinzie, son of Mr. John Kinzie, who had succeeded his father in the Indian trade, and his stock consisted of groceries, Indian goods and supplies for the settlers, and was the store of the village, as essentially as Wentworth's was the village tavern. Across the south branch, on the east side, resided Mark Beaubien, brother of Gen. J. B. Beaubien, who also kept tavern. In 1831 his establishment had risen to a two-story dwelling, painted, with green blinds, and soon attained to the title of the Saganash Hotel—which was the Indian name of Billy Caldwell—and so called in honor of that distinguished chief and man of the times, for he was then one of the prominent residents of Chicago. It stood near what is now the southeast corner of Lake and Market streets. By this time there had been a place of amusement started in a little, low, log shanty, where was set up a billiard table, at which citizens of leisure amused themselves in knocking about three cracked balls. Further up the south branch was the residence of a French Indian trader by the name of Bourissa. In the South Division, near the "slough" that drained the marshes of the south side, and emptied into the river at State street, was the trading house of Medert Beaubien—son of Col. Beaubien—a cabin of small pretensions. Upon the Lake shore, a little distances south of the fort, Col. Beaubien resided in the cabin which he had purchased of the American Fur Company, in 1817—which he had elevated to the dignity of a homestead, and which was now familiarly known among the settlers by the name of the "Wigwam." Near this residence was his store, in which the American Fur Company kept a stock of goods for the Indian trade.

Further south, the old Dean house had started on the way to ruin; the water of the lake had gradually encroached upon the shore, until it had undermined the foundations of the cabin, and it had fallen backward down the bank, where it lay, a type of ruin, an emblem, in the estimation of the croakers (who existed at that time, as well as the present), of the future of Chicago. Another settler about this time had taken up his residence in the suburbs, to be rated with the other "outside settlers," who had linked their fortunes with Chicago, for better or worse—and this was Dr. Harmon, the father of Isaac D. Harmon, who had made a claim a mile and a half south, on the lake shore, on the site of the Indian battle ground of 1812, and was making a fine improvement there. This was the place since known as Clark's, the site of which is now occupied by some of the finest residences in Chicago.

In the year 1804 the United States erected Fort Dearborn upon the south bank of the river, just east of the present Michigan avenue. Mr. Kinzie and his son, John H., Indian traders, were the only white residents until the war of 1812, when the post was abandoned. The small garrison, in attempting to escape, were captured by the Pottawatomies, and massacred at a point now represented by Twelfth street and Michigan avenue. In 1816 the fort was rebuilt, and the Kinzies returned, and the fort served for many years as a resting place for emigrants passing to the West. The inhabitants did not exceed half-a-dozen families, until in 1827 Congress made a grant of land to aid in the construction of a canal to connect the waters of Lake Michigan with those of the Illinois river. In 1829 the State Legislature appointed a commission to mark out the route of the canal, and a surveyor arrived to mark out the town. Beside the garrison at that time, there were eight families, engaged mostly as Indian traders, in the place. Gov. Bond, the first Governor of Illinois, in his inaugural, in 1818, called the attention of the General Assembly to the importance of opening a canal to connect Lake Michigan with the Illinois river. In his valedictory, in 1822, he again urged its importance. The session of Congress, 1821–2, passed an act, granting "permission to the State of Illinois to cut a canal through the public lands connecting the Illinois river with Lake Michigan, and granting to it the breadth of the canal and ninety feet on each side of it," coupled with the condition, "that the State should permit all articles belonging to the United States, or to any person in their employ, to pass *toll free*, forever."

With a hard and protracted struggle by numerous individuals, and especially by Daniel P. Cook, Esq., who was at that time Representative in Congress, and from whom Cook county was named, an act was passed by Congress, March 2d, 1827, granting to the State for the construction of this work, "each alternate section of land, five miles in width, on each side of the proposed canal." We make mention of these facts, because it was from this act of Congress the State acquired the title to those lands which have formed the basis for many of its most important financial transactions; from which originated the titles to the valuable canal lands, on which a large portion of the city is built—on which, too, villages, towns and cities have sprung up, all along its line.

In the autumn of 1829, commissioners authorized the laying out of the "Town of Chicago," on the alternate section which belonged to the canal lands—lying upon the main channel of the river, and over the junction of the two branches. The first map of the original town of Chicago, by James Thompson, surveyor, bears date, August 4th, 1830. This was the *first beginning of Chicago*, as a legally recognized place among the towns and cities of the world—the first official act of organization, which must accordingly be dated as its birth, or real starting point, and the town was comprised within the limits of what are now known as Madison, State, Kinzie and Halstead streets, or about three-eighths of a square mile. Hence this city, with its population of 330,000—the leading mart in the world for grain, pork, lumber, will have arrived on the 4th day of August, 1872, at the precocious maturity of forty-two years. In 1831 Cook county was organized, embracing, in addition to the present county, the territory which now is known by five other large and populous counties. The prospective work on the canal was attracting population, but, in 1832, the cholera visited the incipient city, and was very severe. In 1832 the first public religious worship was held in a log hut erected for that purpose. The tax list for 1832 amounted to $148.29. Lake street was laid out the same year. In 1833 the settlement had increased enough to have a post office and postmaster, and a weekly mail; and late in the year, the *Chicago Democrat*, a weekly paper, was started by John Calhoun. On the 10th of August, the voters of Chicago held an election to determine whether they would become incorporated, and to elect trustees. Every man voted, and the number of voters was twenty-eight, many of whom are now living; and the levy for city taxes, in 1834, was $48.90. In 1834 the number of voters had increased to one hundred and eleven, and a loan of $60 was negotiated for public improvements. In 1835 the number of voters was two hundred and eleven. In 1836 the town applied to the State Bank for a loan of $25,000, and was refused. In 1837 the Legislature incorporated the City of Chicago, and in May following the Hon. William B. Ogden was elected Mayor of Chicago.

Thus, on the first Tuesday in May, 1837, twenty-four years ago, commenced the City of Chicago, which then contained a population of 4,179. The following is a statement of the population of Chicago, for each year since that time:

Year.	Population.	Year.	Population.
1837	4,179	1854	65,872
1838	4,000	1855	80,023
1839	4,200	1856	86,000
1840	4,470	1857	93,000
1841	5,500	1858	not taken
1842	6,590	1859	90,000
1843	7,580	1860	109,263
1844	8,000	1861	120,000
1845	12,088	1862	137,030
1846	14,169	1863	150,000
1847	16,859	1864	161,288
1848	20,023	1865	187,446
1849	23,047	1866	200,000
1850	28,269	1867	220,000
1851	34,000	1868	242,383
1852	38,734	1870	298,977
1853	60,662	1871	334,270

This has been the extraordinary growth of this wonderful city.

The natural line of the site of Chicago, was but a few feet above that of the lake, and there was no drainage, and in seasons of rain the surface was covered with water. In the winter of 1855-6 the city ordered a change of grade, raising the height of the carriage ways an average of eight feet. This placed the lower or ground story of each building several feet below the level of the street; but the inconvenience was rapidly overcome by raising all the buildings, brick, stone and wood, up to the level. All the large buildings, including many hotels, business blocks, warehouses, &c., were raised, by means of screws, from their foundations a height of from six to ten feet, and new foundations built under them. This secured deep, dry cellars and admitted a thorough system of sewerage. The city ordered an effective dredging of the harbor, and the clay thus obtained served to fill the streets to the new grade. For several years, while this process was going on, the passage of Chicago streets was a work of trying difficulty to pedestrians. The expense was great, but was cheerfully borne by the property holders. Then commenced the works of permanent improvement in the city, and how far they had progressed may be seen by the following comparative tables:

	Year 1854.		Year 1871.	
Sewers, ...	6½	miles.	160	miles.
Nicholson pavement, .	600	feet.	40	"
Stone pavement, . . .		"	5	"
Water pipe and drains,	30	miles.	400	"
Sidewalks (plank), . .	159	"	900	"
Sidewalks (stone), . .	500	feet.	30	"

The Chicago Water Works.

Chicago has always had the reputation of a boastful city, but the truth is, its growth, expansion and increase have always exceeded the predictions of its own most sanguine people. This is in nowise more clearly shown than in its water supply, the history of which at once tells the story of an enterprising people and of the city's extraordinary progress. In 1839, a company was chartered to supply Chicago with water. It erected a reservoir on the lake shore at the corner of Michigan avenue and Water street, and with a pump, the motive power of which was a small engine of twenty-five horse power, drew water from the lake into the reservoir, and this water was distributed through logs, having a bore of from three to five inches.

In 1851, a new company was formed, and in the fall of that year a plan was adopted, which was based upon the estimate, considered ridiculous at the time, that in 1866 the city would have 100,000, inhabitants. This company selected a site on the lake shore. A crib made of wood 20 by 40 feet was sunk 600 feet out in the lake, and from this a wooden inlet was constructed, through which the water was introduced to a large well, 25 feet deep. Over this well was erected a pump. This pump, moved by a steam engine, forced the water into the mains. At three points in the city were erected large stone reservoirs, in which the water accumulated and received a head, which forced it through the distributing pipes. A large tower was erected in the engine house, serving the double purpose of a chimney for the boilers, and a chamber for the standing column of water. The engine was of 200 horse power. In December, 1853, the water was first pumped, and in February, 1854, water was first introduced into buildings. In the meantime railroads had been laid down to and from Chicago. The city had three trunk lines of rail communication to the Atlantic seaboard, and as many west to the Mississippi river. A road had been built with two nearly parallel lines southward, the whole length of the State. Immigration was pouring in. In 1862, the length of water pipe laid exceeded 105 miles and the demand was greater. In 1860, the city had exceeded 109,000 inhabitants, and the increase after the beginning of the war had received a new impetus. The commerce on the river or harbor had grown immensely. Simultaneously with the water system, the city had established a system of sewerage. Under the plan adopted the sewerage all found its way into the river. As the water was extended, the closets of all buildings were connected with the sewers. On the banks of the river and its branches were erected large distilleries with their accompanying cattle pens; the drainage all flowing into the river. The packing houses which had become numerous, with extensive business, emptied their refuse into the river. A result was that the river became a horrible nuisance. Its odor was terrific; as the wind happened to blow, so were the various parts of the city suffocated with this fearful stench. The river itself had no current save when the wind blew off shore, when the putrid stuff slowly escaped into the lake where its inky waters might be traced for miles; when there were heavy rains, the current carried out the blackened, sickening water, and for a few days after each of such floods, the river was clean again. The smells of Chicago river had become as historical as those of Cologne. The worst evil, however, was that whenever the wind was from the south or east, the water of the river escaping into the lake was carried up to the crib, through which the water works obtained its supply. It was thence redistributed to the public. At times the stench in dwellings from this fearful liquid was intolerable. It was not only black, with a shocking odor, but was greasy to the touch. It became necessary, therefore, not only to provide better water, but also to provide for a supply commensurate with the growth of the city.

In 1863, the city was authorized to construct a tunnel under the lake to obtain a supply of pure water. A careful survey was made, and such a proceeding was pronounced feasible. On the 9th of September, 1863, bids were opened and the contract awarded to Dull and Gowan, of Harrisburg, Pennsylvania, for $315,139. Ground was broken on the 17th of March, 1864. The shore shaft was first sunk. The original intention to have this shaft exclusively of brick was abandoned because of some quicksands, and a cylinder was sunk, 26 feet, to the bottom of the sand bed. This cylinder is 9 feet in diameter inside, and $2\frac{1}{4}$ inches thick.

From the shore shaft the tunnel is 5 feet wide and 5 feet 2 inches in height, the upper and lower arches being semi-circles. The masonry consists of brick 8 inches thick, laid in two rings, the bricks being laid lengthwise. The bottom of the tunnel where it connects with the lake shaft is 66 feet below the level of the earth, and 64 below the level of the lake. The inclination towards the shore is 2 feet per mile. By closing the gate at the crib, the tunnel will empty into the shore shaft, and can then be inspected and if necessary repaired. The work was prosecuted incessantly by night and by day. Stiff blue clay was first met with in the bore, and with the exception of a few slight pockets of sand, the whole work was carried through the same formation. A railway was laid in the tunnel, and cars were filled with clay and drawn to the mouth by mules; the returning cars carried back bricks and cement. There were several niches or turnouts constructed, having a double purpose of affording convenience and of giving strength to the work.

In July, 1865, or nineteen months after the commencement of work at the shore end, the monster crib, built for the lake end of the tunnel, was launched, and towed safely to its destination, and sunk. It was of large proportions. The dimensions were imposing. It was of a pentagonal form, 40 feet high, with a circle of 98½ feet in diameter was built of square logs having three walls 11 feet distant from each other, leaving in the center a space equal to a circle of 25 feet; in this inner circle or space was sunk and fixed an iron cylinder 9 feet in diameter, extending from the water line 64 feet to the tunnel. The water at that point is 33 feet deep, and the cylinder is therefore 31 feet below the bottom of the lake. To safely anchor this important structure so that it might withstand the fury of lake storms and the incessant beating of the waters, was no easy matter. It contains an equivalent to 750,000 feet of lumber, board measure; 150 tons of iron bolts, and is loaded with 4,500 tons of stone. Its whole weight is 5,700 tons. The structure stands 12 feet above the water line. As soon as this was safely anchored and the cylinder sunk, the whole was covered with a building to protect the workmen. The earth excavated was loaded upon scows, which brought back with them bricks and cement. The work on the tunnel proper did not begin at this end until December, 1865, when the first brick was laid. The whole length of the tunnel was 2 miles. On January 1st, 1865, there had been 4,825 feet of the tunnel built from the shore end. After that time work progressed from both ends. On December 6th, 1866, the wall between the two gangs was broken, the men shook hands, and the last brick was laid by Major John B. Rice. The water was not, however, furnished to the city until March, 1867, when there was a grand civic celebration.

The increase of water supply necessitated an increase of distributing power. The old engine and pump house was greatly enlarged. A new tower of stone, 130 feet high, was erected some distance west of the pump. Within this tower is an iron column, three feet in diameter, to the top of which the water is forced from the tunnel by the powerful pumping machinery, and thence by its own pressure is forced through the mains and distributing pipes of the city. The total cost of this grand work complete, with new engines and all things pertaining to the enlarged works, was about $1,000,000.

CHICAGO WATER-WORKS.

Since then, the laying of water mains has been pushed extensively. In 1854 the first pipe was laid. At the close of 1860, 71 miles of pipe had been laid. When the water was admitted in March, 1867, it flowed through 154 miles of pipe. In 1867 and 1868, 50 additional miles were laid, and on the 1st of April, 1870, the total length of pipe laid was 239 miles 4,763 feet, when the fire occurred there were about 275 miles of pipe laid.

The increase in the consumption of water upon the procurement of a pure quality was surprising. The total amount supplied in 1866, averaged 8,600,000 gallons daily. In 1867, the first year of the pure water, it averaged 11,560,000 gallons daily. In 1869 its average during the whole year was 18,633,278 gallons daily, though on some days it equalled 20,000,000 gallons. In 1870 the average had increased to 21,000,000 gallons daily. In 1871 no official report had been made, but the consumption was fully up to 24,000,000 gallons daily. So greatly had this demand exceeded even the most sanguine expectations, that it was feared the capacity of the works would not be sufficient. So this enterprising people resolved to extend the tunnel from its present shore end, west of southwest in an air-line, a distance of nearly three miles under the city, and under the main river and its south branch, and there erect a duplicate works. It was also contemplated to build another tunnel under the lake to secure an additional supply of water, to be used in case of any accident to the one now in use. The capacity of the present tunnel is 57,000,000 gallons daily.

The quality of the water is most excellent. It is very pure and free of all earthy substances. Even in the most stormy seasons, such are the admirable precautions at the crib, that little or no sand enters the tunnel, and what does enter is caught in the catch basins before reaching the shore wells. The engraving represents the exterior of the works with the tower. The surrounding grounds had but recently been put in order, and the whole presented a handsome landscape, the broad lake spreading far to the eastward an appropriate back-ground.

The annual expense of the pumping works, or operating expenses including repairs and salaries, was about $80,000, and the cost of delivering water per million of gallons was less than $10,000. The annual income from water service was about $650,000, paying the interest on the water debt, all expenses, and leaving a surplus to pay for extensions of the service pipes.

The machinery of the water works was of the most excellent character. It had recently been augmented by an enormous engine, not surpassed in power or excellence of workmanship by any like production in the country. This engine was put in place in September. The fire destroying the supports of the roof, let the burning mass fall upon this machinery. It was then exposed to the intense heat borne by the gale for twelve hours. The effect was damaging. As soon as possible a force of mechanics were put at work, and in eleven days an engine was in operation, again supplying the city with water.

The Streets of Chicago.

The whole length of streets in Chicago numbers 531 miles. Of which there were improved :

By wooden blocks,	37.60	miles.
" boulders,	3.77	"
" McAdam,	11.26	"
" cindering,	2.40	"
" gravelling,	6.43	"
Total miles improved,	61.46	"

The annual assessments upon abutting property since and including 1869, for street improvements, exceeded $2,000,000.

Sewerage.

The total length of sewerage constructed to April 1st, 1870, was 136½ miles; in 1870 and 1871 about 50 miles additional were laid.

Gas.

The North and South Divisions were supplied by the Chicago Gas and Coke Company, whose works were at the junction of Adams and Franklin streets; and the West Division by the People's Gas Company. The former company had just completed new works north of the city, and in six days after the fire, was again furnishing gas to the people, resident in that portion of its territory not swept by the fire.

Bridges and Tunnels.

Communication between the several parts of the city was kept up by pivot-bridges, spanning the river and its branches. During the fire all the bridges on the main river, four in number, were destroyed, and three were burned on the south branch. As these bridges had to be swung open to permit vessels to pass, the interruption to passengers and vehicles was so great that other means were demanded. For this purpose, in 1869, a tunnel was built under the south branch, under the line of Washington street. This tunnel has a double roadway for vehicles, and a twelve feet passage for pedestrians. In September, 1871, another but much better tunnel was constructed under the main river, on the line of La Salle street. In both cases the skill of the engineers and the success of the mechanics have been remarkable. These tunnels were not injured by the fire.

The River and the Canal.

To understand the last grand triumph of the enterprise of the people of Chicago, it must be borne in mind that the river is the receiver of the entire sewerage system of Chicago. Into that river there is forever falling the foul discharges of the hundreds of miles of sewers, and in Chicago all the water closets are connected with the sewers. The washings of the distilleries and of the packing-houses also flow into the river. As the river, though deep, is but in fact an estuary of the lake, there is no current, save when the wind is off shore, and consequently none of this filth was ever carried out, save when continued heavy rains would produce a current. The river, therefore, was offensively odorous; in the winter, when covered with ice, the foul gases did not escape, but at other seasons it was intolerable. The Illinois and Michigan canal was connected with the south branch of the river by a lock, the canal being several feet above the river To supply the canal with water, pumps were erected, and the city was forced to hire these pumps to pump the water from the river into the canal continuously, thus drawing pure water into the river from the lake. But as the sewerage increased, the efficacy of the pumps diminished, and finally the consent of the Legislature was obtained and the city resolved to so deepen the canal as to establish a continuous flow of water *up stream* from the lake, through the river into the canal. Many miles of the excavation was of solid rock, and the first estimate of $2,500,000 was exhausted. Finally, in June, 1871, the work was completed at a cost of $3,750,000, the locks were torn away, the river poured its inky stream of fetid water into the canal, and in twenty-four hours the water in the river was as pure as that of the lake. It continues to work admirably, much to the astonishment of those who insist, even in the face of this contrary demonstration, that the water of a river will not flow up stream. There is a current of several miles per hour constantly flowing to the head of the stream, keeping the river pure and inodorous. During the suspension of the water works, since the fire, water from the river has been pumped into the mains and distributed to the people. It was smoky but otherwise good.

Chamber of Commerce.

In 1864–5 the Chamber of Commerce was built at the southeast corner of Washington and La Salle streets, at a cost including the lot, of $490,000. In this magnificent building, built of marble, the Board of Trade, consisting of 1400 members, met daily for the transaction of business. It contained, also, offices occupied by two banks, insurance agencies, brokers, and commission merchants. The hall where the daily business was transacted was as fine as any in the country, and was the scene of many an exciting event. This building was swept by the fire as if it were made of wood.

The Grain Market.

Chicago had long since become the leading grain market of the world. The growth of this trade is but an illustration of the general growth of the city in all its branches of commerce. After the disastrous events of 1837, Walker & Co., in 1838, commenced as an experiment the shipment of grain, and the shipment of that year was 78 bushels of wheat. Flour was not exported until 1844. The record of corn shipments commenced in 1847. A few statements will show the progress of this trade:

Shipments of Wheat.

Year.	Bushels.	Year.	Bushels.
1838, . . .	78	1860, . .	12,402,197
1841, . . .	40,000	1861, . .	15,835,935
1844, . . .	891,000	1866, . .	10,118,907
1848, . . .	2,160,000	1868, . .	10,374,683
1855, . . .	6,298,155	1870, . .	16,432,585

Corn.

Year.	Bushels.	Year.	Bushels.
1847, . .	67,315	1816, . .	24,322,725
1851, . .	3,221,317	1866, . .	32,953,530
1854, . .	6,626,054	1869, . .	21,580,808
1860, . .	13,700,113	1870, . .	17,777,377
		1871, to October.	

Of all Grains.

Reducing the flour shipped to bushels of wheat, the aggregate of all kinds of grain shipped in both forms is thus shown:

Year.	Bushels.	Year.	Bushels.
1841, . .	40,000	1862, . .	56,484,110
1350, . .	1,830,938	1866, . .	66,736,660
1854, . .	12,932,320	1870, . .	54,745,903
1860, . .	31,108,750		

The receipts and shipments during 1871, promised to exceed by many millions of bushels those of any previous year.

Elevators.

The machinery by which this vast amount of grain was handled was the monster elevators, of which there were seventeen, with a total capacity of holding 11,580,000 bushels in store. The trains were run to these elevators and quickly emptied of their contents, while the business of loading a vessel was proportionately speedy. The elevators were built on the river, thus admitting of receiving from the cars on one side, and delivering to vessels on the other. Of these elevators there were six destroyed, having an aggregate capacity of 2,630,000 bushels. They contained at the time 1,650,000 bushels of grain. The other elevators yet remain. Those destroyed will rapidly be replaced.

Cattle Yards.

Another institution of this city was its stock yards, which were opened in December, 1865. Their area is 345 acres; 100 acres in pens; used for hotel and other buildings 45 acres; 31 miles of drainage; 12 miles of paved streets and alleys; 3 miles of water troughs; 12 miles of feed troughs; 2,300 gates; 1,500 open pens; 800 covered pens; the whole supplied by water from an artesian well. The hotel is large. The establishment has its national bank, telegraph office, newspaper, and is reached by the tracks of 21 railroads and their tributary roads. These yards are uninjured by the fire.

The number of animals received and shipped at these yards during the year 1870 is as follows:

Cattle.	Receipts.	Shipped.
Cattle, ...	532,964	391,709
Sheep, ...	349,855	116,711
Hogs, live, ...	1,693,158	924,483
Hogs, dressed, ...	260,214	171,188

Lumber Trade.

The magnitude of the lumber trade may be briefly stated in the following statement of the receipts:

Year.	Lumber, feet.	Shingles.	Lath.
1867–8,	882,661,770	447,039,275	146,846,200
1870–1,	1,018,998,685	652,091,000	

More than half of these receipts of lumber are shipped hence to all parts of the west by rail and canal.

Other Articles in 1870.

	Receipts.	Shipments.
Pork, barrels, . . .	40,883	165,885
Provisions, pounds, .	52,162,881	112,433,168
Lard, pounds, . . .	7,711,018	43,292,249
Beef, barrels, . . .	20,554	65,529
Seeds, pounds, . . .	18,681,148	6,287,615
Wool, pound, . . .	14,751,089	15,826,536
Hides, pounds, . . .	28,539,668	27,245,846
Salt, barrels, ...	674,618	571,013
Coal, tons, ...	887,474	110,467
Lead, pounds, . . .	14,445,622	7,855,471
Hogs, packed, '69–'70,	2,595,233	

Lake Commerce.

The aggregate number of vessels arriving in Chicago during the year 1870, was 12,739, with a tonnage of 3,049,265 tons. The vessels owned in Chicago in 1870, are thus recorded:

	No.	Tons.
Steamers,	3	467
Propellers,	10	4,256
Tugs,	53	1,752
River steamers,	4	376
Steam canal boats,	14	1,226
Barks,	34	11,753
Brigs,	7	1,553
Schooners,	242	45,201
Scows,	41	2,956
Barges,	8	3,103
	418	72,764
Canal boats,	224	20,564

Railroads.

The number of main lines of railway entering Chicago was 21, including their extensions and branches 45, with nearly 10,000 miles of track through the country tributary to this city. The number of passenger trains arriving daily was not less than 120, and of freight trains, about the same number.

Taxable Property.

The assessment for municipal taxation of personal and private property for the year had just been completed, and was about $287,000,000. This did not include public property, and only so much of the personal as was visible. It was perhaps one-third less than the real or selling value. It did not include the churches, charitable or school property, all of which was valuable.

City Debt.

The debt of the City of Chicago in April, 1871, was $14,103,000, of which $1,500,000 was held in cash intended for the extension of the water works. The increase of the debt was prohibited by the Constitution of 1870.

Manufactures.

The manufactures of Chicago during 1870, produced an aggregate of about $76,000,000. The heaviest of these establishments were destroyed.

Banks.

The City of Chicago had 25 banks, 17 of them national banks, with an aggregate capital of $13,000,000, and of deposits amounting to

$35,000,000, all these banks, save the Prairie Savings Institution, were located within the burnt district, and their buildings destroyed. In no case was any money lost, though most of them lost their books.

The Post Office.

The Chicago Post Office was in general business, the third in the country, ranking next after Philadelphia, but in the number of letters received and mailed, it was exceeded only by that of New York. The building was erected in 1855, and was supposed to be fire proof. It was of Athens marble. The exterior walls are standing. The building also contained the Custom House, United States Depository, United States Courts, and Marshal's offices. All the books and records were destroyed. The gold in the depository was recovered, having melted down, but the $1,300,000 of greenbacks and national bank notes were consumed.

The Court House

Was a large building made of Lockport granite. It was three stories high, with a basement, used as a county jail. During 1870, the city erected a large wing on the west side of the square, and the comely-like structure on the east side. These were occupied in March last for the first time. They had been handsomely and expensively furnished throughout. All the records of all the courts, and of the city and county, including the record of deeds, were consumed in the fire. On the dome of the center building was recently erected a clock, with four dials, and on the belfry was hung a powerful fire alarm bell. The bellman did not abandon his post until the roof of the building was in flames.

The Police.

The police force consists of 450 men, under the general charge of a Board of Police Commissioners. The force is generally effective.

Fire Department.

The Fire Department consisted of four hook and ladder trucks; two hose elevators; 17 steam engines; 54 hose carts; one fire escape, and 11 alarm bells; with 48,000 feet of hose. It was a paid department. Until this calamity, it had proved to be brave, vigorous and prompt, though there was a growing impression that its executive officers were not what they ought to be, neither the Police, nor Fire Department had become political or partisan attachments, though the Commissioners are elective.

The Population.

In June, 1870, the Federal census was taken, and in June, 1871, it was again taken by private enterprise. The following are the results:

Wards.	Year 1870.	Year 1871.
1	6,522	8,103
2	14,320	13,449
3	17,681	17,934
4	12,174	14,022
5	11,566	14,991
6	19,445	22,918
7	13,854	15,590
8	22,911	25,420
9	27,817	30,778
10	13,771	17,292
11	15,065	16,212
12	13,970	15,018
13	8,928	9,740
14	9,035	9,339
15	20,361	25,706
16	14,045	16,380
17	18,078	18,814
18	17,084	18,805
19	8,716	9,237
20	13,628	14,522
Totals,	298,977	334,270

The destruction by the fire was nearly complete in the wards in which it occurred. The fire originated in the Ninth Ward, burning out the northeast corner of that ward. Four blocks of the Tenth Ward had been destroyed the night before It then crossed the river in the Second Ward, burning, leaving but a dozen dwellings in that ward, and destroying twenty-five or more in the Third Ward; it swept every house in the First, Twentieth, Nineteenth, Eighteenth, and Seventeenth Wards, and four-fifths of the Sixteenth Ward. This makes the computation of those rendered homeless, a matter of easy calculation. Taking the census of 1871, as the basis, the following is the population whose habitations were destroyed. We follow the course of the fire.

Wards.	Inhabitants.	Wards.	Inhabitants.
9	2,000	19	9,237
10	250	18	18,805
3	250	17	18,814
2	13,449	16	13,650
1	8,103		
20	14,522	Rendered homeless,	98,860

The First Ward was, with but few exceptions, built of stone or brick; the streets were all paved, but in many cases the board sidewalks had not yet given place to the stone. In this ward were concentrated all the city and county buildings; all the banks; all the insurance brokers, and real estate offices; nearly all the wholesale dry goods, groceries, jewellers, clothing, crockery and glassware, boots and shoes, drugs, oils and paint, and leather dealers; all the hotels, save those built since 1869, the opera house, and all the theatres. During 1869 and '70 State street had been improved by the erection of some thirty or forty marble front business buildings, all six stories high. In this street were most of the large booksellers and publishers. East of State street, and in the same ward, the improvements have been on an equal scale. There were but two churches in this ward, the Second Presbyterian, a stone building, and St. Mary's Roman Catholic. Adjoining the latter was the Convent of the Sisters of Mercy, which included a large boarding house and school. Near by, on Michigan avenue, was the marble residence of Bishop Foley. In the same ward were all the newspaper offices and principal publishing houses, including Callaghan & Cochroft, Law Publishers, who lost the plates of the reports of several States. The Opera House had been refitted at a cost of $90,000, and was to open on Monday night. McVicker's Theatre had been substantially rebuilt, at great cost. The United States Post Office, Custom House and Depository, was in the same part of the city. Though the ward covered a large area, the resident population was comparatively small, those doing business there residing in other parts of the city. It contained large factories, in which were employed many thousands of women. At six o'clock in the evening the various working people, clerks, and others, male and female, would throng the streets in long processions, returning to their homes in various parts of the city. The various horse railways had their common starting point on State street.

Michigan avenue, until within a few years, was the grand place of residence. Built only upon one

CHAMBER OF COMMERCE.

CITY HALL.

side, the dwellings looked out upon the broad lake, with an intervening park. Next to this was Wabash avenue, hardly less desirable as a residence, but the growth of business had become such that residence after residence was abandoned, and business, wholesale principally, was converting once proud private mansions into places of traffic. Not a house stands on either avenue, north of Congress street; there one block was saved, including the Avenue Hotel. To the west of this the fire burned down to Harrison street, the southern boundary of the Second Ward.

The Second Ward contained a large proportion of wooden buildings, which were, however, giving way to those of stone and brick. It included the Palmer Hotel, opened in March; the Bigelow House, just furnished, but not opened; and the Pacific Hotel, hardly completed. These three hotels were intended to surpass any of the other great hotels for which the city was proverbial. In the First Ward was the great Union Passenger Depot of the Illinois Central, Michigan Central, and Chicago Burlington and Quincy Railroads, and all the freight depots of the same roads. In the Second Ward was the magnificent and costly passenger depot of the Rock Island and the Michigan Southern Railroads. The buildings were all of stone.

Crossing the river to the Twentieth Ward, the fire entered a field of more combustible material. For three blocks north of the river the buildings were generally of brick, and for three blocks west of the lake the private residences, most of them costly, were of stone. Along the river were two elevators, McCormick's reaper factory, a freight depot, and various manufacturing establishments. On Kinzie street was the great meat market, to which all the slaughtered meat was brought, and from which most of the butchers got their daily supply. North of these parts and for miles, the buildings as a general thing, were of wood, and were consumed as so much kindling wood by the fire, driven by the furious gale. In this section there were several handsome churches—St. James, Episcopal, stone; Cathedral of the Holy Name, R. C.; St. Joseph's Church, R. C., German; Unity Church, Rev. Robert Collyer's; New England Church; besides numerous frame churches. The Roman Catholic Orphan Asylum, stone, and two hospitals, were also in this part of the city. One stone Public School, of the modern style, and four brick schools were also within the area swept by the fire. To the east, near the lake shore, were the water works already mentioned, and also several large breweries. In the same part of the city were located the supposed fire proof buildings of the Chicago Historical Society and Rush Medical College. The population of this North Division, except along the streets near the lake, was mostly of foreign birth. The Sixteenth and Seventeenth Wards were almost exclusively Germans. The Eighteenth was principally settled by Irish. The Nineteenth and Twentieth had a more mixed population, but the Germans were in the majority. The buildings destroyed in the Ninth and Tenth Wards have been described as wooden. The population dislodged were mainly Irish, but included, also, a settlement of Bohemians in the Ninth Ward.

The Parks and Boulevards.

Chicago had just entered upon a system of parks and boulevards, which, when completed, would have been unequalled by those of any other city of the world.

The first of these was LINCOLN PARK, a tract of land within the n rthern limits of the city, containing one hundred and fifty-three acres, and with a broad front upon the lake. This park had been already comparatively completed and was a great public resort. The plan embraced a boulevard with a roadway 250 feet wide, proceeding from the northern extremity of this park westwardly about four miles, where it entered HUMBOLDT PARK, a tract of 290 acres. This park had only been commenced; it was enclosed and was partially planted. About two miles south of this, and connected by a like boulevard, was CENTRAL PARK, containing 236 acres, and a mile south of this park was DOUGLAS PARK, containing 232 acres. All of these parks were but in their infancy, but with the speed with which all such things progress in Chicago, would in a few years have become handsomely decorated places of resort. From Douglas Park, the boulevard upon the same extended to the south and east, until it reached NORTH PARK, a tract of over 500 acres, just south of the city. A mile and a half to the south and west of this park was SOUTH PARK, which contained nearly 500 acres; both parks containing combined 1,055 acres. The North and South Parks cost over two millions of dollars, for which the bonds of the South Division have been sold. Work on these parks will probably be suspended for years, as the property to be taxed for their improvement and maintenance has been destroyed. When completed, as they would rapidly have been had not this fire occurred, they would have been unequalled. The length of boulevard, or broad paved avenue planted on both sides, would have been nearly twenty-five miles, exclusive of the roadways in the parks. No other equal extent of drives can be found in any other city of this day. The park system will be suspended, but not abandoned, and before five years are over, no other calamity intervening, the work will be resumed. The lands for parks and boulevards have been purchased, and will be held until the city recovers some of her lost greatness and wealth.

The Business of Chicago.

On the 5th of October, only a day or two before the fire, the Chicago *Tribune* had the following editorial concerning the trade of the city:

"Our Washington despatches of yesterday show, that one more obstacle to the shipment of goods from foreign ports direct to Chicago has been removed. This is the permission of the Treasury Department to carry foreign goods, on which there is no duty, in the same bonded cars with goods upon which the duty is to be collected here. Few persons, except those directly engaged in the import trade of this city, are aware of what important changes have resulted from the recent removal of the unnecessary restrictions in regard to cars, and locks, and guards, that were imposed a year ago upon the shipment of goods direct from foreign ports to this city, Our leading dealers in dry goods, ribbons, hosiery, carpets, liquors, crockery, &c., say that they are importing from five to six times as much as they have ever done before at the same season of the year. It is only within a year that Chicago merchants have ever thought of keeping their own exclusive agents in Europe. Now, at least four prominent houses keep either members of their firms or an exclusive agent in Europe, the greater portion of the year, moving from one market to another, now buying German cloths, now at Basle for ribbons and hosiery, and again in England for carpets, &c. During the last four weeks a thousand tons of railroad iron have been received in Chicago, direct from England via Montreal, and we hear of another thousand tons afloat for here, that will arrive within the next few weeks. When we say that our merchants are importing six times as many goods as ever before, at this season of the year, it is not meant that their stock is six times as great —though there is a vast increase also in that respect —but mainly that they are buying six times as many of their goods direct from the foreign manufacturer, instead of buying them of middlemen in New York and other Eastern cities. As far as direct trade with Europe is concerned, this great change has been effected by relieving the Chicago importing merchant from the necessity of doing his warehousing in New York city instead of at home. The Chicago merchant now pays nothing until his goods arrive here, he gives his bond here, the goods are appraised here, and he can withdraw any portion of them from warehouse on any day and have them in his store without the former delays. In this connection it may be mentioned that the increased demand for Government bonded warehouse room has increased so much, that the Michigan Southern Company are now building a bonded warehouse on Harrison street, and the company, in conjunction with others to New York, intend to bond their lines, in order to make a specialty of carrying goods imported direct to Chicago. But it is not only with Europe that the direct foreign trade of Chicago has been so extensively increased this fall. The increase of the tea trade exceeds even that of the dry goods trade. It is a fact of great significance in this connection, that whereas the total quantity of teas in Government bonded warehouses in this city, on September 30th, 1870, was only 2,500 chests, it is now nearly 15,000 chests, all of which has come direct on through bills of lading from Hong Kong and Yokohama, through San Francisco to Chicago, without a day's unnecessary delay, and there are further receipts of teas now via the North Western and Rock Island Railroads every day. This great increase of the direct importing trade of this city has been mainly within the past two months, as will be seen by the following table of the amount of duties paid at this custom house, during each month of the first quarter of the current fiscal year, as compared with the same time last year, viz:

	1870.	1871.
July, ...	$63,141	$70,375
August, ...	76,803	87,608
September, ...	55,909	174,706
Total, ...	$185,853	$332,689

It will be seen that the amount of duties paid during September this year were over three times as great as during the same time last year.

"As regards the tea trade there seems no reason why Chicago will not become the great distributing market for all the central part of the continent, between the Allegheny and the Rocky mountains. As prominent cities as Cincinnati and St. Louis will, of course, do a portion, but the superior facilities of Chicago, in her constantly increasing network of railroads, are practically acknowledged by the New York tea houses, four or five of which have their resident agents here, receive their teas here via the overland route, and distribute them from this point all over the northwest. These agents receive but few teas from New York, and there is no longer any question of competition, as regards the route by which the teas consumed in the States west of Pennsylvania and New York shall come. The trans-continental railroad on the one hand, and the increased facilities for direct importation on the other, are revolutionizing the foreign trade of the United States. We see evidence of this not only in the increased direct importations of Chicago merchants, but in the exports of products. As instances, the steamship Great Republic, which sailed from San Francisco, on October 1st, took 21,000 barrels of flour for Hong Kong; the ship Ringleader, which sailed the same day, took $100,000 worth more for the same port; and every regular Pacific steamer now takes more or less flour. If China and Japan continue to take our breadstuffs, at that rate, it will leave less to go to England, and will have the effect to make a better average of prices for the grain produced in the northwest."

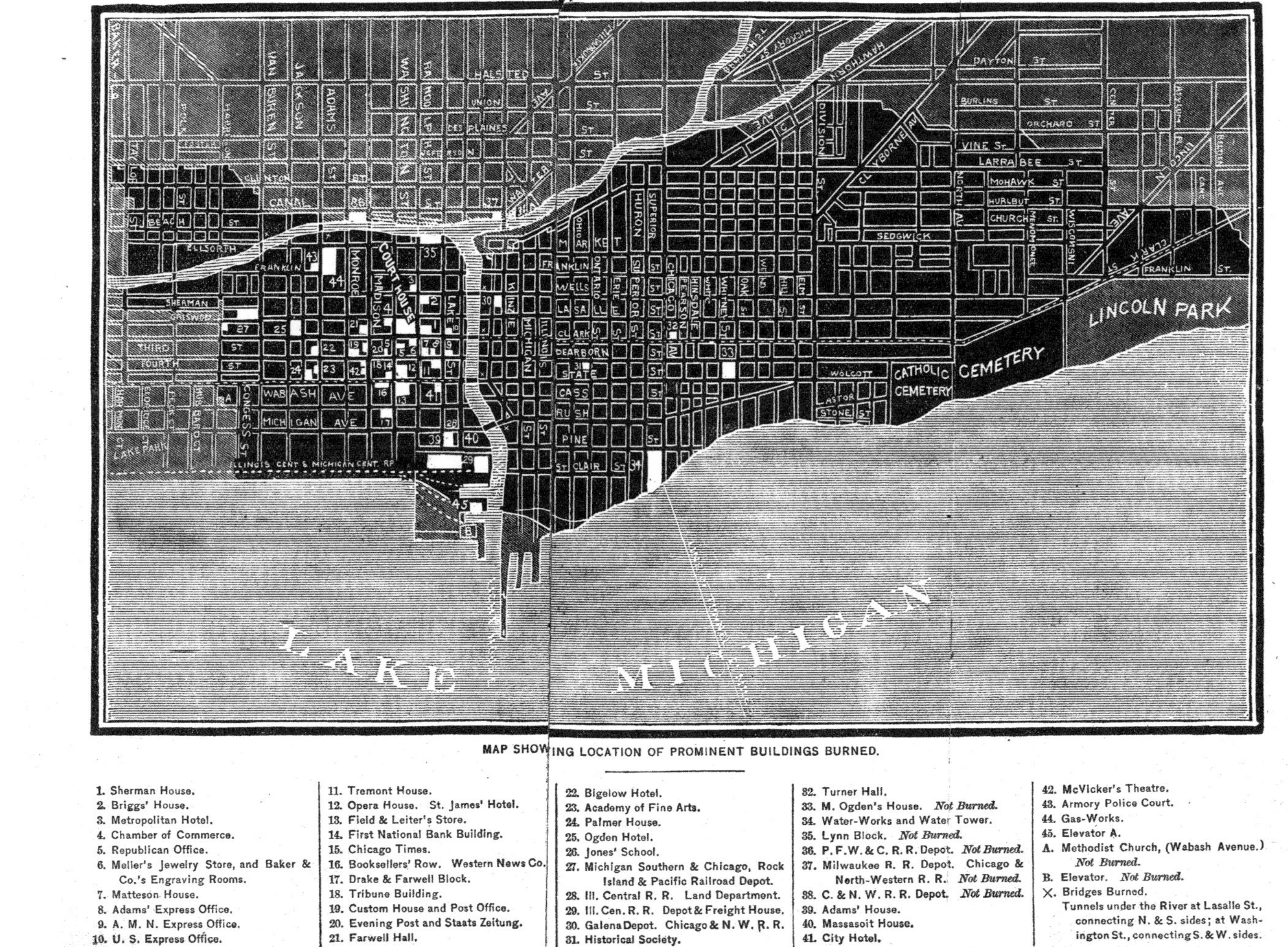

MAP SHOWING LOCATION OF PROMINENT BUILDINGS BURNED.

1. Sherman House.
2. Briggs' House.
3. Metropolitan Hotel.
4. Chamber of Commerce.
5. Republican Office.
6. Meller's Jewelry Store, and Baker & Co.'s Engraving Rooms.
7. Matteson House.
8. Adams' Express Office.
9. A. M. N. Express Office.
10. U. S. Express Office.
11. Tremont House.
12. Opera House. St. James' Hotel.
13. Field & Leiter's Store.
14. First National Bank Building.
15. Chicago Times.
16. Booksellers' Row. Western News Co.
17. Drake & Farwell Block.
18. Tribune Building.
19. Custom House and Post Office.
20. Evening Post and Staats Zeitung.
21. Farwell Hall.
22. Bigelow Hotel.
23. Academy of Fine Arts.
24. Palmer House.
25. Ogden Hotel.
26. Jones' School.
27. Michigan Southern & Chicago, Rock Island & Pacific Railroad Depot.
28. Ill. Central R. R. Land Department.
29. Ill. Cen. R. R. Depot & Freight House.
30. Galena Depot. Chicago & N. W. R. R.
31. Historical Society.
32. Turner Hall.
33. M. Ogden's House. *Not Burned.*
34. Water-Works and Water Tower.
35. Lynn Block. *Not Burned.*
36. P. F. W. & C. R. R. Depot. *Not Burned.*
37. Milwaukee R. R. Depot. Chicago & North-Western R. R. *Not Burned.*
38. C. & N. W. R. R. Depot. *Not Burned.*
39. Adams' House.
40. Massasoit House.
41. City Hotel.
42. McVicker's Theatre.
43. Armory Police Court.
44. Gas-Works.
45. Elevator A.

A. Methodist Church, (Wabash Avenue.) *Not Burned.*

B. Elevator. *Not Burned.*

X. Bridges Burned.

Tunnels under the River at Lasalle St., connecting N. & S. sides; at Washington St., connecting S. & W. sides.

THE GREAT CONFLAGRATION.

The Fire of Saturday.

About 10 o'clock on Saturday night, Octobei 7th, 1871, a fire broke out on South Clinton street, just north of Van Buren street. A fierce wind from the southwest was blowing at the time, and despite the exertions of the firemen it destroyed all the buildings within the area bounded by Adams on the north, Clinton on the west, Van Buren on the south, and the river on the east, excepting a few valueless buildings on the northwest corner of Clinton and Adams, a row of frame buildings on Van Buren street from Clinton to Canal, and Murray Nelson's grain elevator, which was situated east of Canal street, and near Adams street bridge. The buildings destroyed were not very valuable, being mostly two-story frame buildings occupied as laborers' boarding houses. In one of these was a corpse of a woman, and her friends were holding a "wake" over her remains. The friends fled before the fire, leaving the dead body to be consumed. Between Canal street and the river were a number of coal yards, and the extensive lumber ya*r*d of Chapin & Foss. The piles of coal and lumber burned all day on Sunday, and when night set in the sky reflected the brilliant light of the blazing mass below. The loss of property by this fire which swept an area of about sixteen acres was about $300,000. The neighborhood was visited during the day by thousands of persons. About one hundred families were turned out of their homes by the fire.

The Fire of Sunday in the West Division.

At precisely half-past nine o'clock on Sunday evening the fire-bell sounded an alarm, and simultaneously a bright light appeared in the southwest. To the great majority of persons this appeared but a revival of the fire of the previous night. It was just as the churches were out and the congregations were returning to their homes. No special attention was given to the fire, and many hundreds of families, after noticing that it was at a great distance, went to their homes, and later retired to sleep, all unconscious that the demon was unloosed which would disturb and expel them before many hours. Standing to the west of the territory covered by the fire of Saturday, we readily discovered that the alarm was not called for by any revival of the embers of that conflagration. Proceeding directly to the scene, we discovered that it had originated in a cow-shed in the rear of a one-story frame building, on the northeast corner of Dekoven and Jefferson streets. The origin is a mystery. The story that an attempt to milk a cow by the light of a kerosene lamp, had ended in the overturning of the lamp, and the rapid firing of the cow-shed, is now known to be untrue. It must always be borne in mind that for thirty-six hours previously the wind had been blowing with unusual violence from the southwest. The flames immediately spread to the adjoining sheds in the interior of the block, the wind bearing them far in advance. By reference to the map it will be seen that from the initial point of the fire to the water works, the direction is directly northeast, and in the light of what followed from the first outburst, it seemed as if the fire and the gale had united to mow a breadth of desolation from the one place to the other in the shortest possible space of time. From the beginning the fire rushed forward in a varying breadth, directly before the wind in a literal air line, to the destruction of the water works. Before the firemen had reached the scene, the fire had crossed Taylor street, thence into Forquer street, burning a breadth of from fifty to eighty feet, leaving behind it the blazing buildings to spread the conflagration to the right and the left. It then reached Clinton street, just south of Polk street, still confining its breadth to two buildings, sometimes to three; but cutting diagonally through the blocks, it included within its path the ends of many other buildings. The firemen posted themselves in front of the fire, struggling to arrest it, but their labors were in vain; they might as well have attempted to arrest the wind itself because at this time the wind and the fire were the same thing, the blaze often reaching across the streets, and burning brands were carried far in advance of the actual fire. There had been no rain in Chicago, of any account, for nearly six weeks, and the wooden buildings, tenements, lumber piles, and sidewalks, were as dry as paper and burned as readily. Though the wind carried the original fire directly before it, it also, by its eddies and currents, extended it. Though the northwest and southeast corners of the block, where the fire began, escaped destruction, it turned back to Jefferson street at a point two blocks north, and burned all the buildings on the east side of that street to a point one-half a block north of Harrison street. To the east it extended gradually from the point where it crossed Taylor street to Canal street, and thence to the river, which it crossed at Polk street, destroying the bridge, and setting fire to the extensive works of the Chicago Hide and Leather Company.

The main fire—the advance guard after crossing Polk street—soon reached the rear of several planing mills and factories, the buildings being all of wood; these furnished the peculiar aid this fire needed to make it irresistible. It would lift a bundle of blazing shingles and bearing it upon the wind would deposit them on the roofs of buildings far in advance. The line of the continuous fire was thus considerably hastened. The result was as if a corps of men were firing the city at various points simultaneously. As the continuous fire came along before the wind, it found buildings already ablaze and still others in advance already ignited. While this was going on in advance the fire at the base was extending to the east, and as each building caught, the wind carried the flames forward, making the breadth of the destruction forever wider and wider. In this way all the area between Jefferson street and the river north of Polk and south of Van Buren street was soon enveloped in flames. The scene at this time was grand to the spectator. The wind seemed to gain fresh intensity. The blazing brands were thick, and their flights long. Before the fire had reached Van Buren street, blazing faggots, shingles and other brands had commenced falling in the North Division. At 11.30 o'clock the advance of the fire reached Van Buren street, the south line of the fire of the previous night, and here had there been no more than an ordinary gale, it would have stopped. Before it were the broad sixteen acres which had been swept of its combustibles the night before. When the fire enveloped the buildings on Vân Buren street, there was behind it in full blaze a conflagration covering perhaps 150 acres—the food for which was planing and saw mills, dwellings, barns, factories and shops, lumber yards, coal depots, all of the most combustible character. It was, notwithstanding its terrors, a brilliant spectacle. The smoke, except immediately in front, did not obscure the view, but everywhere was a broad sheet of flame leaping, darting, and sending forth, as if from some grand pyrotechnic preparation, the most brilliant, dazzling meteors of living fire.

Here was the grand turning point in the conflagration. Here the fire, under ordinary circumstances, would have stopped; here it had consumed everything that had been in its path. To the north lay the plain laid waste the night before, and having nothing to consume except the coal, already on fire, and the Nelson elevator at its northeast extremity. To the west was the wind; to the east was the river. But afar off to the northeast beyond two rivers, beyond the great structures of hotels, banks and warehouses, beyond the towering walls of marble and of brick, away off in the northwest, two miles distant, were the water works, the only possible human agent that could save the city from annihilation, and to that the grand objective point of wind and fire, this conflagration seemed determined to reach. Precisely at midnight, a blazing board carried by the wind fell upon a cluster of miserable shanties, striking them just at the point where the roofs of several made a sort of junction, affording a secure lodgement. These buildings were on Adams and Franklin streets, east of the river, a third of a mile from any burning building of any size west of the river. In a moment a blaze sprang up instantly, and the wind carried it to the northeast, leaving between the two fires the large building used for police business by the city, and known as the Armory, and the buildings of the south side Gas Company, various coal yards, and numerous other buildings, large and small, in the area between the two fires. The progress of the fire was immediately forward. The blazing torches were carried by the wind far in advance, and where-ever they fell they produced a fire. From that point until the fire crossed Madison street, there were several distinct fires, widely separated, burning simultaneously, with large blocks of buildings between.

But the continuous fire followed, overtaking these advance conflagrations, gathering new strength from them, and forever sending forth its pioneers—forever keeping its due course to the water works, the only hope of the doomed city. The operations of the fire after it had crossed or jumped the river from Canal and Van Buren to Adams and Franklin, belong to the history of the South Division. But, from a point of observation to the windward of the fire, the scene was, perhaps, unequalled. No thought of any serious devastation had occurred to any one, until the fire crossed the river. Until this time no one had supposed it would amount to any more than the destruction of the frame buildings which it had engulfed. All had anticipated that it would stop upon reaching the boundaries of the district burned the night before; but the general alarm which was now rung out in all parts of the city, the blazing lights which marked its path for over nearly a mile in one direction, and half a mile in another, had aroused all Chicago. The people of the comparatively remote North Division were aroused, and for an hour, gazed upon the extraordinary spectacle spread out to the south and west of them, hardly admitting that there was any danger to them. But when the fire burst forth in Franklin street, at Adams; when it rushed as in a field of straw, through the alleys and intervening streets to Wells, and eventually to Madison; when blazing boards and lumps of fire were falling thick and heavy on Lake and Water streets; and far away in the North Division, when fires broke out at intervening distances, far in advance of the main fire; when, standing to the west, there could be plainly distinguished five distinct fires in the route of the wind, each a little in advance of the other, and behind all these a sheet of continuous flame, reaching a mile and a half to the southwest, the effect so far exceeded any previous observation as to defy description. It was sublime, yet terrific; magnificent, yet appalling. Even while the brave watchman in the court house tower made the old bell peal forth its warning notes, the flames had not only reached the stately buildings facing the square, but had broken out on the north side of the river, beyond State street, and were making their way directly to the water works.

In the meantime, the fire on the West Division had gone on in its lateral extensions. Jefferson street runs due north; the wind, in its fury had carried the fire far to the north and to the east; but this did not save Jefferson street. The east side of that street presents remarkable instances of the course of the fire, governed only by the wind. There are a number of houses left on that side of the street, the fire having burned all the adjoining buildings, and then, passing to the rear of these, re

WHERE THE FIRE BEGAN.

OGDEN'S RESIDENCE. ONLY RESIDENCE LEFT ON NORTH DIVISION OF BURNED DISTRICT.

turned to Jefferson street, north of them, again. It was not until eleven o'clock next day, fifteen hours after the beginning of the fire, that the half dozen buildings to the north and east of the one where the fire originated, were burned. The fire had burned back to them in the very teeth of the wind. It is also remarkable, that though Jefferson street in that part of the city is very narrow, not exceeding forty feet, including both sidewalks, not one house on the west line of the street was burned, and none of them were scorched or blistered. The wind in its force had blown back the fire from the street and had also blown back the heat. Until the destruction of the water works, the people in the neighborhood, to the windward of the fire, had fought and resisted it by the use of water, but when the great engines ceased to pump, all means of defence were lost, and the city was at the mercy of the wind. In the reaction of the fire, after it commenced on the South Division, the bridge over the river at Adams street, was burned, and also Nelson's elevator, which had escaped the night before.

The South Division.

There was probably not a person in the South Division who imagined for a moment that the fire would extend beyond the portion of the city in which it originated. Indeed, when it approached the burned district of the previous Saturday night's conflagration, there was a universal sigh of relief, for here certainly it would be stayed, notwithstanding the furious wind. The hope was a futile one. At just twenty minutes past twelve. a huge blazing brand was blown across the river. Onward it sped, like a fiery messenger of doom, and lodged upon the roof of a three-story tenement house, which was as dry as a tinder box. The roof was immediately in a blaze, and almost instantly every part of the building emitted furious jets of flame. The house was about midway between Adams, Monroe, Wells and Market streets, and surrounded by one and two-story wooden houses, and alleys littered with all sorts of inflammable materials. Through this wooden nest, the fire spread with inconceivable rapidity and soon attacked another group of low, wooden buildings known as Conley's Patch, densely covered with saloons, tumble-down hovels and sheds, and peopled by the lowest class in the city. For years this spot had been the terror of the neighborhood beyond it, and had been stained with every conceivable crime. The male residents were absent at the fire in the West Division, and as the flames seized upon it, squalid women and children rushed out in droves. Most of them escaped, but undoubtedly some were overtaken by the fire and miserably perished. Right and left the flames spread as fast as a man could walk, and soon the Gas Works and huge piles of coal in the yard took fire, and a red glare shone all over the doomed city. Down the south line of Monroe street, it sped with lightning-like rapidity. A fearful mass of flames leaped the street, lapping up John V. Farewell's stables and those of the United States Express Company, and burning many of their noble animals. Across Wells street it sped, sweeping everything before it and driving out hundreds of women and children, who fled in all directions without saving a scrap of household property. The fire was now beyond the control of the firemen and henceforth was to go on its way with no one to check it. Northward and eastward the flames progressed crossing Madison street and extending east to La Salle street, at the same time destroying stone, brick and wooden structures alike.

Another column of fire crossed the river further north and now it sped on its way with the same terrible power and swiftness. Great masses of flame from each division leaped far in advance of the main columns, and kindling new fires returned to complete the work of destruction. In almost an inconceivably short space of time the entire tract of the South Division, between the river and La Salle street, was in flames, and south of Van Buren, the fire was working steadily against the wind, taking the splendid depot of the Michigan Southern Railroad for a starting point, south to Harrison street, thence destroying a narrow strip along the river as far south as Taylor street.

The two main columns sent out detachments which entered every street with the regularity of an advancing army. Standing at the lake end of any one of the eleven streets between the river and

Michigan avenue, the spectator saw a furious shower of livid coals and fire brands sweep round the corners, followed by a sheet of dazzling flame, which would suck into the windows and instantly fire the buildings. At the same time the fire entering the alleys burst through the rear of buildings on either side, swept through them, and dashing through the fronts united in one solid, writhing, twisting column of fire, which would shoot up into the air a hundred feet, and then, seized by the wind, leap to roofs in the next block and fire them. The progress was aided by huge, blazing brands, which the blasts would send crashing through windows into the interiors of buildings, or into awnings, setting everything afire adjacent to them. The very goods which were tumbled into the streets aided the march of the destroyer.

The main column of the fire had now crossed Washington street. The Chamber of Commerce, the Telegraph Office and the lofty insurance blocks were all in flames. The Court House bell rung peal after peal, ringing its own knell, for the flames speadily leaped to its dome and fired it. For a few minutes its blazing trellis work, sheeted with flames, stood out against the sky in splendid relief. Then in every window at the same instant, an ominous glare appeared. The flames burst out, the dome fell in, and then a crash told that the interior walls had yielded and the Court House was no more. The Sherman House was the next to go, and crossing Clark street, Hooley's Opera House, Wood's Museum, the Matteson House, the Tremont House and whole squares of palatial business blocks melted away before the destroyer as snow melts in water.

In the meantime, still another column was sweeping over the South Division. The great Ogden House, which covered an entire square, and which was nearly finished, was a mass of flames from basement to roof, and from its towering height and grand proportions, presented a sublime spectacle. The new and beautiful Bigelow House was next wrapped in the flames, and so, on they went, taking successively the new Honore and Shepherd blocks on Dearborn street. At this point, for a time, the solid walls of the post office presented a barrier. Thwarted here, the flames spread down Clark street to the north, and then, turning Madison, came up the south line of the street like a whirlwind, and, turning Dearborn, melted away the Reynold's block almost immediately, bringing them to the north side of the post office; while another column, coming east in Monroe, attacked it on the west side. Before this joint attack, it yielded, and although its walls stood bravely its interior was soon gutted. When the flames turned the corner of Madison and Dearborn streets, a huge column shot across diagonally and fired the Dearborn Theatre, further north, and from this point both right and left destruction spread anew. To the left, it went down to Washington street, and again crossing, caught the roof of Crosby's Opera House. In almost the time it takes to write these lines, that noble building, with the handsomest operatic auditorium in the country, with its wealth of bronzes, paintings, statuary and rich ornamentations, was destroyed, while the St. James Hotel adjoining it on the east, which had two or three times before stood the test of fire, at last yielded and fell. To the right, the flames quickly reached the corner of Madison and Dearborn streets, opposite the *Tribune* office. A vacant lot, formerly occupied by the Dearborn School, intervened, but the fire quickly passed round it and came up on the other side. The *Tribune* building, one of the noblest structures in the city, on the southeast corner of Dearborn and Madison streets, had already stood the test bravely. The fire came down on the south side of it from Monroe street and dashed against its walls in vain. It was the key to that vicinity, and if it should stand, much valuable property it was hoped might yet be saved. But far to the south the flames had seized the huge eight-story Palmer House, and came sweeping northward with fearful rapidity to McVicker's Theatre, separated from the east wall of the *Tribune* building only by a narrow alley. This new onset of the fire was irresistible. From the other three attacks, it had become heated to an intense degree and was ready to kindle at the slightest sparks which should penetrate to its interior. Its roof yielded. The iron shutters on the alley side, bent by the fire, sprung out of place, and speedily the whole interior was in a mass of smouldering ruin. Of the strength of the structure, it may be said that on the day after the fire the walls were still standing. Some of the floors were intact, and in the basement the presses, boiler and engines sustained little damage beyond the burning of the wood work, and a slight warping of some of the iron work.

At Field & Leiter's mammoth establishment, on the corner of State and Washington streets, a determined effort was made to save the building but it was useless. The flames attacked it from the north and eastwardly in the rear, and it soon yielded. There was still a narrow strip bounded by Washington street on the north, Harrison street on the south, State street on the west, and the lake on the east, two blocks in width and about half a mile in length, not yet burned. The fire to traverse it must burn against the wind, and strong hopes were entertained that this tract might yet escape. But all the heavy warehouses at the north termini of these streets were in flames. There was no water to check it, for before this time, eight o'clock on Tuesday morning, the water works in the North Division had been destroyed. Slowly but surely the fire worked up these streets, right and left. West of State street, the fire, hours before, had reached Harrison and stopped. On Third and Fourth avenues buildings were torn down. On State street and Wabash avenue, buildings were levelled to the ground by General Sheridan's orders; and the splendid manner in which the Wabash avenue Methodist Church, one of the oldest structures in the city, resisted, also held the fire in check at the corner of this avenue and Harrison street. On Michigan avenue the fire did not reach Harrison. There were no buildings on the east side of it. The west burned slowly, the last building consumed being the Terrace block. Hon. J. Y. Scammon resided in the extreme south house, and between this and Congress street was a vacant lot. Here the fire was checked, and those living south of Harrison street breathed more freely.

Prominent Buildings.

Let us glance for a moment at the principal buildings destroyed by the south side fire, for in them was contained almost the entire business wealth of Chicago. The list includes the Michigan and Illinois Central Depots, two of the finest passenger structures in the United States, and their adjacent freight depots; the old and familiar Tremont House, Sherman House, Briggs House, Matteson House, St. James Hotel, Nevada House, Adams House, Massasoit House, Girard House, Metropolitan House, all substantial brick or stone hotels, the magnificent Ogden House, covering an entire square, the walls of which had already reached the top story, the new Bigelow House, which had just received $80,000 worth of new furniture, and the new eight-story Palmer House, on State street, which had been in successful operation a few months; every bank building in Chicago except the small Twenty-second Street

Savings Bank. Every insurance building; seven daily and numerous weekly newspaper offices; Crosby's Opera House with its brilliant auditorium, the finest in the United States; McVicker's Theatre which had just been completely renovated and had been open but a few weeks; Hooley's pretty little *bijou* of an Opera House; Wood's Museum with its large collection of curiosities, and the Dearborn Theatre which had been the home of minstrelsy; the great book house of the Western News Company, S. C. Griggs & Co. and W. B. Keen & Cooke; the First Methodist Church; St. Mary's (Catholic); First and Second Presbyterian; Trinity (Episcopal); St. Paul's (Universalist); and the Swedenborgian Church, the Academy of Design, with its fine gallery of paintings, by American and foreign artists, and its splendid collection of casts from the antiques; the Chamber of Commerce, only the day before the scene of busy life and traffic; the Telegraph Office; the Court House, with all the valuable city and county records; the Post Office and Custom House; the Armory, the Jewish Synagogue; such magnificent stone blocks as the Terrace, Armour, Shepherd, Honore, McCormick's Merchant's Insurance, Oriental, Ætna, Birch, Drake, Farwell, Lombard, Sturgess, Stone, Arcade and Hubbard; Crosby's Music Hall, Metropolitan Hall, so intimately associated with the early history of Chicago, in music, literature and art; Farwell Hall, one of the most elegant and spacious auditoriums in the country, and hundreds of other palatial structures.

The scene from the Tribune Office.

The sight from the upper windows of the *Tribune* office, a few hours before that structure was consumed, was one of the wildest and grandest ever seen by mortal eye. About one o'clock, a cloud of black smoke rose in the southwest, which, colored by the lurid glare of the flames, presented a remarkable picture. Due west another column of smoke and fire rose, while the north was lighted with the flying cinders and destructive brands. In ten minutes more the whole horizon to the west, as far as could be seen from the windows, was a fire cloud with flames leaping up along the whole line, just showing their heads and subsiding from view like tongues of snakes. Five minutes more wrought a change. Peal after peal was sounded from the Court House bell. The fire was on La Salle street, had swept north, and the Chamber of Commerce began to belch forth smoke and flame from windows and ventilators. The east wing of the Court House was alight; then the west wing; the tower was blazing on the south side, and at two o'clock the whole building was in a sheet of flame. The Chamber of Commerce burned with a bright steady flame. The smoke in front grew denser for a minute or two, and then bursting into a blaze from Monroe to Madison streets, proclaimed that Farwell Hall and the buildings north and south of it were on fire. At 2.10 o'clock the Court House tower was a glorious sight. At 2.15 o'clock the tower fell, and in two minutes more a crash announced the fall of the interior of the building. The windows of the office were hot, and the flames gave a light almost dazzling in its intensity. It became evident that the whole block from Clark to Dearborn, and from Monroe to Madison, must go; that the block from Madison to Washington must follow; Portland Block was ablaze, while everything from Clark to Dearborn, on Washington street, was on fire. At 2.30 the fire was half-way down Madison street; the wind blew a hurricane; the firebrands were hurled along the ground with incredible force against everything that stood in their way. Then the flames shot up in the rear of Reynold's block, and the *Tribune* building seemed doomed. An effort was made to save the files and other valuables, which were moved into the composing room, but the building stood like a rock, lashed on both sides by raging waves of flame, and it was abandoned. It was a fire proof building; and there were not a few who expected to see it stand the shock. The greatest possible anxiety was felt for it, as it was the key to the whole block, including McVicker's Theatre, and protected State street and Wabash and Michigan avenues, north of Madison street. When the walls of Reynold's block fell, and Cobb's building was no more, the prospects of its standing were good. Several persons were up-stairs and found it cool and pleasant—quite a refreshing haven from the hurricane of smoke, dust and cinders that assailed the eyes.

Meanwhile the fire had swept along northward and eastward. The Briggs House, the Sherman House, the Tremont House, had fallen in a few minutes. The bridges from Wells to Rush street were burning; the Northwestern Depot was in a blaze, and from Van Buren street on the south, far over into the north side, from the river to Dearborn street, the whole country was a mass of smoke, flames and ruin. It seems as if the city east of Dearborn street and to the river would be saved. The hope was strengthened when the walls fell of Honore's noble block without igniting that standing opposite. The vacant lot to the south seemed to protect it, and at 7 o'clock on Monday morning the whole of the region designated was considered saved, no fire being visible except a smouldering fire in the barber's shop under the *Tribune* office, which being confined in brick walls, was not considered dangerous. Every effort was made to quench it, but the water works had burned, and the absence of water, while it announced how far north the flames had reached, forbade any hope of quenching the fire below.

A Turning Point.

There was one remarkable turning point in this fire, in which everything was remarkable; and that was at Madison street bridge, where every one expected to see the fire re-cross to the west side, and commence upon a new path of destruction. Directly across this bridge were the Oriental Flouring Mills, which were saved from destruction by the immense steam force pump attached to the mill, by which a powerful stream of water was thrown upon the exposed property, hour after hour. This pump undoubtedly saved the West Division from a terrible conflagration, for if the Oriental Mills had burned, the combustible nature of the adjoining buildings and adjacent lumber yards would have insured a scene of devastation too heart-sickening for contemplation.

Workings of the Fire.

The scene presented when the fire was at its height in the South Division, is well nigh indescribable. The huge stone and brick structures melted before the fierceness of the flames as a snow-flake melts and disappears in water, and almost as quickly. Six-story buildings would take fire and disappear forever from sight, in five minutes by the watch. In nearly every street the flames would enter at the rears of buildings, and appear simultaneously at the fronts. For an instant the windows would redden, then great billows of fire would belch out, and meeting each other, shoot up into the air a vivid, quivering column of flame, and poising itself in awful majesty, hurl itself bodily several hundred feet and kindle new buildings. The intense heat created new currents of air. The general direction of the wind was from the southwest. This main current carried the fire straight through the city, from southwest to northeast, cutting a swath a mile in width, and then, as if maddened at missing any of its prey, it would turn backward in its frenzy and face the fierce wind, mowing one huge field on the west of the north division, while in the south division it also doubled on its track at the great Union Central Depot, and burned half a mile southward in the very teeth of the gale—a gale which blew a perfect tornado, and in which no vessel could have lived on the lake. The flames sometimes made glowing diagonal arches across the streets, traversed by whirls of smoke. At times, the wind would seize the entire volume of fire on the front of one of the large blocks, detach it entirely and hurl it in every direction, in fierce masses of flame, leaving the building as if it had been untouched—for an instant only, however, for fresh gusts would once more wrap them in sheets of fire. The whole air was filled with glowing cinders, looking like an illuminated snow storm. At times capricious flurries of the gale would seize these flying messengers of destruction and dash them down to the earth, hurrying them over the pavements, with lightning-like rapidity, firing everything they touched. Interspersed among these cinders were larger brands, covered with flame, which the wind dashed through windows and upon awnings and roofs, kindling new fires. Strange, fantastic fires of blue, red and green, played along the cornices of the buildings. On the banks of the river, red hot walls fell hissing into the water, sending up great columns of spray and exposing the fierce white furnace of heat, which they had enclosed. The huge piles of coal emitted dense billows of smoke which hurried along far above the flames below. If the sight was grand and overpowering, the sound was no less so. The flames crackled, growled and hissed. The lime stone, of which many of the buildings were composed, as soon as it was exposed to heat flaked off, the fragments flew in every direction, with a noise like that of continuous discharges of musketry. Almost every instant was added the dull, heavy thud of falling walls, which shook the earth. But above all these sounds, there was one other which was terribly fascinating, it was the steady roar of the advancing flames—the awful diapason in this carnival of fire. It was like nothing so much as the united roar of the ocean with the howl of the blast on some stormy, rocky coast.

Of the destructive power of this fire, Hon. Wm. B. Ogden, in a letter to a member of his family, briefly but very succinctly says: "How it could be that buildings, men or anything could encounter and withstand the torrent of fire without utter destruction, is explained by the fact that the fire was accompanied by the fiercest tornado of wind ever known to blow here, and it acted like a perfect blow-pipe, driving the brilliant blaze hundreds of feet with so perfect a combustion, that it consumed the smoke, and its heat was so great that fire proof buildings sunk before it, almost as readily as wood. Nothing but earth could withstand it."

Language can hardly convey to the reader an idea of the terrible scenes in the streets. The struggle of humanity was more fearful even than the horrors of the fire. In the latter there was an element of the beautiful, even of the sublime, which continually enforced itself, notwithstanding the wide-spread destruction it was causing; but in the various phases developed by this struggling, toiling, and despairing tide of humanity in the streets, there was nothing which would give pleasure.

Street Scenes.

Great calamities always develop latent passions, emotions, and traits of character, hitherto concealed. In this case, there was a world-wide difference in the manner in which men witnessed the destruction of all about them. Some were philosophical, even merry, and witnessed the loss of their own property with a calm shrug of the shoulders, although the loss was to bring upon them irretrievable ruin. Others clenched their teeth together, and witnessed the sight with a sort of grim defiance. Others, who were strong men, stood in tears, and some became fairly frenzied with excitement, and rushed about in an aimless manner, doing exactly what they would not have done in their cooler moments, and almost too delirious to save their own lives from the general wreck. Of course, the utmost disorder and

BOOKSELLERS' ROW, STATE STREET.

CLARK STREET, SOUTH FROM WASHINGTON STREET.

excitement prevailed, for nearly every one was, in some degree, demoralized, and in the absence both of gas and water, had given up the entire city to its doom. Mobs of men and women rushed wildly from street to street, screaming, gesticulating, and shouting, crossing each other's paths, and intercepting each other as if just escaped from a mad house. The yards and sidewalks of Michigan and Wabash avenues, for a distance of two miles south of the fire limit in the South Division, were choked with household goods of every description—the contents of hovels, and the contents of aristocratic residences, huddled together in inextricable confusion. Elegant ladies, who hardly supposed themselves able to lift the weight of a pincushion, astonished themselves by dragging trunks, and carrying heavy loads of pictures and ornamental furniture, for a long distance. Some adorned themselves with all their jewelry, for the purpose of saving it, and struggled along through the crowds, perhaps only to lose it at the hands of some ruffian. Delicate girls, with red eyes and blackened faces, toiled, hour after hour, to save household goods. Poor women staggered along with their arms full of homely household wares, and mattresses on their heads, which sometimes took fire as they were carrying them. Every few steps along the avenues were little piles of household property, or, perhaps, only a trunk, guarded by children, some of whom were weeping, and others laughing and playing. Here was a man sitting upon what he had saved, bereft of his senses, looking at the motley throng with staring, vacant eyes; here, a woman, weeping and tearing her hair, and calling for her children in utter despair; here, children, hand-in-hand, separated from their parents, and crying with the heart-breaking sorrow of childhood; here, a woman, kneeling on the hot ground, and praying, with her crucifix before her. One family had saved a coffee-pot and chest of drawers, and raking together the falling embers in the street, were boiling their coffee as cheerily as if at home. Barrels of liquor were rolled into the streets from the saloons. The heads were speedily knocked in, and men and boys drank to excess, and staggered about the streets. Some must have miserably perished in the flames, while others wandered away into the unburned district, and slept a drunken sleep upon the sidewalks and in door-yards. Thieves pursued their profession with perfect impunity. Lake street and Clark street were rich with treasure, and hordes of thieves entered the stores, and flung out goods to their fellows, who bore them away without opposition. Wabash avenue was literally choked up with goods of every description. Every one who had been forced from the burning portion of the division had brought some articles with them, and been forced to drop some, or all of them. Valuable oil paintings, books, pet animals, musical instruments, toys, mirrors, bedding, and ornamental and useful articles of every kind, were trampled under foot by the hurrying crowds. The streets leading southward from the fire were jammed with vehicles of every description, all driven along at top speed. Not only the goods which were deposited in the streets took fire, but wagon loads of stuff in transit, also kindled, and the drivers were obliged to cut the traces to save their animals. There was fire overhead, everywhere, not only on the low, red clouds, which rolled along the roofs, but in the air itself, filled with millions of blazing faggots, that carried destruction wherever they fell. Those who did rescue anything from the burning buildings, were obliged to defend it at the risk of their lives Expressmen and owners of every description of wagons, were extortionate in their demands, asking from twenty to fifty dollars for conveying a small load a few blocks. Even then there was no surety that the goods would reach their place of destination, as they were often followed by howling crowds, who would snatch the goods from the wagons. Sometimes, thieves got possession of vehicles, and drove off with rich loads of dry goods, jewelry, or merchandise, to out-of-the-way places. A mere tithe of the immense treasures piled up in these palatial warehouses was saved.

Character of the Buildings.

Many of the buildings destroyed were models of their kind. Among these was the *Tribune* office, which was probably one of the most complete and elegant newspaper establishments in the world. It was a four-story stone structure, and having nothing but brick division walls, and corrugated iron ceilings, was supposed to be fire proof. It was completed in April, 1869, at a cost of about $225,000, and its contents, including furniture, two of Hoe's eight-cylinder presses, boiler and engine, several folding machines, and a complete assortment of miscellaneous machinery, tools and apparatus necessary to carry on a great paper at $100,000 more. As we have already stated, it stood the ordeal bravely, hour after hour, until McVicker's Theatre took fire, penetrating its interior with a terrible volume of flame, which speedily consumed all the wood work and badly cracked and twisted the walls. Its honesty and strength of construction, however, assured the safety of every safe within its walls and partially saved its great presses in the basement.

The Crosby Opera House, had been closed during the summer and fall for renovation. Its proprietor had expended $80,000 upon it in ornamentation, upholstery and frescoing. It was to have been reopened to the public on Monday evening, the night after the fire, by the Theodore Thomas orchestral troupe, and on Sunday evening, only an hour or two before the fire, it was lit up for the first time, that its effects might be seen by gaslight. It was a gorgeous auditorium and fairly dazzling to the eye, and its frescoes were exquisitely beautiful. The carpet and upholstery were made expressly for it in France, and the bronzes imported for it alone cost $5000. Its illumination a few hours later was more brilliant and gorgeous, but alas in a few brief minutes the labor of years had gone. In addition to the auditorium proper, there was connected with the house a cozy little music hall, capable of seating about 1500 people, an art gallery from which most of the paintings, including Bierstadt's great picture of the Yo Semite Valley, and Dieffenback's "Christmas Tree," were saved; several artist's studios which were involved in common ruin, the art rooms of Mr. Moore, a well known connoisseur, filled with pictures, and one of the most valuable art libraries in the United States; the Opera House Restaurant, and the three great music houses of Roof & Cady, Bauer & Co., and J. W. Kimball. Mr. Crosby at one time had contemplated devoting the entire house to business purposes, as being more profitable than art, but under the advice of friends, changed his intentions, and then set himself about the work of making it the handsomest temple of music in the country. He had succeeded in it, and was just about to throw wide open its doors to the public when the fire came; and on the night when its beauty was to be admired, and its dazzling auditorium ring with plaudits, it was a heap of smouldering ruins, broken stones, jagged walls and twisted iron.

McVicker's Theatre was probably one of the coziest as well as handsomest dramatic establishments in the country. Like the Opera House it had been closed for the summer and entirely remodelled and refitted throughout at heavy expense. It had been open but a few weeks, when the fire occurred, and was already beginning to repay the management for the large sums expended, when the fire came and swept it away. Wood's Museum, on Randolph street, had a wide-spread reputation, for in addition to the theatre proper, it also contained the largest department of curiosities in the West, embracing a superb ornithological and entomological cabinet, choice specimens of minerals, a considerable number of paintings, and many live animals, all of whom perished. The museum was originally established by Col. J. H. Wood, who, after bringing it to a remarkable pitch of success, retired, leaving its control in the hands of Mr. Frank Aiken, the theatrical manager. Its success, however, falling off considerably, Mr. Aiken had retired from it to take the management of Hooley's new Opera House, on Clark street, and early in the fall, Col. Wood resumed possession. He had just reorganized the curiosity department, and opened the museum with an entirely new company, when the fire closed its doors forever. Hooley's Opera House, owned by the well known Brooklyn manager, was also one of the pleasantest little theatres imaginable. The building was originally known as Bryan Hall, and for many years had been used for concert purposes, and was the scene of some of the sanitary fairs during the war. When Mr. Hooley pu chased the property, he remodelled the entire interior, changing it into a theatre, and like all the others, he had just opened it with a new company, and was in the full tide of success. The Dearborn Theatre, on Dearborn street was the home of burnt-cork minstrelsy, and had no rival in the United States. Indeed, no other company in this country ever enjoyed the advantage of performing in an elegant and thoroughly appointed theatre.

Farwell Hall was the home of the Young Men's Christian Association. It was a spacious and elegant auditorium, and probably one of the largest in the country, as it was capable of comfortably seating 3,500 people. Its ornamentations and frescos were of the most elaborate kind, and a large and handsome organ had just been placed upon the stage. Metropolitan Hall, on Randolph street, was one of the oldest in the city. Sixteen years ago, Adelina Patti, then a mere child, had sung in it, and for many years it was intimately associated with the musical progress of Chicago. For some time prior to its burning, the hall and other rooms in the building had been leased by the Young Men's Library Association, and its destruction involved the loss of their library, which numbered about 20,000 miscellaneous volumes, including a complete set of the British patent office reports, the only set in the country.

The loss of the Academy of Design involved a terrible blow to art. The gallery had in it about three hundred paintings by home and foreign artists. Some of the larger ones, including Rothermel's great historical painting of the Battle of Gettysburg, were saved, but the most of them were lost. Nearly all the prominent artists in the city made the Academy their home, and they consequently suffered heavily in the destruction of their studios. In the art school connected with the Academy was a large and valuable collection of casts of the most celebrated antiques, which had been presented to the Academy by Hon. J. Young Scammon, all of which were lost.

The building occupied by the Academy of Sciences was supposed to be fire proof, but it was utterly destroyed, together with the following valuable cabinets :—

"1. The Audubon Club collection, consisting of 400 finely-mounted specimens of game birds and mammals.

"2. The State collection of insects, recently purchased, of great scientific value for the number of types it contained.

"3. Cabinet of marine shells, purchased of William Cooper, the most complete in the country.

"4. The Florida collection, made by Mr. E. W. Blatchford and the Secretary in two winters, containing a full illustration of the zoology of Florida.

"5. The cabinet of minerals recently purchased by subscription of the estate of Col. G. W. Hughes.

"6. Splendid series of specimens illustrative of the natural history of Alaska.

"7. The Smithsonian collection of crustacea, undoubtedly the largest in the world, which filled over 10,000 jars, and contained types of all species described by Prof. Dana and other American authors, and hundreds of others, described only in manuscripts lost in the fire.

"8. The invertebrates of the United States, North Pacific, the majority undescribed except in manuscripts destroyed.

"9. Collection of Marine shells of the coast of the United States, made in twenty years' dredgings from Maine to Texas.

"10. Herbarium of the late Dr. F. Scammon, consisting of 6,000 species of plants, with numerous duplicates.

"11. The Scammon collection of ancient Central American pottery, and other implements, collected by Dr. Van Peston.

"12. The Arctic collection of the late Robert Kennicott from 1859 to 1861; one of the most important features of the museum.

"The general collection contained 2,000 mammals, 30 mounted skeletons, including 2 mastadons, 10,000 birds 1,000 nests and eggs, 5,000 fishes, 10,000 species of insects with other specimens in proportion.

"The library contained about 2,000 volumes, chiefly the publications of other societies. At the time of the fire the academy was in communication with 15 American, and 100 European institutions. The manuscript department was also valuable."

Of the general character of the business structures destroyed, it is only necessary to say that they were of the most solid and massive description, and many of them exceedingly beautiful in an architectural point of view. The entire portion of the South Division which was consumed was almost exclusively built of stone and brick, but even these substantial structures offered no apparent resistance to the terrific fury of the fire. Indeed the destruction of many of the heaviest stone buildings was much more rapid than that of wooden buildings, as they had become so thoroughly heated that the moment the flames seized upon and swept through them, they melted away and disappeared. The intensity and ferocity of the fire has never had a parallel. It twisted iron into all manner of fanciful shapes. In crockery stores, it fused glass and china together in beautiful forms, and many sight-seers, after the ruins of such stores had cooled, carried away as relics, great masses of glass, china, mortar, brick and earthen ware, cemented together in the most incongruous manner. In some streets it burned the blocks of the Nicholson pavement to the earth beneath them. It twisted many of the rails of the street railroads into perfect U's, which stood inverted on the pavement. In such seething masses of flames, chasing after each other for twelve hours like billows along a beach, the very Pyramids would have yielded had they received the full force of the fire. In the entire burned portion of the South Division but two buildings were uninjured. One was an unfinished stone structure at the corner of La Salle and Monroe streets. There was no wood work in the building at all, the walls being of stone and the partitions and floors of brick. The buildings adjoining it were small wooden structures, while those opposite to it, though of stone, were very shallow, being only about twenty feet in depth and fell almost immediately. The second was the Lind block, which was comparatively isolated.

Of the detail of losses in this division it is impossible to speak with any accuracy. It was the very heart of Chicago and it contained the larger part of the treasures of the city. In its destruction, every newspaper office in the city, both daily and weekly, every public library, every place of amusement, every bank but one, every first-class hotel with one or two exceptions, the two great depots of the city, every insurance office, seven churches, every public building of any size, the gas works, the post office the custom house, the marine hospital, several Roman Catholic charitable institutions, the city hall, the chamber of commerce, every art gallery, the telegraph offices, nearly every lawyer's and physican's office, all the best restaurants in the city, two thriving commercial colleges, thousands of business offices, and all the great warehouses of wholesale business, piled to their utmost capacity with goods laid in for the fall trade, were involved in common ruin. The wreck was as complete as the wreck of Pompeii and Herculaneum.

The Feeling of the People.

And yet in the face of this universal and crushing disaster, when it seemed as if both banks and insurance offices were so crippled that utter bankruptcy and financial ruin must ensue, the faith and undaunted courage of the men who had built Chicago never faltered. While yet the fires were blazing all about them, there was but one expression of opinion and that was that the Garden City must be the Phœnix City. On the very next morning after the disaster, scarcely a pile of bricks that marked where a building had stood, but bore a rudely extemporized sign that Messrs. So and So had removed to No. ——, and would continue their business as heretofore. The newspapers were the first to resume business. On the second day of the fire, the *Tribune*, *Post*, and *Journal* appeared as usual, the others following as rapidly as they could reorganize. The following editorial which appeared in the *Tribune* in its first issue, reflected the universal sentiment of the people:

"CHEER UP.

"In the midst of a calamity, without parallel in the world's history, looking upon the ashes of thirty years' accumulations, the people of this once beautiful city have resolved that,

"CHICAGO SHALL RISE AGAIN.

"With woe on every hand, with death in many strange places, with 2 or 300,000,000 of our hard-earned property swept away in a few hours, the hearts of our men and women are still brave, and they look into the future with undaunted courage. As there has never been such a calamity, so has there never been such cheerful fortitude in the face of desolation and ruin.

Thanks to the blessed charity of the good people of the United States, we shall not suffer from hunger or nakedness in this trying time. Hundreds of train loads of provisions are coming forward to us with all speed from every quarter, from Maine to Omaha. Some have already arrived, more will reach us before these words are printed. Three-fourths of our inhabited area is still saved. The water supply will be speedily renewed. Steam fire engines from a dozen neighboring cities, have already arrived, and more are on their way. It seems impossible that any further progress should be made by the flames, or that any new fire should break out that would not be instantly extinguished.

"Already contracts have been made for rebuilding some of the burned blocks, and the clearing away of the debris will begin to day, if the heat is so far subdued that the charred material can be handled. Field, Leiter & Co., and John V. Farwell & Co., will recommence business to-day. The money and securities in the banks are safe. The railroads are working with all their energies to bring us out of our affliction. The 300,000,000 of capital invested in these roads is bound to see us through. They have been built with special reference to a great commercial mart at this place and they cannot fail to sustain us. *Chicago must rise again.*

"We do not belittle the calamity that has befallen us. The world has probably never seen the like of it—certainly not since Moscow was burned. But the forces of nature, no less than the forces of reason, require that the exchanges of a great region should be conducted here. Ten, twenty years may be required to reconstruct our fair city, but the capital to rebuild it fire proof will be forthcoming. The losses we have suffered must be borne; but the place, the time and the men are here, to commence at the bottom and work up again, not at the bottom neither, for we have credit in every land and the experience of one upbuilding of Chicago to help us. Let us all cheer up, save what is left yet, and we shall come out right. The Christian world is coming to our relief. The worst is already over. In a few days more all the dangers will be past and we can resume the battle of life with Christian faith and Western grit. Let us all cheer up!"

This was the first public announcement by the press, and it had the ring of the true metal in it.

As, a matter of public record, we append the first proclamation of the Mayor of the city:

"WHEREAS, In the providence of God, to whose will we humbly submit, a terrible calamity has befallen our city, which demands of us our best efforts for the preservation of order and the relief of the suffering:

"BE IT KNOWN, That the faith and credit of the City of Chicago is hereby pledged for the necessary expenses for the relief of the suffering. Public order will be preserved. The police and special police now being appointed will be responsible for the maintenance of the peace and the protection of property.

"All officers and men of the Fire Department and Health Department will act as special policemen without further notice. The Mayor and Comptroller will give vouchers for all supplies furnished by the different relief committees. The head-quarters of the city government will be at the Congregational Church, corner of Ann and West Washington streets. All persons are warned against any acts tending to endanger property. All persons caught in any depredations will be immediately arrested.

"With the help of God, order and peace and private property shall be preserved. The city government and committees of citizens pledge themselves to the community to protect them and prepare the way for a restoration of public and private welfare.

"It is believed the fire has spent its force and all will soon be well.

R. B. MASON, Mayor."

The Fire in the North Division.

At twelve o'clock the fire crossed the south branch of the river, and entered the South Division at Adams and Franklin streets. Taking a due course to the northeast, it found the Court House and Sherman House in its path. Precisely at twenty minutes past two o'clock, the roof of the centre building of the Court House fell in, and before that event, and about the time that the Sherman House was ablaze, the fire, carried by the wind, had fallen upon the north side, and broke out just north of the bridge, at State street. North of the bridge was a long viaduct of wood, erected on trestle work. West of this roadway, and near the river, was a long, low building, used as a freight depot by the Northwestern (Galena branch) Railway. To the east was Wright's large livery stable, both buildings of brick, but of shingle or flat roofs. Farther to the east was the Galena elevator, also of wood. The buildings, all within the course of the fire, had been ignited by burning brands. To the west and further north of the freight depot, were rows of small frame buildings, used as cheap boarding houses, all made of wood. In the alleys, and in the rear of these buildings, were stables, all of wood, dry as tinder, and over all of which the intense heated wind had been blowing for hours, and upon which had been falling the blazing brands of the fire during its previous advance. Simultaneously, the fire blazed up in half a dozen places, within a distance from east to west of one hundred and fifty yards. No sooner had these been fairly under way, than the ever-growing fire from the southwest cast its brands still farther on in advance; and long before the fire in the South Division had levelled a path, or was visible in a burning house on the south line of the river, the fire on the north side had gone six or eight blocks through the frame buildings on the north side of the river. As the base of the fire on the south side of the river widened to the west, it crossed the river, to find inflammable materials, all prepared to continue it, and at each new crossing it formed a new line, which swept on with new fury. The work of destruction on the north side was rapid. Though the houses were not built so closely to one another, yet the proportion of them of wood was greater. There was no longer an attempt to stop its progress. It was its own director. In one hour after its first breaking out it swept onward in an unbroken sheet of flame, extending at its base from Rush street westward to Clark street, burning in a due line to the northwest. It rushed onward, sweeping everything before it. At half past three o'clock the great breweries near the water works were ablaze, and soon after, engineers and firemen in the water works building, opening the valves, were forced to abandon their posts to save their lives. The roof, which was of shingles, soon burned, the rafters fell in, the machinery was disabled, and Chicago was left without a drop of water. The fire, in the mean-

PALMER HOUSE, COR. STATE AND QUINCY STREETS.

time, had extended to the eastern point of the South Division, and had burned all on the north side of the river (Rathbone's stove warehouse excepted). On the east everything had been burned to the lake. The wave of fire which had swept the breweries and the water works, had expended itself a few rods farther in the lake. But new lines were advancing on the west flank. The advance of the fire was in the order known in military practice as echelon, with the right in the advance. As the most advanced reached its destination, the next to the left moved forward, and as fire was forever widening and forming new extensions to the left, it was soon obvious that it would leave nothing undestroyed.

Persons living north of Chicago avenue and west of Clark street, considered themselves as safe, because they were out of the line of the wind. But each half hour enlarged the sweep of the wind. When day dawned upon that awful morning, the fire had worked westward along the river to Wells street, destroying the large elevator, and the Galena Passenger Depot at that point. It rapidly swept all before it, each new line of fire going straight through to the northeast, until it struck the lake. Some fugitives from dwellings destroyed east of Clark street, about five o'clock, were kindly sheltered by a lady residing on Oak street, near La Salle, and she prepared a bountiful breakfast for them. By nine o'clock both guests and hostess were alike fleeing for their lives before the roaring, sweeping stream of fire which pursued them. Thus, all day, from morning until midnight of that dreadful day, did the fire rage in that doomed division of the city. Twenty-four hours after it started on Dekoven street, it was igniting fresh fires near the northern limits of the city, having in the meantime consumed all within its scope for a distance of four miles north, in an average belt, seven-eighths of a mile wide.

The north branch of the river shortly after leaving the main river, diverges to the west, and is locked in by the west division, no fire coming from the west, a few tenements near the river were saved, but as a general thing by 10 o'clock in the forenoon, the fire extended from the river on the west to the lake on the east, in a line running from the southwest to the northeast. In this form it continued to advance northwardly, until the west end reached Fullerton avenue, which it did not cross west of Orchard street. East of Orchard street it destroyed everything to the lake, and then during the night, having consumed all that there was to consume, it finished its work by destroying the dwelling of Dr. J. H. Foster. Except some indifferent shanties near the bridges, and some scattered dwellings in the northwest corner of the Sixteenth Ward, not a dwelling was left north of the river, except that of Mr. Ogden.

The principal buildings in this part of the city have been enumerated elsewhere. The width of territory swept in that division was nearly one mile by nearly three miles long. The once teeming place is as silent as the graveyard. To the east there are some fragments of churches and of walls, but these are exceptions,—the whole surface being, as a general thing, as level as the original prairie. The streets were for a large part paved and their grade raised. The few bricks left have fallen into the basements, the sidewalks have disappeared, leaving to the streets the appearance of embankments to permit passage through a marshy region, or like the pathways through the vats of an extensive tannery. Nothing was so desolate—not a sound to break the solitude, nor a building to change the wide-spread, blackened landscape. The north side was highly ornamented with trees, many of them of choice varieties, and of many years' growth. All these have been swept away,—not even a skeleton of them left. One peculiarity of the destruction is, that amid all the ruins there are no charred or half burned boards or timbers; not even in the streets is there anything wooden. The fire in its intense heat destroyed everything combustible, leaving nothing whatever to survive it. Even the floors in the basement of the largest buildings have been eaten up by the fire, leaving not a sign that such things existed.

The Flight of the People.

The residents of the North Division had all retired to sleep long before the fire had assumed any serious proportions. When it had crossed into the South Division from the west, and thus threatened the centre of the town, the incessant clanging of the bells, the gorgeous illumination, the intense heat and smoke, and the unfailing shower of brilliant sparks, fully aroused them. No one, however, stirred. The merchants and bankers crossed to their places of business to do what could be done; but when the court house fell, when the massive blocks of stone and brick opposed the progress of the fire no more successfully than so much straw, and when at last the blaze broke out in a half-dozen places north of the river, there was a preparation for flight. Those within the immediate range of the first advancing column of fire fled with such hastily gathered articles as they could to the lake shore. Those who were fortunate enough to own carriages, put their families and valuables in and drove off to the north. Wagons and teams were gathered and loaded, and furniture and families moved to Washington Park. This small park was at one time packed with furniture and people of every age, including many lifted from beds of sickness. In two hours the fire had got to the west far enough to include this park in its sweep, and then the flight was begun anew. This time all the property that had been rescued was left behind, so close upon them was the fire, and the weary men, women and children on foot took up their precipitate march further to the northward; occasionally they would stop to rest; occasionally some delicate woman would faint from exhaustion or anxiety; occasionally some child would fall to the ground, unable any longer to walk. But the fire followed close. The shower of sparks and blazing fragments never ceased to fall upon them. Time and again the clothes of the women and children would be on fire, and on they had to march, enveloped in a cloud of smoke and fire, and followed by the roar of blazing buildings and the terrible howling of the gale. Thus they were driven from block to block, and street to street, until daylight found them on the boulevard road along the lake shore, far beyond the city limits.

Those who fled directly to the eastward, to the lake beach, passed hardly a less pitiable night. Behind them was the fire, south of them the lumber yards on the beach and pier was ablaze. Hemmed in between pier and lumber yard, were many fugitives, men, women and children, of whom many are known to have perished, and it is feared the number is very great. Along the beach were judges, merchants, doctors, workingmen, women and children; among whom, as they lay on the sand, fell the rain of fire. The clothing of the women was repeatedly on fire, and bundles of rescued articles had to be thrown into the lake to extinguish them. The scorching heat, the falling fire, the horrible roar, the blinding smoke and cinders, the raging thirst, and the hot sand, were terrible to endure, and there these people remained until the next afternoon before they dared turn their faces towards the yet blazing but destroyed city behind them.

Farther to the westward, among the habitations

of the poor, the distress was even more terrible. Quickly dislodged, the flight was precipitate. Each family had its small corps of helpless children. Fathers and mothers struggled against the blinding, burning atmosphere, with their little ones, for safety. Here and there sidewalks would fall in, precipitating all upon them into the vaults beneath. It is assumed, that of necessity, many hundreds perished in this flight. Exhausted women, surrounded by their helpless children, would fall upon the street, the next moment to be shut out from mortal aid by the far-reaching, whirling flames. In every case, so high was the wind, the flames of a burning building extended across the street, consuming everything within their reach.

In a district embracing 75,000 people, there were necessarily many who were upon beds of sickness. These had to be rescued by their immediate friends, or perish, and too often, the only immediate friends were helpless children. The mind shudders to think of what happened to both sick and well. Until the day shall come when the ruins of these 20,000 habitations shall be critically examined, the number of those who thus perished—whole families—will never be known.

During that terrible night the wife of one of the State officers, he being in another part of the State, was in the pangs of labor, when necessity compelled her removal. In that perilous state she was conveyed to the house of a friend a mile north, and far beyond any supposed reach of the fire. She reached there with her babe born during the removal, but three hours later had again to be carried to another part of the city to escape the fire which had followed her. This was but one of many cases equally distressing, though not all so fortunate. Other women in the same condition were removed, who did not survive the fright. There were numerous cases of ladies who trying to escape on foot, were overtaken by the pangs of maternity, and upon the street, or in front yards, or on doorsteps, became mothers. Thus hastily forced by the ever pursuing fire, they fled they knew not whither, away from the roaring, fiendish storm of fire. Some who had escaped into the West Division found shelter in human habitations, and comparative comfort. But throughout the city, in every large group of fugitives, there were painful incidents of the effects of the terror produced by the flight for life.

An ex-member of Congress, fled with his family out on the north pier. The fire followed him, burning the pier and enveloping him in its dense smoke, and burning them with its terrible heat. He remained until the next afternoon, when there was nothing before him but the lake and the skeleton frame of the light house, and the fire fifty feet in his rear, when hailing a tug boat he got on board with his family, and running the risk of destruction, steamed up the river between two sheets of fire, and landed on the west side of the north branch. It was a desperate venture, but rendered necessary to avoid the death which was fast approaching him.

To comprehend the horrors of that flight let the reader imagine a population of 76,000 men, women and children, suddenly driven from their homes, hemmed in by a roaring blaze on each side, with a far reaching fire impelled by a furious gale in the rear; let him imagine these people forcing along in a few streets, trying to keep families together, enveloped in clouds of smoke, and covered at every step with blazing cinders; the horrors of the exodus made more terrible by the wild foray of horses and cattle, terrified by the fire, madly running hither and thither, kicking and trampling, often in herds of a dozen, aimlessly trying to escape and instinctively following or plunging through the human procession.

This terrible flight of 76,000 people during that night and morning, pursued by the relentless fire, and often headed off in their march by a building fired by a brand from the fire behind. There was no shelter, no refuge, no escape, but to push on through the narrow streets to the north. The few bridges to the northwest were thronged, but soon became gorged with broken vehicles, and it was almost death to attempt to pass them. Time, in fact, did not permit their use; the fire was in the rear, roaring, and sending forward its incessant discharge of blazing brands, shingles, and fragments of timbers. Occasionally, above the roar and din, above the shrieks and shouts of the moving mass, above the wild neighing and snorting of the frenzied horses and cattle, would be heard the explosions of drug stores, distilleries, warehouses, and the fall of stone walls. Then would come the shower of fiery projectiles, the horrors of which were often aggravated by the pitiable sight of dismembered portions of human bodies, the victims of explosions. Any one who has witnessed the passage of an army of 75,000 men, moving through the streets in perfect order, discipline, and with the surroundings of a gala show, can get a faint picture of this terrible flight of the inhabitants of the North Division, by substituting for this army of disciplined soldiery, the same number of terrified men, women and children, most of them half clothed, bearing their sick, their dying, their aged, and their helpless, with the sidewalks on fire, the buildings in a blaze in every direction, the horrible roar behind, the stifling smoke and cinders, and all this fearful procession hastening forward as best it could—going no one knew where. When one fell it was almost certain death. The ever surging crowd could not stop to pick up the exhausted or the feeble, but over the fallen bodies rushed on—on, away from the monster that was pursuing them. How many thus perished will never be known; but the next day, when the fire was out, and the scattered families called their rolls, over two thousand children were missing, the most of whom were of an age as to exclude all hope of their safety by their unaided exertions. The horrors of that flight were greatly increased by the fact that men and women could not understand that the fire was irresistible, and delayed their departure until the flames actually drove them forth. Many sought to carry valuables and clothing, but these impediments to rapid movement were soon abandoned, though in many cases they were held too long,—so checking flight, that the blaze which often encircled a block of buildings, crossing the street ahead of the fugitives, and thus destroyed all escape.

One wealthy citizen occupied a costly mansion erected in the very centre of a block. The square was thickly planted with trees and shrubbery, and a large portion devoted to conservatories; the whole enclosed with a board fence ten feet high. Time was wasted in packing valuables, and when the family and servants came out from the building, they found the whole fence in flames, the sidewalks on all four sides ablaze, and the trees already burning. Thus imprisoned within a very wall of fire, with the building, stables, and conservatories all on fire, they rushed wildly about, with no visible means of escape. Rescue from without was impossible. While thus reduced to despair, while thus environed by a circuit of fire, and the trees over their heads in flames, a section of the wooden fence fell down, but still blazing; beyond it was the wooden sidewalk, eight feet wide, also on fire. It was a desperate chance. The old and the young made a speedy rush, bounded over the fallen blazing fence, jumped upon and over the burning sidewalks and thus reached the street, on each side of which there was an equal fire. Rushing with the speed of desperation, men and women reached a few blocks north, when were they compelled to halt to extinguish the burning garments of the women. This was accomplished with great difficulty, and with great injury to all. The flight was continued, and for twenty-four hours these people wandered on the distant prairie, unable to return to the city.

The Intense Heat.

The most striking peculiarity of the fire was its intense, devouring heat. Nothing exposed to it escaped. Amid the hundreds of acres left bare, there is not to be found a piece of wood of any description, and unlike most fires, it left nothing half burned. The innermost timbers, floorings, doors, window sills, were all reached and wholly consumed. From the wreck of the many thousand buildings, there is not a vestige of timber or charred wood. The excavators turn up brick, stone, glass, iron, silver, gold, bronze, brass and all other remnants of merchandise, household goods and building materials, but not a particle of wood. The combustion was complete. The fire swept the streets of all the ordinary dust and rubbish, consuming it instantly. Nothing was left but the incombustible. In repeated instances the popular building stone, the Athens marble, a free limestone, which when first uncovered in the quarry is soft, but rapidly hardens, and which was universally used in the city, when broken and falling upon the bed of burning coal, was of itself on fire—burning as does the ordinary stone in the lime kilns.

But this does not account for the intense heat. Various theories are stated. One is that the blazing fire evolved a gas which was carried on before by the wind; that it penetrated and filled all the buildings on the line; that the blazing brands reaching these buildings, being fanned into flame as soon as they touched the roofs or windows, communicated instantaneously with the gas, producing a fire of the greatest heat, and general in all parts of the building. It is argued that as the gas escaping from an ordinary furnace, if economized and again subjected to flame, produces a heat far in excess of that proceeding from the fuel in its original form, so this gas, escaping unconsumed from the fire, when again brought in contact with flame in large bodies and in comparatively confined rooms, produces not only instantaneous combustion, but intense heat.

Whatever may be the true theory as to the cause of the extraordinary heat, the fact is evidenced by countless examples of its destructive power. It made little or no difference what the material was of which the building was built, whether of brick, or stone. The effect on all was alike — marble structure perishing with hardly less speed than that of the frame shed. The First National Bank was supposed to be fire proof. It was situated on the northeast corner of a block, with north and east fronts. On the south it was flanked by a row of marble front brick buildings, and the same on the west. It had no party walls. It was built after the other buildings, with independent walls, on the south and west; it was protected from the fire and wind by its own walls and those of the adjoining buildings. In front was a street one hundred feet wide. The only result of this double protection was that its walls are standing, but the intense heat, borne by the eddies of the wind, entered the building on the fronts not exposed to the wind; the furniture and window casings were burned, and so great was the heat coming from without, that the monster iron girders expanded upward, breaking the iron ceilings, crashing the exterior walls, and leaving the building a wreck and a ruin. Precisely the same effect was produced in the *Tribune* building, also fire proof. The furniture in the building, if all collected and fired, would not have produced heat enough to seriously damage the room in which it was burned; but the intense heat borne into the building seemed to so feed the blaze of the burning tables, chairs and desks, that the iron girders and ceilings expanded upward and downward to such a degree that they tore down, shattered, or forced outward into the streets, walls that it was supposed nothing short of an explosion of the first magnitude could disturb.

The intensity of the heat may be judged, and the thorough combustion of everything wooden may be understood, when we state that in the yard of one of the large agricultural implement factories, was stacked some hundreds of tons of pig iron. This iron was two hundred feet from any building. To the south of it was the river, one hundred and fifty feet wide. No large building but the factory was in the immediate vicinity of the fire. Yet, so great was the heat, that this pile of iron melted and run, and is now in one large and nearly solid mass.

The effect of the heat is also shown in the cases of the large anchors and cables at the warehouses. These cables of every size were kept upon the sidewalks in huge coils. Since the fire they present a most curious appearance, the coils having melted each into a solid mass, just preserving enough of its original form to show what it had been. Perhaps no city of the country used more of the useful articles known as hand trucks, than this city. They are made of hard wood shafts, fitted into strong iron frames, and every store in this city had its full supply of them in use. They were actively in use during the night in the removal of goods from the stores to the wagons, and were abandoned, many of them on the sidewalks, and thousands of them have been found in the ruins. They are remarkable looking skeletons. The two small iron wheels, the bands, and all the iron work, are perfect, but not a sight of the wood work. A gentleman escaping from one of the hotels with his wife, obtained one of these trucks, and placing on it two trunks hastened to that part of the lake shore occupied by the base ball enclosure. This enclosure was merely a high fence with wooden benches at one end for spectators. He had been there but a few minutes when he was certain the fire would reach him, so hastily digging a hole, he put the trunks in it, covered them with earth and left the trucks exposed. This was in the middle of the base ball diamond, remote from the fence and the seats. When he returned next day, the wooden work of the truck, which could not have come in contact with any fire, was consumed. The intense heat, acting on the iron had fired the wooden parts, and they were burned.

There can be no question that the intense heat was the result of the gale. The fire once under way, the gale gave to it the intensity given to flame by the blow pipe. The heat itself thus generated would have produced an extensive conflagration, had there been no burning faggots. These latter, lodging on cornices, roofs, in crevices on wooden sidewalks, in yards, on wood piles, were kept alive by the wind, forced into flame, and spread the fire with rapid speed. Hundreds of persons, who rushed from their residences in the North Division to look after their stores and warehouses in the South Division, on their return found their dwellings in flames and their families fugitives.

The fire left but little of architectural adornment. The marble mantels were not only broken, but consumed. A gentleman visiting the *Tribune* building after the fire, after climbing over broken walls, and shaking iron stairs to an upper room, discovered one of the carved shields which had ornamented one of the marble mantels. Hastily seizing it, intending to preserve it as a memento, it crumbled in his fingers as so much lime. It had preserved its shape, but the substance had been consumed by the furnace heat. The power of the blow pipe in producing heat from flame, is well understood, and the most rational explanation of the astonishing heat of this fire is that the gale operated on the flame as does the blow pipe, and before that concentrated heat everything combustible was consumed, and all else, melted and destroyed.

Losses and Insurance.

It is impossible, even at this late date, to give the details of losses. A close estimate, however, fixes the loss at about $200,000,000, divided substantially as follows:

	Losses.
City Corporation,	$5,000,000
Churches,	3,000,000
Dry Goods,	10,000,000
Clothing,	5,000,000
Hardware,	4,000,000
Boots and Shoes,	2,000,000
Groceries,	10,000,000
Drugs,	8,000,000
Jewelry,	2,000,000
Elevators and contents,	3,000,000
Hats and Caps,	2,000,000
Shipping,	750,000
Railroad Corporations,	1,000,000
Dwellings,	30,000,000
Stores and Business Blocks,	80,000,000
Offices,	1,000,000
Opera Houses, and Theatres,	2,000,000
Libraries, paintings and miscellaneous,	31,250,000
Total,	$200,000,000

TRIBUNE BUILDING.

UNITY (MR. COLLYER'S) AND NEW ENGLAND CHURCHES.

Products.

The principal losses of products were as follows:

Wheat,	628,900 bush.
Corn,	394,500 "
Oats,	234,900 "
Rye,	115,000 "
Barley,	260,000 "
Total of grain,	1,634,300 bush.

Pork,	6,000 bbls.
Lard,	4,000 tierces.
Cut meat,	1,500,000 lbs.
Broomcorn,	2,400 tons.
Lumber,	50,000,000 ft.
Coal,	80,000 tons.

Churches.

The following is a list of the principal churches destroyed, with their estimated value:

South Side.

First Presbyterian,	$200,000
Universalist,	100,000
Trinity, (Episcopal,)	150,000
Swedenborgian,	75,000

St. Mary's Church and Mission, (Catholic,)	$250,000
Second Presbyterian, ...	60,000
First Methodist Episcopal, ...	400,000
Other smaller churches, ...	250,000
Farwell Hall, ...	400,000

North Side.

North Church, (Presbyterian,)	$75,000
Westminster, (Presbyterian,)	75,000
M. E. Grace Church, ...	150,000
Moody's Mission, ...	125,000
St. James, (Episcopal,)	150,000
Two Catholic churches with nunneries, .	300,000
New England Church, ...	150,000
Robert Collyer's Unitarian Church, . .	100,000

Nearly seventy-five churches, mission schools, etc., were destroyed. The New England church, one of the most elaborate structures in the city, was laid in ruins, as was the home of *every* member of the church. The First and Second Presbyterian churches, the First Universalist, Trinity Episcopal and the New Jerusalem churches were among the ruins. The Roman Catholics suffered greatly, losing as many as seven churches, six convents, eight schools and two hospitals.

Insurance.

It is still more difficult to ascertain the insurance losses, but the following list is sufficiently accurate as a general statement up to the time of writing:

Maine,	$22,500
Boston, Mass.,	3,252,500
Worcester, Mass.,	307,500
Springfield, Mass.,	450,000
Providence, R. I.,	1,985,000
Hartford,	8,500,000
Connecticut,	735,000
New York City,	13,476,500
Brooklyn,	935,000
Buffalo,	1,730,000
Albany,	1,200,000
Philadelphia,	1,590,000
Pittsburgh,	136,500
Pennsylvania,	870,000
Baltimore,	309,000
Cincinnati,	1,241,800
Cleveland,	1,948,000
Columbus,	330,000
Toledo,	10,000
Michigan,	165,000
Chicago,	25,000,000
Illinois,	1,000,000
Wisconsin,	245,000
St. Louis,	462,500
San Francisco,	3,100,000
Foreign,	5,798,000
Miscellaneous,	187,000
Total,	$74,986,800

An approximate statement of losses, as furnished by companies, exhibits the effect produced upon the business by the sudden and overwhelming disaster. Superintendent Miller, under date of November 11th, 1871, gives the particulars relating to the

New York Companies.

The following New York companies have ceased to do business, and gone into liquidation. The gross assets of each, as stated in the annual report of December 21st last, is given in the absence of any present report:

	Gross assets. Jan. 1, 1871.
Ætna,	$442,709
Astor,	405,571
Atlantic,	548,194
Beekman,	261,851
Excelsior,	335,724
Fulton,	359,227
Irving,	321,745
Lamar,	548,402
Lorillard,	1,715,909
Manhattan,	1,407,788
Market,	704,684
North America,	770,305
Security,	1,860,333
Washington,	774,411
Albany City,	397,646
Capital,	293,766
Buffalo City,	370,934
Buffalo Fire Insurance,	473,577
Western,	580,547
Yonkers, N. Y.,	868,933

The following companies sustaining losses are continuing in business.

	Gross assets.	Total losses by Chicago fire.
Adriatic, ...	$261,500	$8,500
American, ...	1,013,393	30,000
American Exchange, . .	280,887	58,000
Buffalo, German, ...	308,716	5,000
Citizens, ...	722,068	35,000
Columbia, ...	468,595	3,400
Commerce, (Albany,) . .	762,000	450,000
Commerce Fire, (N. Y.,) .	253,865	26,000
Commercial, ...	317,451	5,000
Continental, ...	2,847,307	1,400,000
Corn Exchange, ...	359,880	61,000
Exchange, ...	207,374	2,500
Firemen's Fund, ...	182,030	32,500
Firemen's Trust, ...	241,700	5,000
Germania, ...	1,135,332	226,500
Glen's Falls, ...	554,962	13,000
Greenwich, ...	472,070	10,000
Guardian, ...	286,984	45,000
Hanover, ...	750,000	250,000
Hoffman, ...	217,460	30,000
Home, ...	4,813,561	2,139,213
Howard, ...	894,360	473,110
Humboldt, ...	362,786	24,000
Importers' and Traders', .	308,189	22,500
International, ...	1,466,726	546,911
Jefferson, ...	447,391	42,500
Kings County, ...	292,562	31,000
Lafayette, ...	224,643	7,500
Lenox, ...	247,800	32,000
Mechanics', ...	236,356	22,500
Mechanics' and Traders', .	518,062	37,000
Mercantile, ...	292,335	112,000
Merchants', ...	463,864	10,000

	Gross assets.	Total losses by Chicago fire.
National, ...	$300,000	$37,500
New York, ...	389,904	15,000
Niagara, ...	1,321,420	225,000
Pacific, ...	451,405	12,500
Phœnix, ...	1,870,076	350,000
Relief, ...	323,125	40,000
Republic, ...	682,382	208,140
Resolute, ...	254,024	109,927
Sterling, ...	266,581	7,500
Williamsburgh City, . .	531,364	60,000

Other Suspensions.

The following Rhode Island companies have suspended:

	Assets, Jan. 1.	Losses.
American, ...	$374,964	$400,000
Atlantic, ...	326,614	300,000
Hope, ...	211,673	150,000
Providence Washington, .	415,150	550,000
Roger Williams, ...	278,966	100,000

The following Connecticut companies have suspended:

	Assets, Jan. 1.	Losses.
Charter Oak, ...	$251,951	$200,000
Connecticut, ...	400,000	200,000
Merchants, ...	540,096	
North American, ...	456,503	
Putnam, ...	785,783	
Norwich, ...	381,730	350,000

The following Massachusetts companies have suspended:

	Gross Assets, Jan. 1.	Losses.
Hide and Leather, . . .	$419,211	$800,000
Independent, ...	646,050	900,000
New England Mutual, .	1,080,970	700,000

The following Ohio companies have suspended:

	Losses.
Alemania of Cleveland, ...	$500,000
Cleveland, ...	400,000
Sun, ...	100,000

Fourteen Chicago companies were completely prostrated. Their entire assests being swept away, and not amounting to over 10 per cent. of their losses.

Aggregate Losses.

249 American companies, and 6 English doing fire insurance business in the United States, suffered loss. The aggregate loss was as follows:

249 American companies, ...	$82,821,122
6 English companies, ...	5,813,000
Total loss of Insurance Cos., .	$88,634,122

The aggregate assets of these companies are:

American companies, ...	$74,930,216
English companies, ...	71,949,305
Total capital, ...	$145,879,521

The total loss falling upon only a portion of the companies, and upon others only in small sums, has crushed out the losing companies, leaving the insured sufferers to perhaps $50,000,000, on their insured property alone.

The Destruction of City Property.

The following is an estimate of the losses of City Property by the fire, made by the Board of Public Works:

City Hall, including furniture, . . .	$470,000
Water works engines, ...	15,000
Water works buildings and tools, . .	20,000
Rush street bridge, ...	15,000
State street bridge, ...	15,000
Clark street bridge, ...	13,800
Wells street bridge, ...	15,000
Chicago avenue bridge, ...	26,700
Adams street bridge, ...	37,800
Van Buren street bridge, ...	13,470
Polk street bridge, ...	29,450
Washington street tunnel, ...	2,000
La Salle street tunnel, ...	1,800
Lamp posts, ...	25,000
Fire hydrants, ...	15,000
Street pavements, ...	250,000
Sidewalks and crossings, ...	70,000
Reservoirs, ...	15,000
Docks, ...	10,000
Sewers, ...	10,000
Water service, ...	15,000
Total, ...	$1,085,080

Sidewalks Destroyed.

The extent and value of the sidewalks destroyed by the fire has been officially computed. The whole length of sidewalks laid on the 8th of Octo-ober was 680 miles, of which $121\frac{3}{4}$ miles were destroyed. The details of the destroyed work are thus stated:

	Lin. feet.	Cost.
North Division, stone and flag sidewalks, ...	10,194	$58,215
South Division, stone and flag sidewalks, ...	33,050	479,164
Plank sidewalks, ...	599,597	404,000
Total, ...	642,841	$941,379

The Burned Churches.

Within the past ten years Chicago has won an enviable reputation for the number and beauty of her churches. The various denominations have vied with each other in building superb church structures, which have long been the admiration of strangers for their architectural beauty and admirable adaptation to purposes of worship. The fire made no distinction in its destruction. Almost every denomination suffered to a large extent.

The Protestant Episcopal.

The Episcopal denomination lost St. James Church, one of the most elegant in the city, loss $250,000, on which there was a moderate insurance, most of which is available; Trinity Church, loss $110,000, on which there was $40,000 insurance, about half of which is available; the Church of the Ascension, loss $15,000, without insurance; and St. Ansgarius (Swedish), loss $11,000, the insurance upon which is not secure.

Presbyterian.

The Presbyterians lost three churches; the First Church, loss $80,000, with its two mission school buildings, one attached to the church, and the other on La Salle street, both valued at $47,000; the Second Church, not occupied at the time of the fire, the congregation having temporarily united with the Olivet Church, until their new building should be erected, loss $55,000; and the North Presbyterian, loss $65,000, and its mission school, $8,000.

Congregational.

The Congregationalists lost their beautiful New England Church and a small mission school. Total loss $106,500.

Baptist.

The Baptists lost property as follows:

North Church and furniture, ...	$15,000
North Star Church and furniture, . .	20,000
Swedish Church and furniture, ...	7,000
Lincoln Park Association Building, . .	1,000
Publication Society, ...	10,000
Standard stock, ...	25,000

In addition to the above there were other indirect losses in this denomination, which will swell the amount to $200,000.

Methodist.

The Methodist losses were as follows:

Grace Church, one of the most beautiful in the city, loss $100,000.

The First Methodist Church and Block, loss $100,000.

The Wabash avenue Methodist, damaged to the amount of $35,000.

The Scandinavian Methodist, $7,000.

The German Methodist, $7,500.

The African Methodist, $8,000.

The Garrett Biblical Institute property, $90,000.

Unitarian.

Unity Church, over which Rev. Robert Collyer presided, was the only Unitarian Church burned in the city; loss $225,000.

Roman Catholic.

The Roman Catholic denomination suffered more severely than any other. The detailed statement of the losses is as follows.

Church of the Holy Name, 196 by 75 feet in dimensions, costing $275,000; and residence attached, valued at $5,000.

St. Mary's Church, at the corner of Madison street and Wabash avenue, 110 by 50 feet, costing $40,000.

Church of the Immaculate Conception, 110 by 50 feet, with residence, $25,000.

St. Michael's Church, 200 by 80 feet, costing $200,000.

St. Joseph's Church, 130 by 55 feet, $100,000.

St. Louis' Church, 110 by 40 feet, $10,000.

St. Paul's Church, 100 by 40 feet, valued at $15,000, with a $3,000 residence.

The following schools, convents and hospitals were also destroyed:

Christian Brothers' Academy, on Van Buren street, near Fourth avenue, cost $80,000.

St. Francis Xavier's Academy of the Sisters of Mercy, with House of Providence, $120,000.

Holy Name Parish Schools—for girls, $15,000; for boys, $8,000.

Immaculate Conception Parish School, $10,000.

St. Louis' Parish School, $5,000.

St. Paul's Parish School, $5,000.

Redemptionist Convent, $20,000, with parish school for accommodating 1,200 children.

Benedictine Convent, $20,000, with schools costing $11,000.

Alexian Brothers' Hospital, $40,000.

Orphan Asylum, $30,000.

House of the Good Shepherd, $80,000.

House of Providence, under Sisters of Charity, $4,000.

The Bishop's palace, corner of Madison and Michigan avenues, cost $40,000, exclusive of furniture.

Universalist.

The Universalists lost but one church, St. Paul's, on Wabash avenue, loss $75,000.

There were in addition to the above, two Jewish Synagogues burned, loss $40,000; the North Side German Lutheran, loss $30,000, and a few wooden churches of the same denomination, which may swell this amount to $50,000. Probably about twenty-five per cent. of the insurance on the above churches can be made available. The gross losses may be summed up as follows:

Episcopalian,	$360,000
Presbyterian,	255,000
Congregational,	106,500
Baptist,	78,000
Methodist,	347,500
Unitarian,	225,000
Roman Catholic,	1,161,000
Universalist,	75,000
Jewish,	40,000
Lutheran,	50,000
Total,	$2,698,000

This sum represents only the losses on buildings. Other losses of some of the denominations, like the

Presbyterian for instance, will reach a much larger sum.

The Value of Goods Destroyed.

The latest estimate of the losses of goods and stocks on hand, is the following:

Dry Goods, ...	$6,045,000
Groceries, ...	2,452,500
Clothing houses, ...	1,911,000
Stationers, blank books, &c., . . .	1,110,000
Jewellers, watches and clocks, . . .	1,335,000
Hardware, ...	1,280,000
Millinery, ...	1,100 000
Hotels, ...	1,210,000
Church societies and corporations, .	4,240,000
City property, ...	1,005,000
Railroads, ...	2,000,000
Boots and shoes, ...	975,000
Drugs, paints and oils, ...	621,000
Books, ...	864,000
Hides and leather, ...	428,000
Restaurants, saloons, &c., ...	528,000
Furniture, ...	510,000
Music dealers, ...	775,000
Hats, caps and furs, ...	423,000
Glassware, crockery, &c.,.	133,000
Auctioneers, ...	306,090
Tailors and outfitters, ...	178,000
Commissions, &c., ...	128,000

This does not give the losses on real estate, lumber, coal, and many other things; nor does it pretend to state personal losses, accurate information of which never can be obtained. It merely gives the proportions, and will probably be found to err very little in that regard.

Ale Brewing Business.

One of the large branches of business in Chicago was the manufacture of ale and lager beer. Large sales were made to the South and Southwest. With few and minor exceptions, all these establishments were in the range of the fire. The following is a list of those destroyed and their values:

Lill's Brewing Company,	$500,000
J. A. Huck,	400,000
Sand's Brewing Company,	335,000
Bush & Brand,	250,000
Buffalo Brewery,	150,000
Schmid, Katz & Co.,	60,000
Metz & Stage,	80,000
Doyle Bros. & Co.,	45,000
Mloeler Bros.,	20,000
K. G. Schmidt,	90,000
George Hiller,	35,000
Schmidt & Bender,	25,000
Mitinet & Puopfel,	12,000
John Behringer,	15,000
J. Miller,	8,000
William Bowman,	5,000
George Wagner,	5,000
Total,	$2,025,000

Little or no valuable insurance was on these buildings, nevertheless, the majority of the owners have already taken steps to renew their business.

One of the Chicago religious papers, in its first issue after the fire, said, the "fire also fortunately destroyed a large number of breweries and saloons." The brewers deny the morality of this statement.

The Newspapers.

The daily newspaper offices were mostly located in the same neighborhood. The *Tribune*, *Times* and *Journal* were on Dearborn street, in sight of each other. The *Post*, *Mail*, and *Staats Zeitung* were in adjoining buildings, on Washington street, near Dearborn, and the *Republican* was on Washington street, in the same vicinity. The *Tribune* and the *Times* owned the buildings in which they were published. The losses of the several offices may be thus estimated:

Tribune, on building, partially saved,	$150,000
Presses and other property, . .	80,000
Times, building, total loss, ...	50,000
Presses and other property, . .	75,000
Journal, presses, &c., including job office,	75,000
Staats Zeitung, presses, &c., ...	45,000
Post, ...	40,000
Republican, including job office, . . .	60,000
Total newspaper property, .	$575,000

The *Times*' building was a total wreck, but was insured. The *Tribune* building was injured to the extent stated, and there was no insurance. The interruption to the issues of the paper was, under the

FIELD, LEITER & CO.'S BUILDING, COR. STATE AND WASHINGTON STREETS

SHERMAN HOUSE.

circumstances, very short. The *Journal* on Monday evening issued from a job office a little sheet, four by six inches; on Tuesday issued a sheet somewhat larger, and on Wednesday evening a large sheet. The *Tribune* issued on Wednesday morning as large a sheet as the only set of column rules in the city would allow. The next day the *Post* and *Mail* issued papers, and the *Republican* got out its first number of any kind on Sunday. The *Times* issued its first paper about the 18th.

During the week preceding the fire there had been numerous fire alarms, and there was put in type, intended for the Sunday issue of the *Tribune*, an editorial discussing the subject of insurance, and pointing out the criminality of the mode in which insurance companies were taking risks, at ruinous rates, spending their receipts in commissions to brokers and agents, imperilling honest risks in case of fire, and inciting by reckless over insurance incendiarism and false swearing. This article was crowded out on Sunday morning, but was enlarged by some references to the fire of Saturday night, and was actually printed in the Monday morning's paper on the "first side." The second side never got to press, and the whole edition was burned up. Chicago is now reaping in the bankruptcy of all her local companies the fruits of the ruinous policy adopted of taking risks at any rate, and for any amount on any description of property.

The Principal Buildings Destroyed.

The following is a list of the more prominent buildings destroyed.

Academy of Design, Adams, between State and Dearborn.
A. H. Miller's building, corner State and Madison.
Andrew's building, La Salle, between Madison and Monroe.
Andrews & Otis's building, Clark, bet. Monroe and Adams.
Arcade buildings, Clark, between Madison and Monroe.
Berlin block, corner State and Monroe.
Blake's building, Washington, bet. Fifth avenue and Fraklin.
Boone block, La Salle, between Washington and Madison.
Bowen's building, Randolph, bet. Michigan and Wabash ave.
Bryan block, corner La Salle and Monroe.
Burch's block, Lake, bet. Wabash avenue and State street.
Calhoun block, Clark, between Washington and Madison.
Chamber of Commerce building, corner La Salle and Washington.
Chicago Mutual Life Insurance building, Fifth avenue, between Washington and Randolph.
The Chicago Times building, Dearborn, between Washington and Madison.
City Water Works, corner Chicago avenue and Pine.
Cobb's block, corner Lake and Wabash avenue.
Cobb's block, Washington, between Clark and Dearborn.
Cobb's building, Dearborn, bet. Washington and Madison.
Commercial building, corner La Salle and Lake.
Commercial Insurance Company's building, Washington, between La Salle and Fifth avenue.
Court House, Randolph and Washington, between Clark and La Salle.
Crosby's building, State, bet. Randolph and Washington.
Custom House, corner Dearborn and Monroe.
De Haven block, Dearborn, between Quincy and Jackson.
Depository building, Randolph, bet. Clark and La Salle.

Dickey's building, corner Dearborn and Lake.
Dole's building, corner Clark and South Water.
Drake's block, corner Wabash avenue and Washington.
Ewing block, North Clark, bet. North Water and Kinzie.
Exchange Bank building, corner Lake and Clark.
Flander's block, foot South Water.
Fry's building, La Salle, bet. Washington and Randolph.
Fullerton's block, corner Washington and Dearborn.
Gallup building, corner La Salle and Madison.
Garrett block, corner Randolph and State.
Hartford Fire Insurance building, La Salle, between Randolph and Lake.
Holt's building, Washington, bet. La Salle and Fifth ave.
Honore block, Dearborn, between Monroe and Adams.
Illinois Central Land Department building, Michigan avenue, between Lake and South Water.
Keep's building, Clark, between Madison and Monroe.
Kent's building, No. 153 Monroe.
King's block, corner Washington and Dearborn.
Lakeside building, corner Adams and Clark.
Larmon block, corner Clark and Washington.
Lincoln block, corner Lake and Franklin.
Link's block, corner La Salle and Lake.
Lloyd's block, corner Randolph and Fifth avenue.
Lombard block, corner Monroe and Custom House place, between Clark and Dearborn.
Loomis's block, corner Clark and South Water.
Lumberman's exchange, corner South Water and Franklin.
McCarthy's building, corner Dearborn and Washington.
McCarthy's building, corner Clark and Randolph.
McCormick's block, corner Dearborn and Randolph.
McCormick's building, corner Michigan ave. and Lake.
McKee's building, corner Wabash ave. and Randolph.
Mackin's building, State, between Madison and Monroe.
Magie's building, corner La Salle and Randolph.
Major block, corner La Salle and Madison.
Marine Bank building, corner Lake and La Salle.

Mechanics' building, Washington, bet. La Salle and Fifth ave.
Mercantile building, La Salle, bet. Madison and Washington.
Merchant's Insurance building, La Salle and Washington.
Methodist Church block, corner Clark and Washington.
Metropolitan block, corner Randolph and La Salle.
Monroe building, corner Clark and Monroe.
Morrison block, Clark, between Madison and Monroe.
Morrison building, Clark, bet. Madison and Washington.
Newbury block, corner Wells and Kinzie.
Norton block, Nos. 136 and 138 South Water.
Old Board of Trade buildings, South Water, between La Salle and Fifth ave.
Open Board building, Madison, bet. Clark and La Salle.
Oriental building, La Salle, bet. Washington and Madison.
Otis block, corner Madison and La Salle.
Otis building, corner State and Madison.
Pacific Hotel, corner Clark and Quincy.
Pardee's building, corner South Water and Fifth ave.
Phœnix building, La Salle, bet. Randolph and Washington.
Pomeroy's building, No. 160 South Water.
Pope's block, Madison, between Clark and La Salle.
Portland block, corner Dearborn and Washington.
Post Office, corner Dearborn and Monroe.
Post Office building, Dearborn, bet. Madison and Monroe.
Prairie Farmer building, Monroe, between, Dearborn and Clark.
Purple's block, corner North Clark and Ontario.
Raymond block, corner State and Madison.
Republic Life Insurance building, La Salle, between Madison and Monroe.
Reynold's block, corner Dearborn and Madison.
Rice's building, 74 to 81 Dearborn.
Scammon's building, corner Randolph and Michigan ave.
Shepard's building, Dearborn, between Monroe and Adams.
Sherman House block, corner Clark and Randolph.
Smith & Nixon's block, corner Clark and Washington.
Speed's building, 125 Dearborn.

Staats Zeitung building, Madison, bet. Dearborn and Clark.
Stearn's building, Washington, bet. La Salle and Fifth ave.
Steel's block, corner La Salle and and South Water.
Stone's building, Madison, between Clark and La Salle.
Taylor's block, corner Franklin and South Water.
Tribune building, corner Dearborn and Madison.
Turner's building, corner North State and Kinzie.
Tyler block, La Salle, between Lake and South Water.
Uhlic block, North Clark, between Kinzie and Water.
Union building, corner La Salle and Washington.
Volk's building, 197 Washington.
Walker's block, Dearborn, between Lake and Randolph.
Warner's block, 123 and 125 Randolph.
Washington's block, Clark, bet. Washington and Madison.
Wheeler's block, corner Clark and South Water.
Wicker's building, corner State and South Water.
Wright Brother's building, corner North State and Kinzie.
Five Public Schools.

Hotels.

Palmer House.
Sherman House.
Tremont House.
Pacific Hotel.
Adams House.
Briggs House.
Mattson House.
Revere House.
Everett House.
Metropolitan Hotel.
Central House.
Howard House.
City Hotel.
Clifton House.
Clarendon House.
Orient House.
Bigelow House.

Churches.

Episcopal. . . .	3	New England. . .	1
Presbyterian.. . .	5	Congregational. .	1
Methodist. . . .	5	Catholic.	5
Unitarian. . . .	2	Jewish.	3
Swedenborgian.. .	2	Lutheran.	2

Theatres.

Crosby's Opera House.
McVicker's Theatre.
Hooley's Opera House.
Dearborn Theatre.
Wood's Museum.
King's Opera House.
Olympic Theatre.
German Haus.
Turner Hall.

Banks.

Chicago Clearing House Association, 82 Dearborn street.
City National Bank, 156 Washington street.
Commercial National Bank, 55 Dearborn street.
Commercial Loan Company, 44 North Clark street.
Cook County National Bank, Honore block, corner Dearborn and Monroe streets.
Corn Exchange Nat. Bank, room 2 Chamber of Commerce.
Fifth National Bank, northeast corner Clark and Dearborn.
First National Bank, southwest cor. State and Washington.
Fourth National Bank, southeast corner Dearborn and Washington streets.
Germania Bank, 40 South Clark street.
Hibernian Banking Association, southwest corner Clark and Lake streets.
Illinois Mutual Trust Com. 147 and 149 Randolph street.
Manufacturers' National Bank, northwest corner Dearborn and Washington streets.
Marine Company of Chicago, 156 Lake, northeast corner La Salle street.
Mechanics' National Bank, 154 Lake street.
Merchants' National Bank, 108 La Salle street.
National Bank of Commerce, 87 Dearborn street.
National Bank of Illinois, 95 Washington street.
Northwestern National Bank, 1 Chamber of Commerce.
Prairie State Loan and Trust Company, northwest corner Randolph and Jefferson streets.
Real Estate Loan and Trust Company, 105 and 107 Monroe street, Lombard block.

Second National Bank, corner Lake and Clark streets.
Traders' National Bank, 44 Clark street.
Third National Bank, cor. Randolph and Dearborn streets.
Union Insurance and Trust Company, 133 Dearborn street.
Union National Bank, southwest corner La Salle and Washington streets.
J. R. Valentine & Co.

Savings Banks.

Chicago Savings Institution and Trust Company, basement southwest corner State and Washington streets.
Com. Loan Company, No. 60 North Clark street.
German Savings Bank, Nos. 34 and 36 La Salle street.
Hibernian Saving Bank Associations Savings Bank, southwest corner Clark and Lake streets.
International Mutual Trust Company, 135 La Salle street.
Marine Company of Chicago, No. 156 Lake street.
Merchants' Farmers' and Mechanics' Savings Bank, No. 13 Clark street.
Merchants' Saving Loan and Trust Company, southwest corner Lake and Dearborn streets.
National Loan and Trust Company, 92 La Salle street.
Real Estate, Loan and Trust Company, next west of the Post Office.
State Savings Institution, 82 and 84 La Salle street.
Union Insurance and Trust Company, 133 Dearborn street.

Railway Stations.

Michigan Central and Great Western of Canada, Union Depot.
Lake Shore and Michigan Southern.
Illinois Central.
Chicago, Burlington & Quincy.
Chicago, Rock Island & Pacific.
Chicago & Northwestern (Galena division.)

Losses in Literature, Art, Music, and the Drama.

The loss to Chicago in places of public amusement, libraries and art galleries it is almost impossible to calculate. It could only be accomplished by personal reports from every one of the thousands of sufferers who were driven from their homes in the South and North Divisions. An approximate idea, however, may be formed, when it is considered that nearly 30,000 houses were burned, and that many of them on the avenues of the South Division and on the Lake front of the North Division, were among the most elegant in the city, and occupied by citizens whose wealth and culture had combined in the accumulation of rare treasures of literature and art.

The chief places of amusement destroyed in the city, were Crosby's Opera House, Hooley's Opera House, the Dearborn Theatre, McVicker's Theatre, and Wood's Museum. The last four had just been refitted and re-ornamented and opened for the regular fall and winter season, while Crosby's Opera House was to have been opened on Monday evening, October 9th, the second night after the fire, by the well known Thomas Orchestral Combination. During the winter of 1870, Mr. Crosby had hesitated for some time whether to continue in the amusement business, and had even employed his architect to draw plans for changing the auditorium into commercial offices. The persuasion of friends, however, and the brilliant operatic and otherwise musical prospects for the season of 1871-72 induced him to abandon the idea. Early in the summer the house was closed and the work of adornment commenced. Eighty thousand dollars were expended in seating, upholstery, fresco work, painting and gilding, superb bronzes, luxurious carpets and costly mirrors. It was finished on Saturday, October 7th, and when on Sunday evening, October 8th, only an hour or two before the fire, the house was lit up that its effect might be seen under gas light, not one of the few who were present but pronounced it to be the most gorgeous auditorium in America. A few hours after when Theodore Thomas and his orchestra arrived, a pile of smoking ruins was all that was left of this beautiful temple of art. It was formally dedicated to music in April, 1865, and during the six years of its existence had been the *locus in quo* of some of the most memorable seasons of English, French, German and Italian opera, Chicago ever enjoyed.

McVicker's Theatre had also been not only ornamented anew, but completely re-modelled. Nothing remained of the old theatre but the outside walls, and these were raised an additional story by means of a lofty Mansard roof. The entire interior of the theatre was removed and a new one substituted upon an entirely different model. It had been in operation but a few weeks when the fire occurred, having opened to stock business in the most successful manner. Mr. Jefferson (Rip Van Winkle) was to have commenced a season, October 9th, and like Mr. Thomas arrived in Chicago just in time to witness the destruction of the theatre.

Hooley's Opera House was constructed a little more than a year ago, by remodelling Bryan Hall, one of the old concert halls of the city. During the first year of its existence it was devoted to burnt cork minstrelsy. During the summer of 1871, the house was refitted, the stage enlarged and thoroughly equipped, and in September it was regularly opened as a comedy theatre, under the management of Mr. Frank Aiken, who a month or two later associated with himself Mr. Frank Lawlor, and leased the building for five years. It had been in operation but a few weeks, when the fire swept it away.

Unlike Hooley's Opera House, the Dearborn Theatre first opened as a dramatic house, under the management of Mr. Frank Aiken, who after a few months took the management of Wood's Museum. The Dearborn then changed colors and was, up to the time of its destruction, known as the Home of the Dearborn Minstrels, under the management of Messrs. Brand and Van Fleet.

Wood's Museum, which combined the attractions of a theatrical stage and curiosity department, was one of the old established institutions of the city. During its long existence, it had met with many vicissitudes, and was rapidly going from worse to worse, under different managers, when Col. Wood, who for many years had been associated with Mr. Barnum, assumed the management and made it a success. Two or three years ago, however, he retired and Mr. Aiken stepped in. It did not succeed under his management, and last summer Col. Wood once more was prevailed upon to try his fortune with it. He completely refitted it, enlarged the curiosity department, and had just opened with an entirely new theatrical company, under the management of Mr. J. S. Langrishe, when it was burned.

In addition to these regular places of amusement, the following public halls were burned: Farwell Hall, one of the most elegant in the country, the home of the Young Men's Christian Association, capable of seating 3,200 people; Metropolitan Hall, used mostly for lectures; Crosby's Music Hall, adjoining the Opera House; Uhlich Hall, occupied by the Germania Mænnerchor; North Market Hall, occupied by the Concordia Mænnerchor; Turner Hall, erected by the North Division Turn-Vereins; and the German Hall, the home of German drama.

The principal public galleries of paintings were three in number, viz.: the Opera House, Academy of Design and Historical Society's collections. The paintings in the Opera House Gallery had remained without any important changes, as they were at the last annual reception, in the winter of 1870. The most noted picture of the gallery was Bierstadt's "Yo Semite Valley." Nearly every picture in the collection was saved through the energy of the superintendent, Mr. Aitken.

The managers of the Academy of Design were

not so fortunate. The gallery was a large one, containing some two hundred and fifty or three hundred works by the best American artists. Rothermel's historical work, "The Battle of Gettysburg," and some pictures by Bierstadt and the Harts were saved, but the greater number were lost, as the artists, many of whom had studios in the building, had no means of removing them. In addition to the paintings, the splendid collection of casts from the most celebrated antiques, which were in the antique school connected with the Academy, were also lost.

The collection at the rooms of the Historical Society was known as the Healey Gallery, and with the exception of an original Conture ("The Prodigal Son") were painted by Mr. G. P. A. Healey, the eminent portrait painter, now in Rome. Among them were portraits from life, of Daniel Webster replying to Hayne, Clay, Calhoun, Buchanan, Pierce, Louis Phillippe, Marshal Soult (a copy), Miss Sneyd, the famous English belle, and many of the founders and officers of the society.

In the destruction of private libraries, the losses were very severe. Horace White, Esq., the editor of the Chicago *Tribune*, lost a valuable political and classical library. Hon. J. N. Arnold, and Messrs. Perry Smith, George L. Dunlap, Obadiah Jackson, J. T. Jewett, and other residents of the North Division, lost valuable miscellaneous libraries. E. B. McCagy lost one of the most valuable philological libraries, and J. Y. Scammon, one of the most extensive Swedenborgian libraries in the United States. R. M. Moore, a widely known art connoisseur, lost one of the most elegant art libraries in the country. Fifteen or twenty clergymen were burned out, and their libraries were in most cases a total loss. The Sanitary Department has a list of nearly 200 physicians who were burned out. Many, if not all of these, lost their offices, instruments and books; and at least five hundred lawyers lost their libraries also. It is probably a fair estimate to set the loss of theological, medical and law libraries alone at $500,000, while the accumulations in the book stores would swell this amount into millions.

The Young Men's Association Library numbered 20,000 volumes, including a complete set of the British Patent Office Reports, the only one in the country. The library of the Historical Society was one of great historical value and embraced 50,000 bound volumes; 145,000 pamphlets; a large collection of manuscripts and several complete newspaper files. The library of the Academy of Science numbered 5,000 volumes, devoted to the specialties of that institution. The Young Men's Christian Association, during the past two or three years, had accumulated 10,000 volumes, mostly of a theological character. The Union Catholic Library, although commenced quite recently, numbered 5,000 volumes, mostly of a sectarian character. The Franklin Library, which pertained to "the art preservative of arts," was organized two or three years since by a printer, and had already reached the handsome number of 3,000 volumes, many of which were exceedingly old and rare. Placing the libraries of smaller Associations at 10,000 volumes, we have in all a loss of over 100,000 volumes in the public libraries. It may be considered absurd to attempt to form an estimate of the number of books destroyed by the fire, but estimating moderately, we are inclined to think that it will reach between two and three millions—a literary holocaust, compared with which the destruction of the Alexandrinian and Strasburg libraries seem insignificant.

The following is a complete list of the newspapers and periodicals which were burned out: Art Review, the Augustana, Bouquet, Programme, the Lorgnette, Chicago Advertiser, Board of Trade Report, Chicago Collector, Commercial Bulletin, Commercial Express, Chicago Democrat, Dry Goods Price List, Evening Journal, Mail, Evening Post, Home Journal, Happy Hours, Journal of Commerce, Legal News, Homœpathic Magazine, Medical Times, the Lens, Microscopical Journal, the Schoolmaster, Railway Review, Railway Gazette, Republican, Chicago Union, Chicago Cynosure, the Progress, Commercial Report and Market Review, Congregational Review, Chicago Magazine of Fashion, Die Freie Presse, Evening Lamp, Everybody's Paper, the Present Age, the Fremad, Gamla-och Nya, Gem of the West, Soldier's Friend, Heavenly Tidings, Home Circle and Temperance Oracle, Little Corporal, Staats Zeitung, Volk's Zeitung, the Amerikanische Farmer, Lakeside Monthly, Life

Boat, Lyceum Banner, Manford's Magazine, Missionarien, National Prohibitionist, National Sunday School Teacher, Song Festival, Song Messenger, Lyon and Healey's Musical Journal, Northwestern Christian Advocate, the Choir, Northwestern Review, the Bureau, the Examiner, Nya Veriden, Our Boys, Present Age, Real Estate and Building Journal, American Builder, the Arts, the Bright Side, the Catholic Weekly, Chicago Weekly, Chicago Ledger, Chicago Mercantile Journal, Chicago Times, Chicago Tribune, the Chronicle, the Detector, the Family Circle, the Herald, the Independent, the Interior, the New Covenant, the Land Owner, the Landewerth and Hausfreund, the Mechanic and Inventor, the National, the Prairie Farmer, the People's Weekly, the Reporter, the Restitution, the Spectator, the Standard, the Sunday School Helper, the Workingman's Advocate, the Young Messenger, Western Catholic, Western Railway Guide, Rand and McNally's Railway Guide, Western Rural, Young Folk's Rural, Young Pilot and Little Men, the Advance, Bryant and Chase's Commercial College Paper, and Author's Sketch Books. Total 107.

The Florists.

There was one business in Chicago which was utterly burned out, and not a store left in the city. It was that of the florists who were located as follows: Dr. Farrell in the *Tribune* building; Desmond and McCormack on Dearborn street;

Gordon Brothers, on Washington street; Charles Reisig, on Washington street; Samuel Muir, on Lake street; Edgar Sanders, on Dearborn street; Krick Bros., Miller and Sons, Pettigrew and Reid, in the North Division. In curious coincidence, the seed stores of Hovey, Emerson and Stafford, P. S. Meserole, Carpenter and Johnson, the Chicago Seed Co., and Fogg and Son, embracing every seed store in the city were also consumed.

Statement by the Fire Marshal of Chicago.

On the 14th of November a reporter of the Chicago *Tribune* "interviewed" the Fire Marshal of Chicago, when the following conversation took place between them:

Reporter. I desire you to give me a statement in regard to the fire—its progress from the time it commenced until you ceased your attempts to subdue it.

Marshal Williams. I had been to Box No. 28—I cannot tell the exact time. I was just crossing Franklin street, going to my house, when that alarm came in. While returning from 28 I told my driver that we were going to have a "burn," as I felt it in my bones, and I said to him, "I am going to bed so as to get some sleep." I went to bed, and was asleep when my gong struck; that was between half-past 9 and 10 o'clock. When I got to the fire I should think there were some six or seven buildings ablaze

DRAKE AND FARWELL BLOCK, WABASH AVENUE.

ILLINOIS AND MICHIGAN CENTRAL RAILROAD DEPOT.

—sheds and outhouses. We got it under control, and it would not have gone a foot further, but the next thing I knew they came and told me St. Paul's Church, about two squares north, was on fire. I told George Raw, foreman of Hook and Ladder 2, to put his longest ladder on the truck and go to the church, because I knew the wind was blowing so hard that we couldn't raise a stream high enough to strike the roof. The citizens got hold of the ladder, threw it down, and broke it into two pieces. I was on the north side of the fire then, and I went up to the church. When I got there I asked Raw where the ladder was, and he said the citizens had broken it. We surrounded the church fire—I had three engines working on it; the Rehm stood on the corner of Clinton and Mather streets, working that plug, and it was so hot there that the engineer had to put up a door to protect himself. The Gund was on the east side of the church, and the Coventry on the north. We got it checked; it was not gaining any headway; the church had fallen in. There was a drug store on the opposite side of the street—on the northwest corner, and a row of buildings north of it, and these caught fire several times. We held the fire at bay, and the next thing I knew the fire was in Bateham's planing mill. When I got there, I found that the match factory between Bateham's and Clinton street was going, as was the lumber in a yard near by, just north of it. We got two streams in there, but couldn't do any good, as the fire was thick and heavy, and ran along to another lumber yard north, and spread east to the old red mill. I went north then to head it off, and found it was down to Harrison street. Commissioner Chadwick came to me and said: "Don't you know the fire is ahead of you?" I told him, it was getting ahead of me in spite of all I could do; it was just driving me right along. I got down to Van Buren street and was working the engines there, but it was so hot that the men were obliged to run for their lives, leaving their hose on the ground. They came to me and asked, what they were to do about hose, and I said: "God only knows."

Reporter. Hadn't you any hose in reserve?

Williams. Not a foot. Every foot of available hose was in use. The statement that several thousand feet of hose was burned in the Armory is not true. After the Burlington warehouse fire every foot of it was taken out of there and put in service. When the fire was raging on both sides of Canal street, and among the furniture that was piled up in the street —mattresses, bureaus, tables, chairs, and everything of that nature had been piled upon the east side of the street, and helped amazingly to set the buildings on that side of the street on fire—several of the engines were obliged to pull up and leave their hose. The foremen came to me and asked for hose, and I told them I had none to give them, and the steamers were entirely useless. We got the Gund, located on the corner of Van Buren and Canal streets, and led her hose up Van Buren street into an alley running south, and tried to cut off the fire in the rear of the corner building, because I knew, if it came through that building the long row on the north side of the street was sure to go, and it would be hot around there. The flames rolled over the men who were with the engine on the corner, and I told the foreman to get her out or we would lose her. I asked some citizens for help, and we ran up to uncouple the section from the plug, and others commenced to uncouple the hose, and I thought if we got the engine away, we would lose the hose. Just then a wave of flame came rolling over the street, and I was obliged to get away. Hose was afterwards attached to the axle of the Gund, and the citizens pulled her into the sidewalk, where she was burned up. When I got on to Canal street, I met Alec McGonegal, foreman of the Long John, and he told me, there was a fire on the south side. I told him to go for it, and I jumped on a hose cart and went over too. I was satisfied that the fire on the west side could not burn any further north, because of the space left by Saturday night's fire, and that the wind would prevent it from going west. I thought, if the fire had reached the south side, I must go and look after it.

Reporter. Where were the Assistant Engineers?

Williams. Where they were, I could not tell at that time. I had been falling back before the fire, and I didn't know where anybody was. When I reached the south side—I went across Madison street bridge—the Long John was ahead of me. I went south on Market street, and when I got to Monroe street, I found that the gas works were on fire. I took a look around, and saw that the Armory and the block up to Wells street was going fast. We formed a line, and had two steamers fighting the fire on Monroe street, and keeping it from getting into the express barn near Wells street, and another building west. We played on those buildings and kept the fire from spreading west. The Economy's stream was in the block between Monroe and Adams streets, and the men were afraid the gas reservoir would explode and blow everything to pieces. I took a view of the property, and saw it was bound to go, despite our efforts. I ran out of the yard and went over to Monroe street again and got another steamer to work. It was of no use; the fire jumped over our heads and ignited some of the frame buildings in the rear of those fronting on Madison street. I knew, there was no use remaining where we were, so I ordered the foremen to take up. When I reached Madison street. I found that there was fire in the rear of the Oriental Building, in the centre of the block. Prescott's row, on the north side of the street, was not touched; the fire was all in the rear, among the shanties and barns. I got the Economy to work on the corner of Washington and La Salle streets, and led the hose in through the stairway opposite. We were not in there three minutes before a sheet of flame rolled over us and the boys dropped the pipe and ran for their lives. The wind was blowing so heavy at the time that the water would not go ten feet from the nozzle of the pipe. We could not strike a second story window. When we came through the stairway on La Salle street, the Court House was on fire, and the next thing the Board of Trade was ablaze. At this place I learned that Alderman Hildreth was around with powder to blow up buildings. He came to me and said, "We have got to let everything go, and begin to blow up. Where will we make a start?" I said, "I don't know, for the fire is going so fast, we can't have time to make a start and know that everybody is out of the buildings." I said if we did anything then, we had better take the corner building—the southwest corner of La Salle and Washington streets. I told him to be sure to get all the people out, as there were many in it then. I then went to work and got my two engines to play on the Sherman House to keep it from burning, I thought we would be able to save it on account of the open space opposite. But, my God! there was a piece of board six feet long that came over and landed right on top of the *Tribune* building on Clark street, and it was not two minutes before that row was on fire. The flames went from there into Wood's Museum, and from there it went in all directions. A fire then started in the rear of the Sherman House among those stables, and away everything went. I couldn't tell how it did go. It went whichever way it pleased. Miller's jewelry store was set on fire by the awnings in front of the windows; they were regular bags to catch sparks.

From there the fire went as it pleased. The Fire Department got separated; some went east, others west, and others south. Where Hildreth did the blowing up, I don't know. I heard that he tried to blow up Nixon's building, but don't know whether he did or not. While I was wetting down the front of the Sherman House, and was doing well, I was told that the Water Works were on fire. I jumped into my wagon and drove over to see if it was true, and when I got near there I saw that the roof was all on fire, and burning rapidly, and the flames rolling out of every opening of the building. I made up my mind then that the whole city was gone. There was no possible chance for the north side, any more than there was for the south.

Reporter. Do you know what took place on the southern line of the fire?

Williams. No; I had my hands full where I was, so that I could not tell what happened there.

Reporter. Did you see any of the Assistant Engineers?

Williams. I did not see Schank, the First Assistant, during the whole fire. I do not know where he was, but he was around somewhere. I saw Walters on the west side and again in front of the long John's house. Brenner was on the south line of the fire, and can tell you about that.

Statement of Mr. Brenner.

Matt Brenner, the Third Assistant Marshal, was also interviewed, and, after giving an account of his adventures on the west side, which consisted of ordering pipemen in here and pipemen in there to save buildings, and prevent the spreading of the flames south detailed his experience on the south side He and the men under his command had worked hard on the west side, and kept the buildings south of the southern line of the fire damp as long as the water lasted. Everything was considered safe, when he was told that there was fire on the south side. He left one engine on the corner of Taylor and Canal streets, and ordered the others over to the south side. Two got over all right, but the third was detained for nearly an hour, by a train of cars standing across Twelfth street. When he reached the corner of Harrison and Clark streets, he found the T. B. Brown at work. A row of buildings on the northeast corner had just caught fire, and he ordered the pipemen to lead the hose into the rear of them. Water at this time was very scarce, there being hardly enough for a "decent stream." Two leads of hose were put on, but before water could be got into the second lead the Jewish Synagogue, on the corner of Harrison street and Fourth avenue, ignited. An effort was made to pull the plaster off, so that throwing water in the building would do some good, but the ceiling was so high, it could not be done. The fire eat its way east very fast, omitting to gut a block or a building at intervals; and Brenner meeting Schank, the First Assistant, left him in charge there, and went after the fire. He went over to Wabash avenue and found the Rice and another engine forming a line to take water from the basin at the foot of Van Buren street. The hose was not long enough to reach the buildings on fire, which were on the west side of State street. It soon became so hot that the men were driven away from where they were stationed, and the flames came so near the Rice that she had to be moved. Her withdrawal broke the "line," and no more water could be obtained. A lot of hose was also lost, the occupants of the dwellings on Wabash avenue having piled their household goods on it, and these catching fire it was burned up. After this Brenner went over to Michigan avenue, and there saw two young men in a wagon, which was filled with powder in kegs. One of them asked him where he wanted the powder, and he told him to go south to Harrison street, and wait until he came up. He subsequently went after the powder, but could not find the wagon. He then went to the corner of Harrison street and Wabash avenue, and heard "a blow up." He looked around, and presently found Ald. Hildreth and several others, who were about to blow up a brick building on Harrison street, near the church. A keg of powder was put into the basement, but it only shattered the house. Some parties then suggested that the church be blown up, and it was sometime before they could be convinced of the uselessness of it, as the church was strong and well built, and able to stop the fire. Several brick buildings on Wabash avenue were also blown up, and this checked the spread of the flames. In the afternoon it became evident that the fire would not go further south, and everything being considered safe, Brenner went home. He did not learn until the next day that the fire had spread over the north side, and was surprised when told such was the case.

The Patrol Duties.

For several nights after the fire, citizens organized themselves into patrol parties and watched their property. Several very humorous episodes occurred during these night watches.

A great rush was made by the poor for passes out of the city on Wednesday. Among one of the most persevering applicants was an unlucky German. After two days' patient but unsuccessful waiting, without a roof to shelter him and utterly friendless, he was left at night to wander through the streets. His loitering pace aroused the suspicions of one of those Argus-eyed "patrols" whose uneasily-worn honors gave—as it did to too many of the class—an enlarged idea of his own importance, and who, believing that vigilance was the price of safety, exercised his newly acquired authority upon late walkers with no slight exhibition of pride. He startled the sleepy German with the stentorian challenge, "Who goes there?" and with a haste that indicated his dread of a too close intimacy with the "unknown," followed the challenge with, "Halt, and give the pass."

The limited acquaintance of the German with the English vernacular prevented him from making a satisfactory reply, when the excited sentinel sounded the alarm, and the patrolmen coming to his rescue, they unitedly bore off in triumph to headquarters struggling Hans. Not doubting they had caught an incendiary, preparations were made for an immediate court-martial, the German all the while struggling with his captors and his English. The severe cross-examination was about to begin, when the mystery was explained by a lucky speech of the German, who, gesticulating wildly, exclaimed: "Vat for you bring me? Ich bin arm. Ein hundred mensch say in alles strausse, 'Your bass;' and anoder say, 'Your bass;' ven I try ein, und anoder, und drie day to get vun bass to gȯ a little vay, und everybody gives me no bass, und you"—pointing to the vigilant patrolman, imitating his actions—"say, give me ein bass, ven I no get vun bass *for myself*."

The shout of laughter which followed this dramatic defence of the German convinced him of the good-will of his captors, but that vigilant patrolman at whose expense the laugh arose is yet badgered with the question: "By the by, have you got your pass yet?"

One other incident will illustrate another aspect

of this "patrol business," which, while we have no doubt it was as a temporary expedient very necessary to the safety of the city, was also a "war measure," endangering lives almost as much as it protected property.

A bold son of Erin was initiated into the mysteries of a patrolman's duties, and being placed at a dangerous post in a dark and lonesome alley, was told to allow no one to pass if they did not say, "Sheridan," which was the countersign for that night. The night was dark, and the captain of the patrol thought he would go see how Paddy was getting along. Turning into the alley he came suddenly upon the valorous sentinel intrenched behind a wood-pile, who bringing his gun to his shoulder, cocked it and aimed it at the intruder all in the same moment, and only paused before firing to shout at the captain: "*Halt! and say Sheridan!*" His services as a patrolman were no longer required.

Proclamations.

The following proclamations are worthy to be preserved as mementoes of the great fire:

BY THE GOVERNOR OF ILLINOIS.

STATE OF ILLINOIS, EXECUTIVE DEPARTMENT.

JOHN M. PALMER, GOVERNOR OF ILLINOIS, *To all whom these presents shall come, greeting:*

Whereas, in my judgment, the great calamity that has overtaken Chicago, the largest city of the

State; that has deprived many thousands of our citizens of homes and rendered them destitute; that has destroyed many millions in value of property, and thereby disturbing the business of the people and deranging the finances of the State, and interrupting the execution of the laws, is and constitutes "an extraordinary occasion" within the true intent and meaning of the eighth section of the fifth article of the Constitution.

Now, therefore, I, John M. Palmer, Governor of the State of Illinois, do by this, my proclamation, convene and invite the two Houses of the General Assembly in session in the city of Springfield, on Friday, the 13th day of the month of October, in the year of our Lord 1871, at 12 o'clock noon of said day, to take into consideration the following subjects:—

1. To appropriate such sum or sums of money, or adopt such other legislative measures as may be thought judicious, necessary, or proper, for the relief of the people of the city of Chicago.

2. To make provision, by amending the revenue laws or otherwise, for the proper and just assessment and collection of taxes within the city of Chicago.

3. To enact such other laws and to adopt such other measures as may be necessary for the relief

of the city of Chicago and the people of said city, and for the execution and enforcement of the laws of the State.

4. To make appropriations for the expenses of the General Assembly, and such other appropriations as may be necessary to carry on the State government.

In testimony whereof I have hereunto set my hand and caused the great seal of State to [SEAL.] be affixed. Done at the city of Springfield, this 10th day of October, A. D. 1871.

JOHN M. PALMER.

By the Governor,

EDWARD RUMMELL,

Secretary of State.

BY THE GOVERNOR OF WISCONSIN.

To the People of Wisconsin:

Throughout the northern part of this State fires have been raging in the woods for many days, spreading desolation on every side. It is reported that hundreds of families have been rendered homeless by this devouring element, and reduced to utter destitution, their entire crops having been consumed. Their stock has been destroyed, and their farms are but a blackened desert. Unless they receive instant aid from portions not visited by this dreadful calamity, they must perish.

The telegraph also brings the terrible news that a large portion of the city of Chicago is destroyed by a conflagration, which is still raging. Many thousands of people are thus reduced to penury, stripped of their all, and are now destitute of shelter and food. Their sufferings will be intense, and many may perish unless provisions are at once sent to them from the surrounding country. They must be assisted now.

In the awful presence of such calamities the people of Wisconsin will not be backward in giving assistance to their afflicted fellow-men.

I, therefore, recommend that immediate organized effort be made in every locality to forward provisions and money to the sufferers by this visitation, and suggest to mayors of cities, presidents of villages, town supervisors, pastors of churches, and to the various benevolent societies, that they devote themselves immediately to the work of organizing effort, collecting contributions, and sending forward supplies for distribution.

And I entreat all to give of their abundance to help those in such sore distress.

Given under my hand, at the Capitol, at Madison, this 9th day of October, A. D. 1871.

LUCIUS FAIRCHILD.

BY THE GOVERNOR OF MICHIGAN.

STATE OF MICHIGAN, EXECUTIVE OFFICE,
LANSING, *October* 9.

The city of Chicago, in the neighboring State of Illinois, has been visited, in the providence of Almighty God, with a calamity almost unequalled in the annals of history. A large portion of that beautiful and most prosperous city has been reduced to ashes and is now in ruins. Many millions of dollars in property, the accumulation of years of industry and toil, have been swept away in a moment. The rich have been reduced to penury, the poor have lost the little they possessed, and many thousands of people rendered homeless and houseless, and are now without the absolute necessaries of life. I, therefore, earnestly call upon the citizens of every portion of Michigan to take immediate measures for alleviating the pressing wants of that fearfully afflicted city by collecting and forwarding to the Mayor, or proper authorities of Chicago, supplies of food as well as liberal collections of money. Let this sore calamity of our neighbors remind us of the uncertainty of earthly possessions, and that when one member suffers all the members should suffer with it. I cannot doubt that the whole people of the State will most gladly, and most promptly, and most liberally respond to this urgent demand upon their sympathy; but no words of mine can plead so strongly as the calamity itself.

HENRY P. BALDWIN,
Governor of Michigan.

BY THE GOVERNOR OF IOWA.

To the People of Iowa:

An appalling calamity has befallen our sister State. Her metropolis—the great city of Chicago—is in ruins. Over 100,000 people are without shelter or food, except as supplied by others. A helping hand let us now promptly give. Let the liberality of our people, so lavishly displayed during the long period of national peril, come again to the front, to lend succor in this hour of distress. I would urge the appointment at once of relief committees in every city, town, and township, and I respectfully ask the local authorities to call meetings of the citizens to devise ways and means to render efficient aid. I would also ask the pastors of the various churches throughout the State to take up collections on Sunday morning next, or at such other time as they may deem proper, for the relief of the sufferers. Let us not be satisfied with any spasmodic effort. There will be need of relief of a substantial character to aid the many thousands to prepare for the rigors of the coming winter. The magnificent public charities of that city, now paralyzed, can do little to this end. Those who live in homes of comfort and plenty must furnish this help, or misery and suffering will be the fate of many thousands of our neighbors.

SAMUEL MERRILL, *Governor.*

DES MOINES, *October* 10, 1871.

CITY HALL, AFTER THE FIRE

BY THE GOVERNOR OF OHIO.

CHICAGO, *October* 12.

To the People of Ohio:

It is believed by the best informed citizens here that many thousands of the sufferers must be provided with the necessaries of life during the coming winter. Let the efforts to raise contributions be energetically pushed. Money, fuel, flour, pork, clothing, and other articles not perishable should be collected as rapidly as possible—especially money, fuel, and flour. Mr. Joseph Medill, of *The Tribune*, estimates the number of those who will need assistance at about 70,000.

R. B. HAYES, *Governor of Ohio.*

BY MAYOR MASON.

Whereas, in the Providence of God, to whose will we humbly submit, a terrible calamity has befallen our city, which demands of us our best efforts for the preservation of order and the relief of the suffering.

Be it known that the faith and credit of the city of Chicago is hereby pledged for the necessary expenses for the relief of the suffering. Public order will be preserved. The Police, and Special Police now being appointed, will be responsible for the maintenance of the peace and the protection of property. All officers and men of the Fire Department and Health Department will act as Special Policemen without further notice. The Mayor and Comptroller will give vouchers for all supplies furnished by the different Relief Committees. The head-quarters of the City Government will be at the Congregational Church, corner of West Washington and Ann streets. All persons are warned against any acts tending to endanger property. All persons caught in any depredation will be immediately arrested.

With the help of God, order and peace and private property shall be preserved. The City Government and committees of citizens pledge themselves to the community to protect them, and prepare the way for a restoration of public and private welfare.

It is believed the fire has spent its force, and all will soon be well.

R. B. MASON, *Mayor.*

GEORGE TAYLOR, *Comptroller,*
(By R. B. MASON.)

CHARLES C. P. HOLDEN,
President Common Council.

T. B. BROWN,
President Board of Police.

CHICAGO, *October* 9, 1871.

1. All citizens are requested to exercise great caution in the use of fire in their dwellings and not to use kerosene lights at present, as the city will be without a full supply of water for probably two or three days.

2. The following bridges are passable, to wit: All bridges (except Van Buren and Adams streets) from Lake street south, and all bridges over the North Branch of the Chicago river.

3. All good citizens who are willing to serve, are requested to report at the corner of Ann and Washington streets, to be sworn in as special policemen.

Citizens are requested to organize a police for each block in the city, and to send reports of such organization to the police head-quarters, corner of Union and West Madison streets.

All persons needing food will be relieved by applying at the following places:

At the corner of Ann and West Washington; Illinois Central Railroad round house.

M. S. R. R.—Twenty-second street station.

C. B. & Q. R. R.—Canal street depot.

St. L. & A. R. R.—Near Sixteenth street.

C. & N. W. R. R.—Corner of Kinzie and Canal streets.

All the public school houses, and at nearly all the churches.

4. Citizens are requested to avoid passing through the burnt districts until the dangerous walls left standing can be levelled.

5. All saloons are ordered to be closed at 9 P. M. every day for one week, under a penalty of forfeiture of license.

6. The Common Council have this day by ordinance fixed the price of bread at eight (8) cents per loaf of twelve ounces, and at the same rate for loaves of a less or greater weight, and affixed a penalty of ten dollars for selling, or attempting to sell, bread at a greater rate within the next ten days.

7. Any hackman, expressman, drayman or teamster charging more than the regular fare, will have his license revoked.

All citizens are requested to aid in preserving the peace, good order and good name of our city.

R. B. MASON, *Mayor.*

October 10, 1871.

BY LIEUT.-GEN. SHERIDAN.

CHICAGO, *October* 9.

To GENERAL BELKNAP, *Secretary of War:*

The city of Chicago is almost utterly destroyed by fire. There is now reasonable hope of arresting it if the wind, which is yet blowing a gale, does not change. I ordered, on your authority, rations from St. Louis, tents from Jeffersonville, and two companies of infantry from Omaha. There will be many houseless people, much distress.

P. H. SHERIDAN, *Lieut.-Gen.*

CHICAGO, *October* 9.

W. W. BELKNAP, *Secretary of War:*

The fire here last night and to-day has destroyed almost all that was very valuble in this city. There is not a business house, bank, or hotel left. Most of the best part of the city is gone. Without exaggerating, all the valuable portion of the city is in ruins. I think not less than 100,000 people are houseless, and those who had the most wealth are now poor. It seems to me to be such a terrible s-fortune that it may with propriety be considered a national calamity.

P. H. SHERIDAN, *Lieut.-Gen.*

WASHINGTON, *October.* 10.

LIEUTENANT-GENERAL SHERIDAN, CHICAGO:

I agree with you that the fire is a national calamity; the sufferers have the sincere sympathy of the nation. Officers at the depots at St. Louis, Jeffersonville, and elsewhere, have been ordered to forward supplies liberally and promptly.

WM. W. BELKNAP, *Secretary of War.*

HEAD-QUARTERS MILITARY DIV. OF THE MISSOURI,
CHICAGO, *October* 11, 1871.

GOVERNOR JOHN M. PALMER, SPRINGFIELD:

Seven companies of United States troops are here or coming, and a regiment is being organized for twenty days' service, from the old soldiers in the city,—which I think will be ample. Shall keep your volunteers for a day or so. Thanks for them.

P. H. SHERIDAN.

HEAD-QUARTERS MILITARY DIV. OF THE MISSOURI,
CHICAGO, *October* 12.

TO HIS HONOR THE MAYOR:—

The preservation of peace and good order of the city having been entrusted to me by your Honor, I am happy to state that no case of outbreak or disorder has been reported. No authenticated attempt at incendiarism has reached me, and the people of the city are calm, quiet, and well-disposed.

The force at my disposal is ample to maintain order, should it be necessary, and protect the district devastated by fire. Still, I would suggest to citizens not to relax in their watchfulness until the smouldering fires of the burnt buildings are entirely extinguished.

P. H. SHERIDAN, *Lieut.-Gen'l.*

HEAD-QUARTERS MILITARY DIV. OF THE MISSOURI,
CHICAGO, ILL., *October* 11, 1871.

GENERAL F. T. SHERMAN:

DEAR SIR:—With the approbation of the Mayor of this city, Lieutenant-General Sheridan directs that you organize a regiment of infantry, to consist of ten (10) companies; each company to consist of one (1) Captain, one (1) First and one (1) Second Lieutenant, and sixty (60) enlisted men, to serve as guards for the protection of the remaining portion of the city of Chicago, for the period of twenty days.

Very respectfully,
Your obedient servant,
JAMES B. FRY,
Assistant Adjutant-General.

The regiment was partly composed of companies of the State militia ordered by Lieutenant-General Sheridan, or some of his subordinates, to report to him or them, and of recruits enlisted under their authority. An extract from the order of Lieutenant-General Sheridan, mustering these troops out of service, will show its organization:

HEAD-QUARTERS MILITARY DIV. OF THE MISSOURI,
CHICAGO, ILL., *October* 24, 1871.

General Orders, No. 5.

The First Regiment Chicago Volunteers, raised with the approbation of the Mayor, and in pursuance of orders dated October 11th, 1871, from these head-quarters, is hereby honorably mustered out of service, and discharged.

This regiment was constituted as follows:

Colonel Frank T. Sherman, First Chicago Volunteers, commanding.

Major C. H. Dyer, Adjutant.

Major Charles T. Scammon, Aid-de-Camp.

Lieutenant-Colonel H. Osterman, First Regiment National Guards, Illinois State Militia.

Major G. A. Bender, First Regiment National Guards, Illinois State Militia.

Captain Fischer's Company (A), First Regiment National Guards, Illinois State Militia.

Captain Pasch's Company (D), First Regiment National Guards, Illinois State Militia.

Captain Cronas' Company (G), First Regiment National Guards, Illinois State Militia.

Captain Paul's Company (H), First Regiment National Guards, Illinois State Militia.

Captain Kelter's Company (I), First Regiment National Guards, Illinois State Militia.

Captain Rogers' Company (B), First Chicago Volunteers, Lieutenant Adams, commanding.

Captain Merrill's Company (C), First Chicago Volunteers.

Captain Baker's Company (K), First Chicago Volunteers, recruited by Captain Whittlesey.

Captain Colson's Company, University Cadets.

Captain Crowley's Company, Montgomery Light Guards.

Captain McCarthy's Company, Mulligan Zouaves.

Captain Ryan's Company, Sheridan Guards.

Captain Sulter's Company, Chicago Cadets.

Captain Williams' Company, Hannibal Zouaves.

The Norwegian Battalion of National Guards. Major Alstrup, commanding.

Ole Bendixen, Adjutant.

Captain Paulsen's Company (A).

Captain Eck's Company (B).

Captain Johnson's Company (C).

Captain Beutzen's Company (D).

HEAD-QUARTERS MILITARY DIV. OF THE MISSOURI,
CHICAGO, *October* 25, 1871.

To the Adj. Gen'l of the Army, Washington, D. C.:

Sir:—The disorganized condition of affairs in this city produced by and immediately following the late fire, induced the city authorities to ask for assistance from the military forces, as shown by the Mayor's proclamation of October 11th, 1871. [Copy herewith marked A.] To protect the public interests, entrusted to me by the Mayor's proclamation, I called to this city Companies A and K of the Ninth Infantry, from Omaha; Companies A, H and K of the Fifth Infantry, from Leavenworth; Company I, Sixth Infantry, from Fort Scott; and accepted the kind offer of Major-General Halleck to send to me Companies F, N and K of the Fourth, and Company E of the Sixteenth Infantry, from Kentucky. I also, with the approbation of the Mayor, called into the service of the city of Chicago, a regiment of volunteers for twenty days. [Copy of this call enclosed herewith, marked B.] These troops, both regulars and volunteers, were actively engaged during their service here in protecting the treasure in the burnt district, guarding the unburnt district from disorders and danger by further fires, and in protecting the storehouses, depots and sub-depots of supplies, established for the relief of sufferers from the fire. These duties were terminated on the 23d inst., as shown from letters herewith (marked C, D and E), and on the 24th inst. the regulars started to their respective stations, and the volunteers were discharged, as shown by special order No. 76, and general No. 5, from these head-quarters. [Copies herewith.] It is proper to mention that these volunteers were not taken into the service of the United States, and no orders, agreements, or promises were made giving them any claims against the United States for services rendered. I am, very respectfully,

Your obedient servant,

P. H. Sheridan,
Lieutenant-General Commanding.

BY THE MAYOR OF NEW YORK.

Mayor's Office, New York,
Afternoon of October 9.

A disaster has fallen on the great city of Chicago, which not only has destroyed the best part of its dwellings, and paralyzed its industry and its business, but threatens the gravest consequences to the commerce and prosperity of our country. It has also reduced thousands of people to houselessness and privation. A despatch from the Mayor of Chicago comes in these words:—"Can you send us some aid for a hundred thousand houseless people. Army bread and cheese desirable." I have responded that New York will do everything to alleviate this disaster; and I now call upon the people to make such organization as may be speediest and most effective for the purpose of sending money and clothing and food. I would recommend the immediate formation of general relief committees, who would take charge of all contributions, in order that no time may be lost in carrying relief to those of our fellow citizens who have fallen under this dispensation of Providence. I suggest that the Chamber of Commerce, the Produce Exchange, the Board of Brokers, and the united presidents of the banks, and all religious and charitable associations immediately call a meeting of their respective members, and from them select independent relief committees, who shall solicit subscriptions of money, food, and clothing within their appropriate spheres of action. In the meantime, I am authorized to state that contributions of food and clothing sent to the depots of the Erie and Hudson and Central Railroads (under early and spontaneous offers of Jay Gould and William H. Vanderbilt), in even small quantities, from individuals or business sources, will be at once forwarded through to Chicago free of expense. I cannot too strongly urge upon our citizens immediate attention to this subject.

A. OAKEY HALL, *Mayor.*

BY ALLAN PINKERTON.

OFFICE OF PINKERTON'S POLICE.

Orders are hereby given to Captains, Lieutenants, Sergeants, and men of Pinkerton's preventive police, that they are in charge of the burning district, in the South Division. Any person stealing, or seeking to steal any property in my charge, or attempting to break open the safes, as the men cannot make arrests at the present time, they shall kill the persons by my orders. No mercy shall be shown them, but death shall be their fate.

ALLAN PINKERTON.

INCIDENTS.

CONCERNING the incidents of that fearful night in the streets of the South Division, volumes might be written. Of course the most exaggerated reports and startling incidents were forwarded by the correspondents of Eastern papers to their respective journals, and for a time the whole country believed that incendiaries were hanging by the scores to lamp posts; that bridges were swung, filled with the hurrying crowds, who were thus suspended over the river and burned to death; that hundreds of women rushed from dwellings with their clothes in a blaze; that the prisoners in the jail and Bridewell, were left in their cells and burned to death; and so on through the gloomy catalogue of horrors.

Leaving out what may be attributed to excited imaginations, and the mere desire to furnish sensational letters, there was still much that was startling and many striking incidents of heroism and suffering that are true. In the pages immediately following we have grouped together a number of these incidents and general facts, which will prove of interest to the reader.

Bookseller's Row.

On State street was the fine row of five-story marble front buildings known as "Bookseller's Row." These buildings were 190 feet deep, and including the basements were filled with books and stationery. Griggs & Co., besides a large stock of imported works, had whole floors of school books. The Western News Company, besides its immense salesroom, had a force of sixty persons engaged in packing goods. All these stores were elaborately finished, and of course included heavy stocks of paper and other stationery. An exploration of the ruins failed to discover a book, or a sheet or a quire of paper. The only legible thing found was a single leaf, badly scorched, of a Bible and this is said to have contained, though we did not see it, that part of the first chapter of Jeremiah which opens:

"How doth the city set solitary that was full of people, how she became as a widow."

"She weepeth sore in the night, and her tears are on her cheeks."

That is all that was left of the more than a million of books contained in all these immense stores.

The rescue of the Dead.

On Saturday, a man residing in the North Division died, and the body was prepared for burial on Sunday. In the meantime the fire came along, and a brave son seized the coffin, and struggling under the load slowly tried to escape. The fire moved faster than he did, and getting help he hastened to the lake shore. But the coffin was reached by the heat, and to save it and the body from burning, it was thrown into the lake, with a large stone attached to keep it from being carried away.

The horrors of the dreadful night were intensified by the painful exhibitions of relatives bearing away from the advancing flames, the bodies of children, mothers and fathers who had died during the twenty-four hours preceding. All other things were abandoned in order to rescue these bodies of their loved ones. In most cases the work had to be performed by the family unaided; and in a majority of such cases, the corpse had to be abandoned at last, even after having been carried a mile or more through the rain of fire. The grief and wailings of the survivors was piteous in the extreme; often men threw away such of their own property as they were saving to aid these afflicted sufferers, but as a rule, and without any actual selfishness, each family had as much as it could possibly do to get beyond the range of the stifling smoke and the ever gaining heat and blaze.

The story is told, but it needs more confirmation before being accepted as true, that a German woman being ill and near death, when the fire reached the premises, the family, unable to remove her, decided not to let her burn, and placing her on a mattress, dropped her into the neighboring river, when she was instantly drowned. It was a choice of deaths, and the decision was one of loving hearts, who unable to save, sought to lessen the horror and physical pain of the last moment.

Destruction of Trunks.

The destruction of trunks during the fire was very great. Almost every person who had one endeavored to carry off a trunk full of the best things he had. As a result the majority of these trunks were unusually heavy, and more than any but a practiced hand could carry alone for any distance. Thousands of trunks were removed from houses and dragged some of them a short and many a long distance, but taking the city as a whole, it is safe to say, that not over half of these trunks escaped destruction in the owner's hands. Those who were so fortunate as to depart early and secure the aid of vehicles, of course saved their trunks, provided they moved beyond the final range of the fire; but hundreds who escaped before daylight, were overtaken again before noon, and obliged to fly, leaving this time to be burned up all that they had rescued in their earlier flight. Owners of express and other wagons in some instances kindly aided in the escape of families and removal of baggage, but avarice was too powerful for others. $50 and $100 were demanded in advance before they would remove a single trunk. One of the government officers after having done his duty at the office returned to his residence to find it threatened by fire. He found an express wagon, and offered to pay $30 for carrying three trunks a few blocks to a railroad depot. When the trunks were in the wagon, he demanded his money, and though he knew the

VIEW FROM HARRISON STREET NORTH ON WABASH AVENUE.

officer personally, threw the trunks out when the latter said he had but $25 with him. As the fire progressed, the sums demanded increased. The clerks of a law publishing house rescued the electrotype plates and a number of works, and piled them on the sidewalk. $100 was demanded to move them out of the range of the fire, and because the clerks could not pay him that sum in advance, he drove away, and $10,000 worth of electrotypes were, an hour later, melted into a mass.

This avarice soon degenerated into dishonesty, and drivers refused to hire on any terms and coursed the streets picking up abandoned trunks, and other property which they carried off as their own. Still the amount of property stolen on that night and the day succeeding was comparatively insignificant. There was no time for stealing. The thief lingered behind the fugitive owner to appropriate what the latter had left, but the fire was immediately at hand. No article of bulk could be stolen without the aid of a horse and vehicle, and these, in order to reach a place of safety, had to make circuitous journeys so long that no second trip was possible. That much was stolen by rogues on foot and rogues in drays, wagons and other vehicles is most true, but it was of little profit. Except in the case of money or jewelry or other like light valuables, all such stolen property was in the main abandoned, and both robber and robbed joined in the race for life and safety beyond the reach of the flame, and beyond the influence of the consuming heat.

Eccentricities.

It was amusing, if it were not too painful, to notice the strange tastes and feelings shown by those who sought to save some portions of their property. The children, of course, were first in order; next a trunk, in which were packed so many things as often to render the trunk too heavy to be moved. Others, having neither children nor trunks, would carry a looking glass, a joint of stove pipe, a pine table, one or two chairs, a child's cradle or cup, a water pitcher, or some other article of the least possible value. On Monday at noon, we saw a young woman, who had fled before the fire from four o'clock in the morning. Over the left arm she had a small bundle of clothing and in the right hand, held between the fingers, were three small wine glasses. These were all she had saved, and these wine glasses she had carried on her long journey for eight hours.

One of the favorite articles which the thieves who had use of vehicles appropriated, was pianos. Hundreds of these were got out of the houses, but were necessarily abandoned for want of transportation. The thieves seeing these, would back up, put the piano on the dray or wagon, and drive off with it. What was done with them? Many of them of course were deposited temporarily in open lots, and were afterwards overtaken and destroyed by the fire. Others were held for ransom, but we have no doubt that scores were secreted to be sent elsewhere, in time, to be sold by the thieves. The same dishonest gentry were special admirers of the fine arts, and boldly entered houses and tore down valuable paintings, of which there were very many in Chicago. These were packed in wagons. The art galleries were also extensively robbed, under the pretence of saving, and in time these pictures will teem up in other parts of the country for sale.

The Domestic Animals.

The number of horses in Chicago was very great, far in excess of the proportion owned in most cities. The work of filling the streets an average depth of seven or eight feet, had built up here an immense business in the way of two horse wagons designed for that business. These wagons were of a peculiar construction. The part above the running gear was a skeleton. When this wagon was to receive a load, one or two boards are placed on the edge at each side, against the posts, giving a depth of two feet or more. Other loose boards, about six inches wide each, are then arranged compactly for the bottom. A tail board serves the double purpose of keeping the side pieces in their places, and of completing the temporary box. The work of unloading is very expeditious. The tail board is removed, then one of the side pieces, and then the bottom boards are turned on edge, one after the other letting the load fall under the wagon.

The great business done here in lumber, and in hauling sand from the lake, in addition to the wants of an active commercial city, gave employment to many thousands of horses. A result was that a stable or barn was a necessary appendage to the great majority of houses, including the unpretending domiciles of the teamsters. Large numbers of these teams were put in use on the night of the fire, removing goods and persons, but a much larger number of the horses were let loose or broke loose. They were uncontrollable. The fire and heat, and the terrible roar, seemed to madden them, and they rushed at full speed through the streets, turning round corners, and forever returning as near to their old places of shelter as the fire would permit. Even those in harness felt the excitement, and their terror was paiuful to witness. Many sunk to the street, overcome by fear. The heat, the blaze, the incessant fall of fire, the smoke and cinders, and above all, the fearful roaring of the gale of fire, seemed to paralyze many of these faithful animals. Of those who were loose, and madly careering through the streets, large numbers perished, being hemmed in by the fire, or rushing frantically into alley ways and courts were caught in the flames, and life extinguished almost instantly.

True to their natural instincts, the cats refused to leave the houses, and many which were forcibly rescued escaped, and went back again into the burning buildings.

Chicago has been notorious for its rats. The

wooden sidewalks have been conducive to their increase. Beneath these structures they were safe from dogs and men, and burrowing deep were protected even in the coldest weather. This fire spared nothing that came within its reach, and it is not at all extravagant to say, that on that night five millions of rats of all ages were destroyed. The dogs, save those unfortunates which were chained, shared the retreat of their owners. Though many of them were lost by being shut up in the houses. The howlings of the poor animals chained or otherwise detained, added to the horrors of that eventful night.

On Madison street, opposite Farwell Hall, was a store in which were kept a large collection of birds of many varieties. Parrots, macaws, mocking birds, sparrows, and an immense collection of imported singing birds, especially of canaries. There were also in the same store three or four monkeys, and in the basement specimens of various choice breeds of poultry. The fire attacked the building suddenly and fiercely. The time was barely sufficient for the human inmates to escape. But from the imprisoned inmates there was a combined appeal, seemingly an agonized shriek that was piteous in the extreme. Had they been released they would have perished in the atmosphere without, and as soon as the glass front of the store was broken, the heat and smoke rushed in, extinguishing the life of every breathing thing within as if done by magic. Chickens, birds, monkeys, parrots all became instantly silent, the hot air had literally consumed them.

The Grave Yards.

A mile or more north of the water works and extending to within 200 yards of the lake, was the Roman Catholic grave yard, and next it was a German grave yard. Interments had ceased in these some years ago, but all the bodies had not been removed to the new cemeteries farther up the lake. These cemeteries had been contemporary with the city. A large part of them was donated to the graves of the poor and strangers. As a general thing surviving friends, who had the means, long since removed the bodies of their kindred; those who remained had been the husbands, wives and children of the poor, but were none the less dear. These graves were marked with wooden boards, upon which were painted or cut the initials of the dead, and occasionally some beyond. In the one yard, the inscriptions were in German. Even in these abandoned cities of the dead, hundreds would spend the long summer afternoons trimming the sandy mounds, straightening the loose boards, and bringing water from the lake to refresh the parched plants and flowers which affection had planted upon the graves. Into these grave yards many fugitives had fled during that Sunday night and Monday morning. With them were carried some household goods. Stands, beds, chairs, tables, the whole presenting a strange collection. The occupants were of all classes. Strong men, hard working able bodied men; weak and delicate women; many of the occupants of fashionable dens of vice; refined and cultivated women; merchants, lawyers and bankers; servant men and women, but the great bulk were the families of small tradesmen, and working people of the neighborhood. Of course there were troops of children, all huddled in groups, with backs to the fire, to protect their eyes from the blinding smoke and consuming heat. Incessantly there fell among them the flying sparks and cinders. In vain did these poor fugitives seek to cover their packages of clothing with sand. The fire would fall upon them and set them ablaze. At last the fire approached them; it seized upon the long wooden sidewalks of the streets beyond, and with the speed of lightning traversed block after block, encircling every place with a cordon of fire. The fences one after another caught, the twigs, and scattered lumber, with here and there a house, a stable, or a shed seemed to furnish food enough to carry that fire along. At last it reached the grave yard, the fences caught and blazed; the heat prepared everything for the advancing column of fire. Group after group fled before the flame; the straw beds, chairs, tables, the trunks, the bundles of clothes and the household goods, soon were on fire; head board after head board blazed as a brazen mirror reflecting light. The little fences around the burial lots, the scanty trees and shubbery all took fire, and each fed the rapacious flames. The living had to abandon even the desolate grave yard, and the fire swept from above the earth everything that was consumable. Stout trees were burned down below the ordinary level of the soil in which they grew. These cemeteries before the fire were desolate—one-half the dead having been disentered, and the monuments and valuable adornments removed, and now came the fire to make desolation more desolate, not a vestige remains of anything in these silent cities of the dead save the blackened embers of the once erect grave signs, and of the little property carried there for safety and then overtaken and consumed by the insatiable fire.

Weddings and Marriages.

The fire played sad work with a number of weddings which were to be celebrated within a day or two after the date of the fire. In one case the daughter of one of our most celebrated clergymen was to have been married on Tuesday. The circle of her acquaintance included the majority of the respectable people of all sects in the city. The groom was equally respected. In anticipation of the marriage, a house had been built for the new couple, and had been furnished throughout. Everything was in readiness, and upon their marriage they were to commence housekeeping the same day. These young people had fondly watched the erection of that home, had visited it together during its progress, and after its completion had selected the furniture and directed its arrangement throughout. Tuesday was to begin a new era for them. The fire came on Monday morning. It destroyed the new house and its contents; it destroyed the home of the groom and of his parents and relatives. It destroyed the church in which they were to be married, and then the house of the expectant bride and of her father; all the wedding clothes were carried off by the flames; all her other clothing save the few articles she had put on in her hasty flight were in like manner destroyed. It was night on Monday before these close bound neighbors could find one another, but the wedding was not to be postponed. Though the fondly anticipated assemblage of friends and joyous house warming had to be abandoned, the marriage itself—the union of hearts and of hands, was still to go on. So on the next morning, at the same hour originally fixed upon, in plain attire, the marriage took place. The only serious difficulty in the case was in the matter of under clothes for the lady. That line of goods was a luxury in Chicago for several days. But very few who saved any clothes it seemed saved these; there were none to be borrowed and none to be bought, and it is said that the whole of Tuesday was consumed before proper garments for the lady could be found. The young couple, however, in sight of the smoking ruins of their promised home, commenced life, happy in the consciousness of mutual affection, and grateful that in their large family circle all had been saved and protected from that loss of life and health which had befallen so many thousands of others.

Other weddings fixed for that eventful week, and which would have been accompanied with all the fashionable display so general at this day, were celebrated under improvised homes, in borrowed clothing, but with no less happy hopes and charming anticipations.

Not so happy, however, was the result in all cases. One bright blooming girl of nineteen years was to have been married on the Thursday following the fire. She was the daughter of a wealthy merchant, and her intended was a member of a large business firm. In that dreadful night she with her father's family escaped on foot, and in the tumult and the confusion of the prolonged flight before the fire, she was separated from her friends. In her ignorance of the localities she wandered from place to place, but forever pursued by the fire, until at last it is supposed she got beyond the northern limits of the city. In vain did her friends seek for her; no one had seen her, nor could any inquiry be prosecuted amid the universal separation of friends and families. Finally, on Thursday morning, about daylight, the citizen's patrol, in a part of the city far remote from where she had been lost, discovered a woman but partially clad, walking listlessly along; occasionally she would in feeble voice call as if for help, again she would mutter unintelligible sentences, and again recite in plaintive tones some little verse or childish song. She made no resistance to the gentlemen when they kindly asked her to go with them. They carried her to a dwelling near by when she was passively placed in a warm bed, and a physician summoned. She would gaze upon the kind faces of those around her, as if in search of some familiar features, but beyond this betrayed no intelligence. She was kept for a few days and every attention given to her, but she grew no better. In changing her clothing a photograph was found with a well known name upon it. This person was informed, and with his wife hastened to embrace their daughter. She failed to recognize them. The long exposure and want of rest, combined with the protracted terrors of that fearful night, had destroyed her reason; and this beautiful and accomplished girl, whose marriage had been so joyfully expected, is now insane, though it is hoped, that time and care and affectionate ministrations may bring back the intelligence that seemingly has gone forever.

The Ogden Mansion.

One of the great objects of interest in the city is the house of Mahlon D. Ogden. Its escape is a marvel. In every direction as far as the eye can reach is the blackened prairie. It stands an oasis in the desert. On the night of the fire the family was absent from the city, but two or three gentlemen were there. They fought to save the building. They tore up the carpets, and used all the blankets on the premises. These they spread over the fronts of the house and of the barn exposed to the fire; with brooms and buckets of water they kept the roofs free of falling fire. In front of the house and between it and the approaching fire was a small park—just one vacant block. But this park early in the night was filled with fugitives and their furniture. In time the fire came, driving out the refugees, and seizing upon the beds and bedding and furniture and household stuff, burned them as if they were so much straw. On the north and on the south flanks of Ogden's house the fire raged with fury, and in front was the grand blaze from the accumulated furniture of fifty families. So long as the water works continued to furnish water, those in charge of Ogden's premises easily kept the carpets and blankets and other woollen protections wet. But when the hydrant ceased to furnish water they were driven to a cistern which they knew was not inexhaustible. Several barrels of cider were used to saturate the carpets, and to throw upon the burning cinders. In the meantime a house in the rear of Ogden's caught fire. It was thus surrounded on all sides by blaze, and the heat borne down upon it by the relentless gale. Yet it was saved. A dozen times did the fences catch, but a ready bucket of water or cider put it out. The wooden sidewalk burned on one side of the building but the wind carried the fire beyond the house. The fire in the park soon burned out. Everything between the house and the wind was rapidly consumed, and when day dawned, after three or four hours of hard labor, the blazing torrent had passed on to the north, leaving nothing but this solitary building in an area of 2,600 acres. On Sunday Mr. Ogden lived in the centre of a densely populated city. The immediate district in which he lived contained 75,000 persons. In the early dawn his nearest neighbor was miles away, and standing in his doorway the view was as unbroken by habitations as it was fifty years ago when it was a trackless prairie. Next to the ruins, and to many far before the ruins, in popular interest is the house that the fire did not burn, the house from which the fire turned to the right and the left to avoid, closing again in its rear, and carrying everything as before in its fearful destruction.

A Courageous Banker.

A remarkable instance of courage and presence of mind is told of Mr. E. I. Tinkham, of the Second National Bank. On Monday morning, before the fire had reached that building, Mr. Tinkham went to the safe and succeeded in getting out $600,000. This pile of greenbacks he packed into a common trunk, and hired a colored man for $1,000 to convey it to the Milwaukee depot. Fearing to be recognized in connection with the precious load, Mr. Tinkman followed the man for a time at some distance, but soon lost sight of him. He was then overtaken by the fire storm. and was driven toward the lake on the south side. Here, after passing through several narrow escapes from suffocation, he succeeded in working his way, by some means, to a tugboat, and got round to the Milwaukee depot, where he found the colored man waiting for him, with the trunk, according to promise. Mr. Tinkham paid the man the $1,000, and started with the trunk for Milwaukee, and the money was safely deposited in Marshall and Illsley's bank of that city.

A Faithful Clerk.

Mr. Nathaniel Bacon, of Niles, Michigan, student at law with Messrs. Tenney, McClellan & Tenney, slept in their office. On waking at about one o'clock, and seeing the Court House on fire, he saw that the office, which was immediately opposite, would surely go. Judging that one of the safes in the office would not prove fire proof, he promptly emptied the contents of his trunk on the floor of the doomed building, and, filling it with the interior contents of the safe, books, valuable papers, money, &c., shouldered the trunk and carried it to a place of safety on Twenty-second street—losing thereby all his own clothing and effects except what he had on.

A Baby Rescued.

In Ontario street, near Clark, where the fire suddenly leaped across westward through the North Division, a baby ten months old was thrown from a fourth-story window, and caught in a blanket by men congregated below. It started head downwards, like Sam Patch in his last leap, but gradually regained the perpendicular, and alighted on its feet like an athlete. The infant was somewhat worried for breath at first, but it gradually recovered equilibrium, and in five minutes was serenely sucking its thumb. The father climbed down by the tin water pipe at the corner of the building.

Safe Vaults.

A vase of wax flowers was taken from a vault on Dearborn street, and was found perfect—not having been injured in the least. From another safe on Dearborn street was taken a box of matches, as new in appearance as when turned out of the factory. The vault of the *Tribune* also yielded all its contents in perfect order, even to a box of matches.

A Deranged Woman.

One of the most pitiful sights was that of a middle aged woman on State street, loaded with bundles, struggling through the crowd singing the Mother Goose melody:

"Chickery, chickery,
Craney crow,
I went to the well to wash my toe," &c.

There were hundreds of others likewise distracted, and many rendered desperate by the whisky or beer which, from excessive thirst, in the absence of water, they drank in great quantities, spread themselves in every direction, to the terror of all they met.

Roche the Teamster.

James Roche, a teamster, lived at 40 Glen street. While attempting to save his furniture a faggot fell in the wagon he was loading and lighted the straw bed in which his wife had deposited $300. While he was trying to save something from the wreck of the load she came rushing out of the house in a blaze, and ran up the street. Roche made chase, overtook her, thrust her into a door, and stripped her of every remnant of her flaming garb. Nothing was left upon her. This house was on fire in another minute. Roche rushed into the street and seized a horse-blanket, which he gave to his wife, and then returned to his house. Here he met another woman in flames, and handled her with similar roughness, and discovered that she was his only daughter. He sent her after her mother down the street, as nude as my lady Godiva, and let us hope that every eye similarly respected her. She found her mother, and the two, in one horse-blanket, crept under the sidewalk and made their way thus to North avenue bridge, where they lay secreted all through the rainy night and far into the next day, until relief was brought.

THE GREAT CONFLAGRATION, AS SEEN FROM THE PRAIRIE.

What Cider accomplished.

One building that remains, an oasis in a bleak and black Sahara, is a small, white, wooden cottage on Lincoln place. A policeman named Bellinger lived here. He hauled up the sidewalk, raked up the leaves and burned them, hewed down the fence and carried it into the house in pieces, and notified his neighbors that, live or die, he would stick to that house. The fire advanced and gave battle. It flung torches into his porch, it hurled them through the windows. It began and kept up a hot bombardment of flaming shot upon the roof. He met it at every point; with hands and boots, with water and wet blankets, and finally as the last wave of fire enveloped the building in a sirocco and whirled through the crackling tree-tops and gyrated madly over the adjacent walls and wavered and whirled over the smoking roof, Bellinger cast a pale into his cistern and it was dry. The blankets were on fire. Then the Bellinger genius rose triumphant. He assaulted his cider barrels, and little by little, emptied their contents on the roof. It was the *coup de guerre.* It gave him victory. His blankets were scorched, his hands blistered, his boots distorted, and his cider spilled, but his house was saved.

The Post Office Cat.

One of the features of the post office was the official cat. This notorious feline may or may not have had a name; at any rate it is not now known, she (or he) had been once before burned out, and was, therefore, in a measure prepared for this calamity. On the night of the fire the cat was present and assisted in the removal, though she did not go herself. Nobody invited her, and she was too much of a public spirited employeé to go without permission. When the work of removing the safes was in progress, the tearing away of a partition revealed the faithful public servant in a pail partially filled with water. She had rented this as temporary quarters and apparently enjoyed the cool shelter which it afforded. From her position it appeared impossible that she could have gone away and returned after the fire, and so she may be set down as the only living being who passed Sunday night and Monday in the burnt district.

Fire Humors.

It was a remarkable feature of the fire that it developed humor as well as pathos. One merchant, who found his safe and its contents destroyed, quietly remarked that there was no blame attached to the safe; that it was of chilled iron, and would have stood, but that the fire had taken the *chill all out.*

A firm of painters on Madison street bulletined their removal as follows, on a sign-board erected like a guide-board upon the ruins of their old establishment:

MOORE & GOE,
HOUSE AND SIGN PAINTERS,
Removed to 111 Desplaines ct.,
Capital, $000,000.30.

An editor of a daily paper received several poetical effusions suggested by the late disaster; but he declined them all, on the ground that it was wasteful to print anything which required every line with a capital, when capital was so scarce.

A bride who entered the holy married state on Tuesday evening determined to do so in a calico dress, in deference both to the proprieties and the necessities of the occasion. But she desired that her *toilette de chambre* should be, if possible, on a more gorgeous scale. Being destitute of a *robe de nuit* of suitable elegance, she sent out to several neighbors of her temporary hostess to borrow such a garment, stipulating that it must be a *fine one.* So peculiar is the feminine nature, however, that her request excited no enthusiasm in her behalf among the ladies to whom it came.

A signboard stuck in the ruins of a building on Madison street, read: "Owing to circumstances over which we had no control, we have removed," etc.

A Narrow Escape.

The following thrilling episode is narrated by an eye witness:

A woman was seen at the window of a building, shrieking for assistance. The building was on fire within, and the only hope of escape, the staircases, had been destroyed. The walls were still safe, and a short ladder was procured. A man with long silvery hair mounted a box and cried out: "A hundred dollars to any brave man who will go to her rescue!" A dozen men sprang forward, and the leader said: "We don't want your money, but we will try!" Throwing off his coat, the stranger seized a rope, ran up the ladder, and entered the lower window. He was lost from view for a moment, but soon returned, his shirt blackened with the smoke and burned by the falling embers. "Let some one come up," he shouted; "I want some help." Another followed, and the ladder was drawn in and pushed up through the burning flames at the staircase. They mounted to the story above and repeated the process. They were now within one story of the poor woman. She meanwhile had been caught by the flames, and to save herself had been obliged to tear off her outer clothing. Not a moment was to be lost, and when the men appeared at the window—with hair curled with the intense heat, their clothing in rags and partially burned—

and sent down the coil of rope for a new ladder, (theirs having been broken by a falling timber) all hope seemed gone. But by great efforts they raised the ladder to where they were, and once more essayed to reach the hapless woman above them. But the flames were too hot, and they were forced back from the interior to the window. Here they essayed to throw the rope to the woman, but in the excitement of the occasion they could not succeed.

The leader, however, was a man of resources, and lowering the rope again, he started for the hook. One was attached, and when drawn up he managed to hand the rope to the woman, and shouted to her to make it fast and to descend to them. She tied the rope to some place, still strong enough to sustain the strain, but could not, in her weakness, risk herself in the descent. All seemed lost; but the crowd soon beheld the first of the men slowly ascending the rope, hand over hand. Cheer after cheer hailed him as he drew himself into the window. In a moment the woman was lowered to the story below, where she was seized by the second brave rescuer, who drew her into the room and waited for the descent of his companion. The rope was not long enough to reach from where it was attached to the pavement, but a second was produced, and a piece of twine attached to a stone, was thrown in, which enabled them to haul it up. The two then lowered the woman, almost "in *natura puribus*," to the street and the first lowered the second and then came down himself.

A Scene in the Tunnel.

While the fire was raging in the South Division, a thrilling scene occurred in the Washington street tunnel. Several of the bridges over the South Branch being on fire, the tunnel was resorted to by thousands of people who desired to pass from one division into the other. At a moment when the passage way was filled with pedestrians, rushing wildly in either direction, the gas suddenly gave out and all were left in total darkness. A terrible panic, a collision, and the trampling to death of the weaker by the stronger, seemed inevitable. But, strange as it may seem, everybody in that dark recess seemed at once to comprehend the necessity for coolness and courage; not a man lost his presence of mind; but all, as with one accord, bore to the right, each calmly enjoining upon others to be cool and steady, and to march steadily on till the end of the tunnel could be reached. Rapidly, but without confusion, the two columns moved on through the thick darkness with almost military precision, the silence being broken only by frequent shouts of "right," "right." There was no collision, and no one was harmed, but all reached the ends of the tunnel in safety, and then, for the first time in almost ten minutes, breathed freely.

Puritan Relics Unharmed.

The beautiful New England Church, in the North Division, was one of the most perfect Gothic structures in the country, was utterly destroyed, with the exception of the Scotch granite columns at the entrance, some Puritan relics from Scrooby Manor, and a piece of the Plymouth Rock, which were inserted in the main archway, above the door. With genuine Scotch persistency and Puritan firmness, these refused to yield to either wind or flame, and still remain there. In a similar manner, all that remain of St. James' Church is the memorial monument to her sons who fell in battle.

Advertisements.

Taking up the first issue of the *Chicago Tribune*, after the fire, the advertisements are singularly suggestive of grief, uncertainty and penury. Many begin as follows: "Wanted to find, Swedish girl Sophia, formerly living in my family;" "A lost cow can be found at," etc.; "Two stray trunks can be heard from at," etc.; "Taken out of the flames, a dark bay mare;" "Ten dollars reward, and no question asked, for a pailfull of dental instruments taken from," etc.; "If the grey-whiskered man who was seen removing trunks from," etc.; "Mr. ———, please call at ———, and get your boy 'Georgie;'" "Mr. ———, go to number ———; your father is there." "Agnes ——— will find her father at ———." And so on for two long, closely-printed columns. There is also a fearful number of "missing" notices, and a column of the very finest type is devoted to a record of those who are "lost and found."

An Heroic Old Woman.

A young lady who escaped from the burning city, in the course of a graphic account of the great fire, tells the following: "Two blocks beyond where I lived in Halstead street lived an old German, an almost helpless cripple, whose sole support was his wife and young son. The latter went away in the morning and did not return. The fire rapidly approached with deadly omen, and the old couple were not only distracted at the absence of the boy, but fearful of their possible fate. At last the flames came so near that they must fly or die. In the strength of her affection the old woman seized the poor cripple, placed him upon her back, and thus staggered along for a distance of two blocks, when some men placed him in a grocer's wagon and drew him to a place of safety."

Coolness.

Another writer says: "I met a friend on Tuesday, walking thoughtfully around with a piece of lead pipe. As I approached and saluted him he stopped, slapped the lead pipe down on a brick wall, it smashed flat, and then said, 'Joe, that pipe's all I've got in the world, but I begin again to-morrow.' I met a man on the night of the fire who had lost first his store and then his handsome residence on Michigan avenue. He was lugging around a marble mantel with the heavy sides attached. He laughed as he saw me, and remarked, 'That's all there is now; but I'm going to see if I can't find another and build a house to fit.' "

Unfortunate Benevolence.

An Iowan heard of the fire on Monday morning and took passage to Chicago to succor the family of his son, who was living there. At a wayside station not far from Chicago he heard that the water works were burned, and that there was a scarcity of water. Not being familiar with the geographical position, he purchased a cask and brought it full of water to Chicago. A philanthropic expressman charged him $50 dollars for carting that barrel to his son's residence.

A Plucky Merchant.

A Chicago merchant who was in New York when the great fire destroyed his store and stock of merchandise, at once bought a large invoice of sugars and syrups and started for home, telling his merchants that by the time the goods reached Chicago he would have his store rebuilt to receive them. He kept his word. On the 19th inst., he telegraphed his New York friends:

"We enter a new store to-morrow, made since the fire, and resume payment in full and at maturity."

Fire Proof Buildings.

Horace White, Esq., the Editor in Chief of the *Chicago Tribune*, in an extremely interesting communication to the *Cincinnati Commercial*, thus clearly shows the reasons why the supposed fire proof buildings in the city succumbed to the flames.

"The Post Office was lost by defective internal construction. There was hardly any wood work in it except furniture. The floors were of stone or clay tiles, the window-casing of iron, and all the outer doors iron. But then there were no interior walls, or next to none. In place of these were upright iron columns and girders, these supporting iron beams, and these again furnishing the resting places for the brick arches which held the several floors. The building itself was surrounded on the four sides by streets, though one of these was narrow as Nassau street, New York. It had no point of contact with any other building. But the heat from the narrow street set the furniture on fire. This warped and sprung the great iron columns which supported the floors, and so the whole interior came down into the cellar. The *Tribune* building was constructed with a view to avoid this defect. There were no iron columns in the interior except where they were employed to give greater strength to the brick walls. Consequently the interior is nearly all standing, the two eight-cylinder presses uninjured to all appearance, except by the burning of the tapes and feed boards, the beautiful engines, whose noiseless strength I have so often admired, scarcely soiled, the boilers perfectly intact, and most wonderful of all, two or three barrels of printers' ink under the alley not burned or upset. For all this, the heat generated by a whole square of combustible, five-story buildings, of which the *Tribune* was one corner, was greater than that of an ordinary blast furnace. It was more than sufficient to melt cast iron. Our brick walls were a great protection, but the exterior wall on the south side, eighteen inches thick, next to a wholesale stationery store, is bulged inward at one place near the bottom fully two inches. This was not enough to let the wall down, and as it was braced with iron beams all the way up it was kept from falling on our printing machinery. A small segment fell out of the front of the building on Madison street. This was caused by the weight of an immense iron safe belonging to the Charter Oak Life Insurance Company, which stood against a wall in the second story. The iron beams getting more or less displaced by the expansive power of the heat, the weight of the safe was brought to bear upon them with a leverage which pried a hole ten or fifteen feet wide out of the Madison street front, and of course every thing which rested upon it came down.

"These two buildings are types of all the so-called fire proof structures of the city, seven or eight in number. It is ascertained that no stone ever used in the business part of the city is worth a farthing in such a fire. Brick is the only thing that comes out whole, and is ready to try it again. The future Chicago will be a city of bricks. But it is not fair to say that an absolutely fire proof building cannot be erected. I think it can be. At all events, the architects of the world should come here and study."

What a Determined Man did.

The manner in which Mr. John G. Shortall, of the firm of Shortall & Hoard, saved their numerous abstracts and indices of real estate transactions, which in the destruction of the public records are invaluable as evidences of title, shows what a determined man can do in an emergency. Mr. Shortall had returned from church to his home in the southern part of the city, and from some unaccountable impulse went down to the fire and watched it for an hour or more, when he began to fear that his office in Larmon block, opposite the court house, might be in danger. His own account of his experiences from this point on is as follows:

"On reaching the office I found great danger existing from the awnings, which were outside the buildings, the embers dropping down very thick on the roofs of the buildings, and on the front, and signs, and awnings. I ran up stairs, got into the office and tried to cut away the awnings in front of our building, and that of the building adjoining; but, owing to the absence of anything adequate, I had to give that up, and simply press them up close to the wall, that the embers might drop off them, and not be caught in them. Even then I scarcely believed it possible that the Larmon block could take fire, and I requested the men in the upper portion of the building, with buckets of water, to put out any embers that might fall there and endanger the building. In another half hour I felt more apprehensive, and went in the street to find an express wagon. This must have been an hour and a half before the building actually burned. I stopped, probably fifteen different trucks and express wagons, offering them any pay to work for me in saving the books. Seven of them, at least, I engaged, one after another, they faithfully promising me that they would come back when they had carried the load and done the work in which they were engaged; but no one came back. At this juncture, I met a friend, Mr. Nye, who was looking out, as I was, for the danger. I told him I needed him, and he answered me promptly that he was at my service. We both watched some time longer for express wagons; but could find none. At last, when the court house cupola took fire, I told my friend that we must have an express wagon within the next five minutes or we were utterly lost. He stood on Clark street and I on Washington, determined to take the first expressman we could find. The first one happened to come along on his side. He seized the reins with one hand; and, taking a revolver from his pocket with the other, "persuaded" the expressman to haul up to the sidewalk, notwithstanding his cursing and swearing. When I came back from my unsuccessful watch, I found the expressman there, and my friend, handing the lines and revolver to me, went up stairs to help our employees, who were then in the office, to carry down the volumes. We got round with the wagon to Washington street entrance, and after filling the wagon, found that we had but about one quarter of our property in it.

"Just at that critical moment I saw a two horse truck drive up to where I was superintending the packing of the books, and my friend Joe Stockton, who was so covered with smut and dust that I did not recognize him until he spoke, turned over the truck and driver to me, with the remark, 'I think, John, this is just the thing you want.' I never felt so relieved or so thankful as I did at his appearance with that substantial aid at that moment. We unpacked our impressed expressman immediately and set him adrift with $5 in his pocket for his five minutes' work, and commenced to pile our property on friend Stockton's truck. Meanwhile the flames were roaring and surging around us. Six of our boys were carrying down the volumes as rapidly as they could, and I, standing on the truck, was stowing away the books economically as to space. About that time they told me the court house bell fell down. I lost all idea of time. It must have been about two o'clock. I never heard the bell fall, I was so excited. Toward the last, when we had got our indices all safely down, and were trying to save other valuable papers and books, many of which we did save, it was stated that Smith & Nixon's building was about to be blown up. Our truck was headed toward that building. The sky was filled with burning embers which were falling around us thickly. As soon, I think, as the information was given that that building was to be blown up, the crowd rushed past us down Washington street, toward the lake, terribly excited, shouting and warning everybody away. My driver was very nervous, and on one pretext or another would start his horses up for a rod or two, swearing that he would not be blown up for us or for the whole country; but I succeeded in stopping him eight or ten times during the terrible excitement. In the meantime our men were coming down the stairs laden with our property, and returning as rapidly as they could. I was standing on the books, packing them in the truck, and the embers were flying on them, and I picked them off as they fell and threw them into the street, until a rod at a time, we reached the corner of Dearborn and Washington. Messrs. Fuller and Handy were the last to leave the office, and they did not leave until Buck & Rayner's drug store was on fire. The store, as we believed, was full of chemicals and explosive matter. At that time the court house was a mass of flames, our building was burning, and other buildings in the immediate vicinity were entirely destroyed.

"Three of us then started with the truck for my house, which we reached about three o'clock that morning. I had our property unloaded and placed securely within; and, after giving the driver and others some refreshments, I started again for the fire to see what aid I could give other sufferers."

A Fearful Trotting Match.

On the morning of the fire occurred the most fearful trotting race on record. It was a race between the flames and Mr. Fred. Blackmar, with his brown mare "Kittie." Mr. Blackmar was a junior partner in one of the largest publishing houses in the city, and his little brown mare had won a reputation as one of the fastest roadsters in the city. A correspondent tells the story of the race as follows:

"Kittie, who had become a well known equine to all those who frequented the boulevards, was stabled in a barn on Dearborn street, almost opposite the post office. The fire had eaten far into the heart of the city, and was rapidly swallowing building after building in its rapacious jaws. Southward and northward along famed Newspaper avenue, as Dearborn street was sometimes called, the fire was driven by the fierce gale, which swept in eddies from over the prairies.

BURNING OF THE CENTRAL GRAIN ELEVATOR AT THE MOUTH OF THE CHICAGO RIVER.

"Blackmar, who lived in the West Division, had gone down early in the fight to assist in saving property from the store, and it was not until late on Monday morning he thought of Brown Kittie. Then he started for the barn only to find the front of the building was one vast sheet of flame. Nowhere could he see the hostler. Through a back door he rushed into the stable, and there stood his pet shivering in every limb. With a cry of joy she recognized her master, and while he was unfastening her halter the grateful creature placed her nose against his face and gently rubbed his cheek. A moment later and the mare was hitched to the light road wagon, the back door was thrown open, Fred sprang into his seat, and while the burning hay dropped down upon him in fiery flakes he drove forth into a perfect hell of flame. There was a narrow alley with buildings on fire on either side of it for him to drive through, and faster than Kittie ever went before went she through that gauntlet of flame. Once a tongue of flame reached across the alley and scorched poor Kittie's handsome mane, and almost burnt out one of her bright eyes, which were almost human in their expression, but Fred spoke gently to her, and with never a skip she went onward and onward across State street, and no chance to turn to the right or left, with buildings blazing up in front and Death with the double team crowding him closely in the rear. Now Wabash avenue was reached, and like lightning the little darling turned the corner and flew with the speed of thought southward along the broad thoroughfare, whose western side was already one long row of flame. With a straight road before him, perfectly level and laid with Nicholson pavement, Fred sent the mare faster and faster. Away off toward Jackson street he could see the black smoke and the red flames reaching across, trying to seize upon the opposite side of the way, and should they succeed before he passed the spot, then all escape was impossible. 'Gently, Kittie, gently!' They were the first words he had spoken for some time. 'Now, then my little lady,' and for the first time in all his life he touched her with the whip. The mare broke into a run, and there was no stopping her. Like a thoroughbred she sped before the wind, and almost in a trice she had cleared the fire and was still running desperately toward the southward. Presently Blackmar succeeded in pulling her down to a trot, and finally he jogged her along at a pace so slow no one would have supposed her the best little equine in all Christendom."

Fatal Leap for Life.

Just north of Madison street, on the east side of Dearborn street, stood Speed's block, consisting of five four-story brick buildings, with stone fronts. The upper parts of the buildings were occupied as offices, and some of the occupants slept in the rooms. When the fire had reached Madison and Dearborn streets, from the west, a man, who had evidently taken full time to dress himself, appeared at a window in the rear. He coolly looked down the thirty feet between him and the ground, while the excited crowd cried to him to "jump!" and then some of the more considerate searched for a ladder. No ladder could be had, but a long plank was found and placed at once against the window, and the man seating himself on it, slid safely to the ground. But before this was accomplished, another man appeared at a window of the fourth story, in the adjoining building; there was no projecting balcony—the wall was flush to the ground for the distance of four stories and a basement. All escape by the interior was cut off—the building being then on fire within, and he looked out in seeming despair. The crowd was helpless, so far as doing anything for his rescue, and grew frantic in their excitement. From the *Tribune* office the whole scene was visible, lighted up by the blaze of a hundred buildings, and by the never-ceasing shower of fire. Senseless cries of "jump! jump!" went up from the crowd; senseless, but full of sympathy, for the sight was absolutely agonizing. Then for a minute or two he disappeared, perhaps even less, but it seemed so long that the supposition was that he had fallen suffocated by smoke and heat; but no, he appears again. First he throws a bed, then some bed clothes apparently; why, probably even he does not know. Again he looks down the dead, sheer wall of fifty feet below him. He hesitates, and well he may, as he turns again and looks behind him. Then he mounts to the window sill. His whole form appears, naked to the shirt, and his white limbs gleam against the dark wall in the bright light as he swings himself below the window. Somehow—how none can tell—he drops and catches upon the top of the windows below him, of the third story. He stoops and drops again, and seizes the frame with his hands, and his gleaming body once more straightens and hangs prone downward, and then drops instantly and accurately upon the window sill of the third story. A shout, more of joy than applause, goes up from the breathless crowd, and those who had turned away their heads, unable to look upon him as he seemed about to drop to sudden and certain death, glanced up at him once more with a ray of hope, at this daring and skilful feat. Into this window he crept, to look, possibly, for a stairway, but appeared again presently, for here was the only avenue of escape, desperate and hopeless as it was. Once more he dropped his body, hanging by his hands. The crowd screamed and waved to him to swing himself over to the projection from which the other man had just been rescued. He tried to do this, and vibrated like a pendulum from side to side, but could not reach far enough to throw himself upon its roof. Then he hung by one hand and looked down; raising the other hand, he took a fresh hold, and swung from side to side again to reach the roof. In vain; again he hung motionless by one hand, and slowly turned his head over his shoulder, and gazed in the abyss below him. Then, gathering himself up, he let go his hold, and for a second a gleam of white shot down full forty feet to the foundation of the basement. Of course, it killed him. He was taken to a drug store near by and died in ten minutes.

Who this person was no one knows. What became of his remains has never been ascertained. The drug store to which he was taken was burned within a few hours after, and every other building for half a mile south, and it was impossible to carry the body, if taken away at all, in any other direction. He had evidently been asleep, and was not awakened until the building was on fire.

A Wedding Postponed.

A wedding fixed for the week after the fire, was postponed by a letter of the lady to her lover, who was in an Eastern city. She was the daughter of a wealthy merchant, and in the letter after telling him of the fire, she wrote:

"Our wedding will have to be postponed for at least one year, as I am in no condition at present to be married; not that I love you less than ever, for you know that better than I can tell you, but that we have no house to live in and my father is rendered almost destitute by the fire. His place of business was, as you know, in the burnt district, and was swept away in company with a number of others the second night of the fire. We expect to have a new house built in a few weeks, just around the corner from where we formerly resided, near —— street and —— avenue. I am very glad you did not come to this city when you intended, for then you would be as the rest of us, half scared to death. Father was up at the time, and saved two suits of clothes—the one he had on and another—but we, that is, Mar, Jeneatte, and I, were less lucky. You would have been surprised to see me, the morning after we were driven out of the house, with a pair of Jim's old pants on, one slipper, one shoe, and a waterproof cloak. This was, indeed, my complete outfit, and it was not until yesterday that I received some other clothes from my cousin Mary, who sent them from Cincinnati. That would have made a splendid wedding suit, wouldn't it?

"The city is building up lively. Work is plenty, but a number of laborers have left this, the doomed city.

"Frank, please come on and see us as soon as you can; I want to see you very badly."

It is not likely that Frank declined that invitation, or that he consented to postpone the wedding a year, or any longer than a new outfit could be provided. Such a man would be out of place in a city which in three days after having been destroyed, was "building up lively," or worthy of the fair lady, who, notwithstanding she had no house to live in and her father was destitute, had time to note in her distress the cheering fact that "work was plenty."

Unprofitable Servants.

A prominent lady of Wabash avenue had been deserted by her servants as soon as it became certain that the house was doomed; they had gone off, taking with them whatever they could lay their hands on. She, her daughter, and her invalid husband, were alone in the house, and the flames were rapidly approaching. There was not a moment to spare, and the two women actually carried away in their arms the sick man, and brought him in safety beyond the reach of the fire.

Deep Grief.

Men, driven by that blind instinct which makes them, though hopeless, return to the scene of that disaster which has ruined them, sought the spots where once their homes had stood, and sitting down on some pieces of fallen timber, actually wept and wrung their hands in anguish.

One of these wretched beings sought his home, and, in stepping on a half-charred beam, caused it to spring up, and from beneath it came a sickly odor. He madly turned and pried away the timber, and saw beneath it the dead body of his son, a young man of about twenty years of age, who, probably returning to the house to save something he prized, had fallen in the flames and been burned to death—roasted alive.

At another point a strong man sitting upon a

wayside box, weeping like a child, his wife meanwhile cheerily boiling coffee with some bits of the unlaid Nicholson pavement, and his children playing hide and seek among the cast-out wares.

The Children.

The most pitiable sights were the sick children half dead, lying crouched on the sidewalks, in many cases with barely any covering on them. A pathetic scene was noticed on the corner of La Salle and Randolph streets, where two little girls were lying terror-stricken by the side of their dead sister, whose remains presented a harrowing spectacle. She had been too late to escape from under a falling building on Clark street, and had been extricated and carried to the corner by her almost dead sisters.

At the Tremont House the elevator became useless, and the sleeping guests, with a large number of babies, hurried down stairs. The removal of trunks and the hurrying of domestics impeded the passageways. Several persons, in their eagerness, jumped over the banisters and limped away. Others in their haste left beneath their pillows, watches and money, only discovering their losses, when they had reached the Michigan Central Depot—then supposed to be a perfectly safe place. A crowd of persons hastened thither, some carrying beds, some sewing machines, and one lady had six canary birds in a cage in one hand, and an immense family Bible in the other. She said: "I was determined to bring these off, if I lost all the rest." Another young woman was seen carrying two large paintings, evidently those of her father and mother. She was but partially clad, and amongst all her household wealth, sought to preserve these filial mementos as being to her most precious.

The Ludicrous.

Several incidents combine the pathetic with the ridiculous. An Irish woman was seen tugging along a half-grown pig, which kicked and squealed with all its might, until the panting female, overcome by the flames, abandoned the animal to its fate. A colored woman shouldered her week's washing in a huge wicker-basket, and grabbed with the other hand a frying-pan and some muffin-rings. Huge cinders fell on the clean, starched clothes and set them smoking. In this way the woman, already half-beside herself with terror, trudged along for several blocks, until the burning rags fell upon her neck and caused her to look around. With a howl of dismay and an expression of horror that can never be reproduced, she dropped her burden and fled for dear life. An immense Dutchman trundled a wheelbarrow along, loaded with a keg of lager beer, some sausages and clothing. His wife and children followed, all laden with sundry articles, two dogs bringing up the rear. He toiled and puffed along until the approach of the flames rendered more rapid flight necessary. The wheelbarrow was then abandoned, but not until the beer-keg was opened and a parting drink was taken all around.

Through the Tunnel.

At 2 o'clock on Monday morning, the people were fleeing in desperate fury from the death fiend pursuing in hot haste on flaming wings. The bridges on both sides were on fire, and the flames were writhing over the decks of the brigs in the river, and winding their fierce arms of flame around the masts and through the rigging, like a monstrous, luminous devil-fish. The awful canopy of fire drew down and closed over Water street, as the shrieking multitude rushed for the tunnel—the only avenue of escape. The gas works had already blown up, and there was no light in any house, save the illumination, which flamed up only to destroy. But into the darkened cave rushed pell-mell, from all directions, the frenzied crowd—bankers, thieves, draymen, wives, children—in every stage of undress, as they had leaped from burning lodgings, a howling, imploring, cursing, praying, writhing mob, making their desperate dive under the river. It was as dark in the tunnel as it is in the centre of the earth, Hundreds of the fugitives were laden with furniture. household goods, utensils, loaves of bread and pieces of meat, and their rush through the almost suffocating tunnel was fearful in the extreme. They knocked each other down, and the strong trod on the helpless. Nothing was heard at the mouth of the cavernous prison, but a muffled howl of rage and anguish. Several came forth with broken limbs and terrible bruises, as they scattered and resumed their flight under the blazing sky to the North Ward.

The Court House Bell, Chicago.

The court house bell, which for so many years had given hourly warning of the flight of time rung forth joyous peals in honor of military and civil victories, told of the presence of fire in the city, and sounded the death toll of the distinguished dead, now lies an almost shapeless mass, surrounded by heaps of brick, mortar and stone, in the east wing of the court house. On the fatal Sunday night, the old bell, even while surrounded by fire, sounded a solemn, continuous and final peal; and those who heard it above the din produced by falling walls, the hoarse roaring of the flames, the crackling of falling embers, and the shouts and screams of alarmed citizens, say they will never forget how awful the sound appeared. Scarcely had the bell cooled after the fire, when hundreds of curiosity hunters went in search of it, armed with cold chisels and hammers. As a consequence, about two-thirds of the metal has disappeared. Pieces of it have sold at high figures, while others have found their way by mail to neighboring cities, to be converted into rings, scarf pins, brooches, etc.

Labors of Love.

Amidst all the ruins and sufferings there were many acts of love and charity to soften the hard fate that had fallen upon the people. Many noble-hearted ladies, bred to scenes of luxury and ease, went about doing good with a zest rivalled only by the energy of the men who resolved to rebuild their city and their manufactories.

Grace Church, on Wabash avenue, is one of the few buildings left standing, and with a true Christian zeal the congregation turned it over to the Relief Committee, for such uses as were deemed necessary. Here, under the able management of the Rev. Dr. Locke, were groups of ladies, delicately reared, acting as the almoners of the world's rich bounty. Most of the people who thronged about the church had been fed quite exclusively, since the fire, on bread or crackers; the reception, therefore, of cooked meat, baked beans, and other plain condiments, was peculiarly acceptable. Porters were constantly entering, bearing in hats, aprons, pillow-cases, baskets and barrels, supplies of food, which were deposited in convenient places for distribution. Generally the applicants represented families or groups of friends, and though they solicited heavy supplies, there was, thanks to the benevolence of sister cities, a goodly portion for each.

This latter class hastened away to the temporary lodgings, while others, who came for themselves, received their share, and walking quietly from the church, ate their food on the street.

There we saw Germans, Irish, Scandinavians, Jews, Italians, and representatives of other nations, laboring men and women, and children of all classes of life, now reduced by hunger and poverty to a common footing.

While this ceremony was attracting the attention of the unfortunate in the church proper, the spacious chapel was filled by day with another party of ladies, working into sandwiches the fresh bread and sweet ham that had been received. These ladies were principally Sabbath school teachers and the daughters of leading citizens; but their fine round arms were bared to the work, and they shaved and sliced as if their very lives depended on their activity. In front of them filed a steady stream of little children, with empty stomachs and ragged clothes, who in regular turn received a hearty meal. These soon after disporting themselves amid the adjacent ruins.

In the evening, however, we witnessed spectacles in the chapel of the church which seemed more touching than those of the day. As the sun went down, and the air grew chilly little squads of men and women, leading by the hand or bearing on the arm, babes and children, marched timidly to the porch, and asked permission to lie down during the night. Many of the benches had been removed, and on the bared portion, cushions were stretched, and the careworn visitors invited to make themselves as comfortable as possible. Here, during hours that appeared lengthened beyond measure, these distressed people endeavored to catch a few moments of repose. Some who had been vainly seeking shelter for many days, slumbered heavily; others groaned and started as delirious dreams grew in their brain; while here and there, babes uttered shrill cries for nourishment, and the sleep that came tardily to them. At all hours of the night pilgrims approached this Mecca, and by the time the sun glanced through the windows, one would have made slow progress in passing about the chapel.

Reflections and Suggestions.

Major D. C. Houston, of the Engineer Corps of the U. S. army, published the following interesting paper on the situation of Chicago.

"The spirit displayed by the business men of this city in rebuilding is astonishing, and deserving of the highest praise after a calamity so terrible as the recent conflagration. That Chicago will rise again, and not only resume her old position, but become in time the first city on this continent, seems to me to be as certain as the perpetuation of our government and the increase of our population.

"It should be borne in mind at this time, that there were certain defects in the plan of Chicago, arising from the rapidity of its construction, which seemed beyond remedy, except at enormous cost; but now it is possible, by considering the subject in time, and taking advantage of the experience of other cities, to make such re-arrangements as will make the plan and accommodations of this city suitable for the metropolis of America.

"The present burnt district, on the south side, is, by universal consent, to become the centre of the city, and every consideration indicates that it should be so. Were the whole city to be laid out anew, the natural features of the country and the railroad communications would point to the south side as the centre. The business operations will commence here, and radiate, as heretofore, to the south, west, and north, but more to the south, owing to the fact that the communication is uninterrupted by natural obstacles. Into this centre hundreds of thousands of people will pour daily, coming from the residence portion of the city, the suburbs, and the whole country.

"There is always, in great cities, an immense amount of time lost in going to and fro from business, and in the absence of proper accommodations for doing business, after the business centre is reached. Persons familiar with the city of New York understand this fully. Two or three hours of the day are consumed in travelling to and fro, and, owing to the crowds in the streets, the contracted markets and places of exchange, the time required to transact business is doubled and trebled.

"Now the points which seem to me to be considered at this time and to be fully provided for, are:

"1. The laying out of certain lines for steam communication from the centre of business to the suburbs, to be so arranged as not to obstruct the street travel, or be interrupted by it. This most essential element of a modern metropolis can never be secured or arranged for, so well as at present.

"2. The arrangement of commodious and central depots for the great lines of railroads centring in the city.

"3. A commodious levee along the river for public docks, a grand market, a grand plaza, where all can go without paying tribute. Instead of having buildings built close down to the river bank, let there be an open space on each side of the river devoted to the above purposes.

"4. The great leading lines of business should be consolidated or concentrated on certain streets running north and south. There should be a financial centre, a dry goods centre, a hardware centre, etc.

"5. An open square for public meetings and out-door business. The Court House square suggests itself at once. Let the court house go further south and leave the present square open.

"Let it be surrounded by banks, brokers' offices, etc., and there will be room for everybody. These suggestions are hurriedly thrown out, but they should be considered, and a committee representing all interests, should be appointed to draw up a scheme by which these desirable results can be secured. In the rebuilding of the city these matters can all be arranged for the benefit of all.

"The business portion of Chicago had already become overcrowded with the street cars, omnibuses,

MASONIC TEMPLE, DEARBORN STREET.

other vehicles, and foot passengers. The limit of capacity had almost been reached.

"You believe in Chicago's future, and a few minutes' reflection will convince any one that more space is needed for the future, and that concentration and co-operation on the part of business men is necessary, to make the best use of the ground now available."

After the Fire.

On Friday, October 15th, 1871, people had so collected themselves as to remember the ludicrous scenes which occurred around them in the awful hours of the burning. Then were called to mind the man who fled with a single joint of stove-pipe under his arm and left his papers to the flames; and the other man, who, abandoning his pictures escaped with a feather dusting broom; and that tenderer picture of the little girl who passed up Michigan avenue, barefooted and bareheaded, struggling under the weight of a box containing four new-born puppies. An eye-witness told us of the attempt to blow up the building occupied by a clothing establishment, Brown & Hammond's, if I am not mistaken. By some accident the fuse did not communicate with the powder intended to do the work. Just after the fuse had gone off, four thieves issued from the building and deliberately walked away with their arms full of clothing. Among the stories of extortion, we have heard this one. An undertaker with a hearse attempted to charge fifteen dollars for conveying a coffin from the burnt district over on to the west side, and the corpse put his head out and remonstrated. An enterprising Chicagoan, it appears, had formed a plan of getting across the river at a reasonable rate; and so terrified was the undertaker that the *ruse* succeeded beyond expectation. The coffin was "dumped out" at its destination, and the driver of the hearse never waited for any pay at all.

Saturday after the fire a rain-storm set in, followed by a terrific gale at sunset. All night long the trees under our window rocked and wailed. There can have been little sleep in the city until toward morning, when the wind abated. Some of the most picturesque, and at the same time the most dangerous, of the ruins were blown down. Sunday opened a bright, cool day. The burnt districts were early thronged with people in carriages, express-wagons, omnibuses, and on foot. Every one, with scarcely an exception, that I can remember, had a clean, washed-up appearance. It must be that the poorer sufferers by the fire did not visit the ruins on Sunday, or else the charity of the outside world has been swift to clothe and cleanse them. So admirable, indeed, have been the arrangements of the relief committees, that one has to go to the churches or other place of refuge for the homeless, to come face to face with positive suffering.

The churches were thronged on this Sabbath morning. Denominations and creeds were forgotten. Societies whose regular places of worship had been burned, met and were cordially received at the churches yet standing. In some instances services were held in the open air, in front of the ruined sanctuaries. Just outside of what was once his church, Robert Collyer is said to have spoken as only he can speak. We could not get there until the afternoon, when the neighborhood was almost deserted. We were fortunate enough, however, to be present at the services in front of one of the Methodist churches. Nothing in modern times, I think, has come so near to primitive Christianity in circumstance and spirit, as this preaching of mutual helpfulness in the face of universal loss and in that desert of ruins.

Chicago by Moonlight.

Only the moon, just rising in the east, casts an uncertain lustre over the scene. The busy men are gone. Nothing is heard but the steady footfall of the patrolman, or the quicker steps of some one hurrying to reach his home. The ruined wall and shattered masonry are softened and refined by the clear, mild light. Dark nooks and deeply-shaded recesses, which by daylight would lose their secrecy, and be nothing but waste blanks, are in the evening full of the charm of mystery and of darkness. Fancy peoples those secluded spots with the creatures of her imagination, and they seem fitting homes for ghoul and afrit—creatures who lurk among the ruined tombs and devour the belated wanderers there. The long, black lines of pavement stretch out into the infinite dim distance as if they led to the quiet homes of the dead. Here and there the vast bulk of undestroyed buildings tower up, silent and uninhabited, like the watch-towers which Vathek saw at Istakhar. Through their open windows streams the moonlight, and half hides and half reveals the fallen walls and shattered floors within. There are inscriptions on them, but it is too dark to spell out the names of supervisors who tried to secure immortality, and have passed successfully through this ordeal of fire.

In this indefinite light all things are old, and all things are strange. It is no longer Chicago, the sky above is clear and starry enough to look upon the Rhine and Arno, instead of the Chicago river. Telegraph posts are transfigured into burned and branchless trees, and in this blue land of supreme fancy, the prosaic and the commonplace have disappeared forever. There are slight, faint sounds, which may be the imagined voices of the night, or the pulsations of the lake, or the sighing of the wind; but there is no hum of myriads, no many-voiced utterances of men.

Yonder, burnt and bruised and blackened, stands the church, its pealing organ stilled forever. Through its gaping portals no more wedding parties shall pass. It has buried its last dead, and there it remains its own monument. Those who have been baptized there are scattered far and wide, and have forgotten the font over which they were once held. The young men who, in the intoxication of first love, followed their sweethearts there, and endured the sermon for the sake of being near the beloved, have outlived the passionate ardor of them, and will not regret the ruined sanctuary, which, to them, was the temple of Cupid, and not of Jehovah. The light glancing through the wide window, falls full upon the untouched memorial of marble. All the artificial aid to devotion, the cushioned pews, the soft foot stools, the elegantly bound books, have disappeared, but it remains, unmoved, while all around is in ruins. The monuments of the dead outlast by far the homes of the living. Here there is no feeling of newness. It might be a page taken from middle age history. Cowled and girdled monks, or corpulent friars, might have dwelt there, and the odor that one perceives might be a reminiscence of frankincense and myrrh, consumed in swinging censers, rather than that peculiar smell which follows a fire. It is so dark that one cannot see the ivy on the walls, but one knows that it is there, and if it were not so hackneyed, one would be apt to quote certain lines concerning Melrose Abbey. But on such occasions people do not express their feelings in the words of another. They do not seek to express them at all, but float along idly, borne by the current of their thoughts, like a boat drifting on the bosom of the river.

At another point one can faintly distinguish twisted and distorted iron beams, half covering and half covered by massive blocks of stone. There they lie, in one chaotic mass, dumb witnesses of some terrible conflict. By the light of day we could tell how recent had been their overthrow; but now, by the uncertain beams of the moon, we cannot tell but what they are as venerable as the world itself, and sitting there, we can reconstruct them as we will. Story by story rises the airy pile. Bright lights gleam from its windows, and strains of music mingle with the tread of the feet that cross its marble floors. But the flickering flame, still fitfully burning in the centre of the ruins, suddenly dies out, and the lights disappear, and the building goes down as suddenly as it rose; and with it, the guests that thronged its halls. Beyond it is something that was once a pile of wheat. Now it is a hill which dwarfs those in Lincoln Park, and from its sides come intermittent jets of fire and smoke. Were it only higher, then imagination could easily convert it into a new Vesuvius. Its flames serve to light up the building beyond, and cast a dim, uncertain glare upon the river, a rival of the lighthouse, and an unsafe guide for sailors.

It is a great pity, for purely artistic reasons, that there are not more walls standing. These poor half-story remnants have not half the pathos of a building, which, destroyed within, still uprears itself and bids defiance to fate. It is a blind Samson, but a Samson still powerful for good or evil; and the architect will come along in the morning, and will scan the vast, though scarred proportions, and will dose him with bricks and mortar, and whitewash him, and restore his flowing locks—to wit, put a

Mansard roof on him, and he will look about as good as new, though the traces of the wounds are still visible, if you only know where to look for them; or else the Fire Marshal will order the walls to come down, and, in the act of doing it, two or three Philistines will be slain, and the coroner will be called upon to hold an inquest, and will find a difficulty in doing so, since the county is too poor to pay twenty-five cents per head to jurymen, and there are no more inducements to accept the position. For office seeking is at an end for the moment, and when the court house was burned, more than half the candidates promptly withdrew. To these buildings, thus left partly standing, there is a wonderful expression, varying with their condition. There are those which seem to implore, and those which seem to threaten. Some are weary of the contest with fortune, while others are still obdurate, and unwilling to give way; but about these odds and ends of brick and mortar there is no expression whatever. No life remains in them, and nothing can lend them the power to charm. But the eye lingers fondly over hanging cornices and projecting pinnacles, one moment bright with the moon, and then shading away into darkness.

Over to the left there is nothing. There no walls remain, and the eye can distinguish nothing but a succession of slight hollows and slight elevations. It might have been anything—a water-washed field, or a space of ground, on which had been deposited dust heaps or the refuse of a furnace.

Beyond that lies a black chasm where the river flows, and as one gets nearer, the gleam of the moonlight upon the waves at once changes the character of the scene. Then there was a dark abyss, beyond which grimly rose a long vista of half-destroyed and threatening walls. Now, the glancing and sparkling waters have dispelled the loneliness and wildness of the spot. For who can feel solitary when he is near a stream that is pure enough to mirror the firmament in its bosom, and whose slight, inarticulate noises furnish him company, and invite him, like the song of the sirens, to come nigher and nigher? While the brook is a child, with which one laughs and babbles, the river is a full-grown man, wherewith we can hold reasonable converse, and wherefrom we can gain rare information, to be found nowhere else. For a moment the moon is eclipsed, and the powers of night have fully resumed their control. By the dim starlight, one can see only the vaguely outlined forms of objects near at hand. The river has gone from sight, and the buildings beyond are swallowed up in the darkness. Far away are the blazing coal heaps, burning up like mimic volcanoes, and farther yet, the gas lamps of the west side; but they seem infinitely remote, and on the verge of the horizon of the night. All other sights, all sounds, have died away, and there remains only a sense of desolation and ruin, so great and terrible that one can linger no longer, but gropes his way as best he can back to the light, and the homes of men.

The Spine of Chicago.

A son of Mayor Mason was engaged in the stove business and was at Troy, New York, at the time of the fire, he returned to Chicago, arriving Tuesday morning. The *Troy Times* tells what he did in view of the calamity:

"He is a young man and just commenced business life. Married a little over a year ago, he was established in a prosperous stove trade, and had just completed a new house for himself and wife. Everything was swept away, except his wedding presents, which were at the house of his father. This house was saved. The fires were hardly out before young Mason gathered these presents together and started with them for New York. He sold them to Tiffany & Co. for $5,000 With this money he will now re-establish himself, opening a store, at present, in the basement of his father's elegant residence. A car load of stoves was shipped to him on Saturday. The young man shows the real Chicago pluck."

Another instance is shown in the following dispatch of a merchant whose wife and family were in New York. The telegraph was not in operation until Tuesday, when among the first business was the following:

"Mrs. ———,
"——— Hotel, N. York.

"Store and contents, dwelling and everything lost. Insurance worthless. See ———, immediately; tell him to buy all the coffee he can get and ship it this afternoon by express. Don't cry."

Wanted to see the Ruins.

The following story is said to be literally true, and serves to explain how the dashing enterprise of this city is appreciated in the rival cities:

At the East St. Louis depot on last Monday evening, considerable confusion occurred among the passengers who were boarding the passenger train for Chicago, by an individual, carpet-bag in hand, and very much excited, shoving and pushing the crowd in his desperate efforts to reach the cars. He crowded aside and elbowed men, women, and children, making a nuisance of himself generally. Finally a gentleman whose ribs had been crushed by the excited man's elbows, and his temper ruffled by the unceremonious manner in which he had been bustled, inquired in sharp tones:

"What the devil is the matter with you, old fellow?"

Individual in a hurry. "Must get that train."

Other Man. "Well, there is plenty of time—the train does not start for ten minutes; and, besides, there are several other people here who want that train."

Excited Individual. "I *must* get that train, and that's fixed. I'll get that train if it costs me my life."

Other Man. "What in h—l is the necessity of your reaching Chicago by this train, anyway?"

Man in a Hurry. "I must get to Chicago to-morrow on this train, or those people up there will have built up the whole d——d town again, and I won't see them ruins—— !"

ANOTHER.

On the Monday morning of the fire, at about 6 o'clock, at which hour the *Tribune* Building was considered safe, and the people began flocking into Dearborn street, a man was observed carefully examining the bricks of the ruins of Reynolds' Block, picking them up carefully and "feeling" them.

An observer asked him to explain his conduct, when he replied:

"I was just seeing if they were cool enough to build with again!"

Announcements.

Following the fire, the sense of ruin and prostration soon gave way to that other spirit which makes the best of every thing. During Wednesday, and the few days that followed, boards were stuck by each man amid the ruins of his place of business with a sign, stating where he would be found "*until* this building can be rebuilt." Some of the signs were facetious. One of them by a real estate dealer read:—" Everything lost but wife, baby and energy. Office, No. —— Canal street."

Wood's Museum was wholly destroyed, and conspicuously upon the bricks was placed a sign, inscribed:

"COL. WOOD'S MUSEUM.

STANDING ROOM ONLY.

R. MARSH,
Treasurer."

Another sign read:

" *Owing to circumstances over which we have no control, we have removed.*"

Carl Pretzel, the publisher of the broken English-German Magazine, had upon the ruins of his place of business this legend:

"Carl Pretzel, gon avay."

A Mournful Case.

One of the numerous correspondents of Eastern papers, writing from this city, relates the following incident, which is substantially true:

"But by far the saddest case here was that of a beautiful and refined woman, known, I understand, in art and operatic circles, whose husband is missing, and who escaped herself in only a night-wrapper, was driven to distraction by the terrors of the wild flight, and was picked up in Lincoln Park in a state of more than half insanity. In the direst need of care from her own sex, ready to die, almost, from extreme exhaustion, and wandering in mind most of the time, she had received last night only the nursing and help which two men could give, and now lay on a pallet upon the church floor, directly behind the rear pew on one side.

"A young woman cared for her during the day, but at night female imagination lent partial insanity too great terrors, and care which should have fallen to womanly sympathy devolved on the rude though kind and skilled hands of men. The man whose brave and clear head gave him chief charge had had experience in a hospital; but it was pitiful that womanly protection should not be at hand, and that the couch of such a sufferer should not be tenderly spread under a private roof. Unhappily, the entire length of burnt Chicago intervened between all these sufferers, on the north side, and that part of the city where suitable care could have been secured for them."

This accomplished lady was carried from her residence in delicate health, and eventually found refuge in a German Lutheran Church, spared by the fire, several miles from her residence. A gentleman residing in that neighborhood discovered her among the destitute, who had fled to the building for shelter. He carried her to his own house, where she had every care and attention that kindness and skill could provide. But all was unavailing. On Sunday morning she died. The shock to her mental faculties had been too severe, and kindness and care had come too late. Her husband was not at home when the fire attacked her residence, nor did he find her until Thursday. This lady belonged to a gifted family—one historically identified with the opera in the United States.

Mrs. Lander.

The accomplished Mrs. Lander, who was stopping at the Sherman House on the night of the fire, was forced to fly. She procured the assistance of a friend, and together they dragged or carried a couple of trunks from the burning hotel, and a few hours later, found a safe resting place a mile distant. In a letter to a lady friend, written on the Sunday after the fire, she thus sketches the dreadful night, and gives an exposition of the indomitable energy of the people of the city:

"My Dear Friend:

A word from me, with an assurance of my mother's and my own safety, will perhaps be welcome. In the hurry of the alarm, at the dead of night, the sparks and flakes of fire, thicker than the heaviest flakes of an Eastern snow-storm, cared for by an entire stranger, we escaped to the shelter of a friend's roof, a mile beyond, where at last the fire was checked; and now a week has passed, yet our nerves are not quieted. Constant alarms of fresh fires keep us anxious and excited. Every block provides its own patrol guard. Every passerby, after nightfall, is stopped and questioned, such is the dread of incendiarism. We have no gas, but none is needed; the immense piles of grain (2,500,000 bushels) in what were the limits of great grain elevators, and the heaps of coal in the storeyards, the smaller heaps in each coal cellar, with their respective yellow and blue flames reflected in the clouds over the burned and unburned streets, light with a fearful red glare, suggesting, where the clouds hang low and heavy, new cause for alarm.

"Think! Four square miles of thickly populated, and on the business side, densely-built streets. First the business offices of the great merchants of this great electric business-mart, then their luxurious homes on the north side, homes in which treasures of the Old World were collected, pictures, sculpture, books, and gems, combined with the workmanship and products of the New World; costly carving, rich furniture, carriages, horses—the estimate in all cannot fall short of one thousand millions—all swept away by the accidental overturn of a lamp in a little Bohemian shanty or cow-shed. It seems inconceivable how the fire could at first have been fed. Amid low one or two-story buildings, through two blocks on the west side, it began, the wind helping from the southwest. It scorched, but left the larger buildings, to return when reinforced by flames from the bridge and shipping, and lumber and coal yards. Then the big flakes of fire and flame crossed the river, taking a diagonal course over the south side, seizing all in its way to the court house, passing the new Pacific Hotel (nearly finished), and sweeping the Sherman House and all between the square and the river. Crossing the street, the whirlwind of flame drew into its circle block after block to the right. Hooley's Opera House to Dearborn street, First National Bank, showered its flakes on the Tremont House, followed on to the Illinois Central depot and the lake, seizing on the lower end of State street and Wabash and Michigan avenues. Then came the marvel: in the teeth of a hurricane of wind, the fire-fiend ate its way in great swirls of flame backward, where people had rested and goods were heaped to the windward 'of all harm.' It pushed back and back, until men, women and children, the sick and the aged, teams, carriages drawn by horses or men, laden down with goods, were fleeing away, many never stopping until the southern limits of the city were reached. Wild rumors of the rapidity of the coming flames caused doubt a mile from the fire. At last, by trusting to Sheridan, and blowing up a few insignificant buildings, the scourge was stopped to the south. But, in the meantime, what had it done

CHAMBER OF COMMERCE AND COURT-HOUSE.

POST-OFFICE AND CUSTOM-HOUSE.

north? While the men had been fighting the flames round their business houses, and the few, comparatively few, houses of their friends, the flames had recrossed the river, burning away all the bridges, forming impassable volcanoes of fire to their homes, surprising, in many instances the unguarded inmates. If at the south the horror was felt, it yielded in all respects to the terrors of the north side of the city; here it was striven against—there it revelled unchecked.

"Nothing but the destruction of Pompeii can outline the savageness and rapidity of its career. It fed on everything—the Nicholson pavement of the streets, the sidewalks, the fences; for example, one instance in many, a lady and her children took refuge four times, and four times that flaming sword pointed "onward!" until she found shelterless safety, with hundreds of others, five miles from home, on the open prairie, where they passed the fearful night. Others were surrounded by the fire and rushed into the lake, where, by plunging under the water as the heat became unbearable, they saved their own and children's lives. Again, delicate women fled along the streets, their footsteps licked by the dogging flames, igniting their hastily-donned clothing. A cry! a stop! and the fire is put out by some friendly hand; that brief stop is almost fatal, and the utmost speed is needed to regain lost ground in this race for life. Into the old graveyard—over the graves of the dead—fled the living, as through the dry grass and over the fences and trees crept or leaped their enemy, beyond all houses, into Lincoln Park, on to the barren lake shore; and there, exhausted, they sank thankful on the sand.

"But in this struggle what became of the weak, sick and infirm among the thousands of families turned out on that pitiless night, separated, and lost—how many forever in time? Weeks must be past before the sad list can be completed. What stayed the fire on that side God knows.

"And now, after this visitation—in which court house, churches, water works, gas house, depots, hotels, theatres, post office, telegraph, wholesale and retail stores, grain elevators, breweries and over 30,000 houses were destroyed, and 150,000 people left homeless—see the hopefulness, energy, and cheerful determination of everybody. Men have sketched plans for their new buildings by the light of the element destroying their old ones. No despondency, even with a conviction of bankrupt insurance companies staring them in the face. Even the most sanguine repudiate the idea of insurance money for destruction on so large a scale; and imagine how their hearts warmed and throbbed when communication with the outer world was re-established, when the sympathy and aid of the whole nation—the whole world—was theirs. The first telegram flashed over the restored wires from St. Louis was followed by others from city after city; before the fires had ceased raging, trains laden with food and clothing arrived, and now relief is pouring in a steady stream.

"To-morrow morning at 10 o'clock all the banks resume business. Insurance offices are ready to pay all demands, the ruins are being cleared off, a hundred wooden buildings are already a story high for temporary use; on Thursday water is promised, in a week gas; and while the city will be rebuilt, the Chicago Aid and Relief Society will supply shelter in wooden barricks, and administer to the needy and sick the funds so lavishly bestowed.."

Escape and Death.

The clearing away of the debris has disclosed the fact that the loss of life has been much greater than was supposed. Nothing but business blocks have yet been searched, and the number of bodies found exceed 300. When the sites of the many thousand of dwellings shall be explored, the additions to this number, it is now feared, will be astounding. Recent facts disclose the tragic end of a well known citizen, the particulars of which are in themselves but the history of hundreds of cases.

Mr. John E. Donovan removed to Chicago some years ago from Sauk county, Wisconsin, where he had served as sheriff of the county, and where he was well known. In this city he had for several years been known as the lessee of Pope's Block, adjoining the new Open Board Building. At the time of the fire he was stopping with his wife and child (a little girl about two years old) in the Post Office Block, on the corner of Dearborn and Monroe streets, east of the post office. During Sunday night Mr. Donovan had watched the burning of the main portion of the business centre of the city; had witnessed the burning of Pope's Block, Farwell Hall, Board of Trade, Court House, Sherman House, etc., having in his own mind concluded that the Post Office Block would not burn. But in the morning the fire had assumed such a shape that it at once became apparent that the block could not be saved. He then removed his wife and child to a place of safety on the corner of State and Monroe streets, while he returned to his room to secure some papers. What followed will appear from the following letter from Mrs. Ackley, the last person, so far as is known, who saw Mr. Donovan:

WYOMING, JONES COUNTY, IOWA,
November 19, 1871.

MRS. DONOVAN: *Dear Madam*:—I regret that your letter was not received sooner, I sympathize with you, and would be glad to give you something definite regarding your husband if possible. All I can say is that, just before the building burned, I went up to my room, leaving my son Jesse on State street to watch my trunks. In a few minutes a man came up and told me to leave the building immediately, saying, "Those old stables are all on fire." I supposed he meant those wooden buildings in the rear of the block, but looking out I saw no fire, and did not think he meant the buildings opposite, on Monroe street. I then stepped into your room, No. 29, seeing Mr. Donovan there, and said to him, "that man is more scared than hurt," to which he replied, "that is just what *I* think—I don't see any fire." The man, speaking as he did, using the word "stables," is what deceived Mr. Donovan, as well as myself. This is all the conversation I had with him. I cannot tell positively whether he had anything in his hands or not—he was standing or walking in about the middle of the room. I saw him no more. On going to my room, my boy came running in perfectly wild with fright, saying, "Mother, you will be burned alive here!" We ran down the Monroe street stairway; in the excitement I never thought to stop at your room and ought to have called to Mr. Donovan, but you know how it is at such times. We ran to The Tribune corner, and found ourselves in a situation where suffocation seemed inevitable. When we went on Monroe street it was black with smoke. Jesse says it was when he came up, and he says he did not see any one either in the building nor in street. I did not see any one. I did not think of anything but being burned alive. The fire was coming on us from the opposite side of Monroe street. I cannot tell whether our building was then on fire, but Jesse said: "We cannot go to the trunks —we must go down Dearborn street." It was hot on the street. We kept on our side of Monroe street, ran around the corner, and down the east side of Dearborn street until we reached The Tribune office. Jesse says he looked back when in range of McVicker's Theatre, and he says (but you must not rely too much on it) that he thinks that the Post Office Block was then on fire—at least, he says, there was a fearful body of fire back of us. I cannot remember as well as he can. The only way of escape for us from THE TRIBUNE corner was along Madison street to the Madison street bridge. This was a fearful journey—beyond description. All this distance, of about seven blocks, had just been burned down, and the smoke and heat and wind, and sometimes the flames, were terrible. I saw no one but men, and their faces were as white as this paper. I do not give up easy, but if a gentleman, escaping the same way had not helped me, I should never have got over the hot piles of brick burning my feet, and the hot coiled telegraph wires tripping me at every step. I lost everything but the clothes I wore. Mrs. Donovan, my heart aches for you! I presume this letter does not contain one grain of anything satisfactory; if you do find your husband, please write to me the particulars.

Very truly,

MRS. ACKLEY.

Nothing further was known concerning the fate of Mr. Donovan until Saturday, November 18th, when the workmen in THE TRIBUNE Building found the remains of two men. Their bodies lay under the pavement, on the north side of the building, and about thirty feet east of Dearborn street. About five feet from the door which led into this "News boys' room," lay the body of Joseph P. Stubbs, a young man who had recently come to the city, and who was associate editor of one of our daily papers at the time of his death; and beyond him, about ten feet to the east, was found the body of John E. Donovan. Both men were found with their heads to the east, their hair burned, features destroyed, and limbs consumed. The broken pavement fell on these bodies, and the watch taken from Mr. Donovan's pocket was crushed, and stopped at 18 minutes to 10. Under this pavement then, these men had been driven for safety—where, doubtless, they were secure, until the expanding of the iron joists caused the north wall of THE TRIBUNE Building to fall, crushing them instantly.

Mr. Donovan was held in high esteem by all who knew him. A friend informs us that he often heard him express his confidence that THE TRIBUNE Building needed no insurance, because it could not be destroyed by fire. Driven to the corner of Dearborn and Madison streets, as he must have been very soon after Mrs. Ackley's escape, in that awful moment he chose the protection of this building to the desperate chance through burning ruins for the distance of more than half a mile.

The Petroleum Stone.

Since the fire there have been numerous publications of a statement to the effect that a large proportion of the stone used in building in Chicago was charged with petroleum; that this exuding from the stone presented an inviting material to the fire, and that the sudden wreck of the buildings was occasioned by the consumption of this inflammable petroleum stone. A writer in Chambers' Journal of Science relates that an immense deposit of this kind of stone lies within a few miles of Chicago, and that the quantity of ore contained in a few square yards of the rock is great. This paragraph in Chambers, has been made the most of by the sensationalists. A city built of stone from which petroleum is forever exuding! It would be a marvel, if true; it would be intensely disagreeable if the fact was as stated, and it would be an admirably devised means of spreading fire from house to house. Now for the facts.

The stone used in building in the city was mainly what is known as Athens, or Illinois marble. It is found in large quantities between this city and Joliet, and large quarries have been opened along the canal. This stone is used for ordinary walls, for curbing, for flagging for sidewalks, and for the polished and ornamented fronts of buildings. It is easily worked, is abundant, admits of a handsome polish, and was the general material used. There was used also, but not until lately, a somewhat similar stone, a shade or two darker, and known as the Cleveland stone. A few buildings were constructed of a harder stone, brought from Lockport, New York. A half dozen others were made of a stone manufactured by machinery, and there were two others going up, which were using a deep red sandstone from Lake Superior.

There was but one building of any size built of what has now been called petroleum stone. This was the Second Presbyterian Church, on the corner of Wabash avenue and Washington street. The petroleum part of the story is due to the fact that the rock is deeply mottled, from a strong gray to a deep dull black. The obscuration of the natural color is owing to what seems to be an exudation of dark matter. If this be an exudation, it is inexhaustible, for this church has been built nearly twenty-five years, and there has never been any change in its appearance.

The quarry from which this stone is obtained is situated in the northwestern part of the city, and the stone was used largely for foundation walls. When the oil wells were discovered in Pennsylvania, it occurred to some persons that this exudation upon the stone might be an indication of oil. As a speculation the property was purchased, and boring commenced. At a depth of several hundred feet the drill struck water! and from that well, ever since, during the six or more years that have intervened, there has been a copious flood of pure water, but not the slightest indication of oil! Not a grease spot has ever been discovered. Another well was subsequently sunk, and to a greater depth, but water and not oil has been the result. The petroleum theory was thus effectually exploded, and was forgotten until it was revived by the sensationalists after the fire.

Another fact, showing the absurdity of the story of petroleum-bearing rock spreading the flames, or occasioning the instant melting down of stone walls, is that the walls of the only large building in the city, built of that stone, did not crumble or fall down under the heat, but survived the conflagration in all their integrity.

The true cause of the destruction of the stone walls was that the gale operated with the force of the blow pipe, intensifying the heat to that degree, that nothing could resist it.

Generous in Danger.

Mr. Kerfoot, son of the late Dr. Kerfoot, of Pennsylvania, gives the following graphic account of his escape from the fire with his wife and children: "Being the owner of a horse and carriage which I used to go to and fro from my business, when I became satisfied that my house would soon be enveloped, I brought my horse and carriage before the house, and placed my wife and children in it. There was no room for me, so I mounted the back of the animal and acted as postilion. While driving through the flame and smoke which enveloped us on all hands, I came across a gentleman who had his wife in a buggy, and was between the thills hauling it himself. I shouted to him to hitch his carriage on behind mine, which he did, and then got in beside his wife. I then drove forward as fast as I could, for the flames were raging around us. After proceeding a short distance, another gentleman was found standing beside the street, with a carriage, waiting for a horse, which was not likely to come. I directed him to fasten on behind the second carriage, which he did, and in this way we whipped up and got out of the way of the flames with our wives and children, thank God."

The Views of an Expert.

Frederick Law Olmstead, Esq., writes a long letter to the *N. Y. Nation* under date of November 2d, from which we take the following:

"I have had an opportunity of looking at Chicago at the beginning of the fourth week after the fire, and, as you requested, will give you a few notes of my observation.

"Chicago had a central quarter, compactly built, mostly of brick, stone, and iron, and distinguished by numerous very large and tall structures, comparable to, but often more ostentatious than, Stewart's store in New York. They were mostly lined, to the fourth, fifth, or sixth floor, with pine-wood shelves, on which, or in pine-wood cases, a fresh stock of—larger at the moment than ever before—dry goods, or other inflammable materials, was set up, with plentiful air-space for rapid combustion. This central quarter occupied a mile and a half square of land. On one side of it was the lake; on the other three sides, for the distance of a mile, the building, though irregular, was largely of detached houses, some of the villa class, with small planted grounds about them, and luxuriously furnished, but generally comfortable dwellings, of moderate size, set closely together. There were also numerous churches and tall school buildings, and some large factories. At a distance of two miles from the centre, and beyond, houses were much scattered, and within a mile of the political boundary there was much open prairie, sparsely dotted with cabins and a few larger buildings. It will be seen that a much larger part of the town proper was burned than a stranger would be led to suppose by the published maps.

"The fire started half a mile southwest, which was directly to windward, of the central quarter, rapidly carried its heights, and swept down from them upon the comparatively suburban northern quarter, clearing it to the outskirts, where the few scattered houses remaining were protected by a dense grove of trees. The field of ruin is a mile in width, bounded by the lake on one side and mainly by a branch of the river on the other, and four miles in length, thus being as large as the half of New York City from the Battery to the Central Park, or as the whole of the peninsula of Boston. The houses burned set ten feet apart would form a row over a hundred miles in length. I judge that more than a third of the roof-space and fully half the floor-space of the city, the population of which was 330,000, was destroyed.

"Familiar with these facts and comparisons before I came here, and having already seen many who had left the city since the fire, I now feel myself to have been able but slightly to appreciate the magnitude of its calamity. Besides the extent of the ruins, what is most remarkable is the completeness with which the fire did its work, as shown by the prostration of the ruins and the extraordinary absence of smoke-stains, brands, and all *dêbris*, except stone, brick, and iron, bleached to an ashey pallor. The distinguishing smell of the ruins is that of charred earth. In not more than a dozen cases have the four walls of any of the great blocks, or of any buildings, been left standing together. It is the exception to find even a single corner or chimney holding together to a height of more than twenty feet. It has been possible, from the top of an omnibus, to see men standing on the ground three miles away across what was the densest, loftiest, and most substantial part of the city.

"Generally, the walls seem to have crumbled in from top to bottom, nothing remaining but a broad low heap of rubbish in the cellar—so low as to be overlooked from the pavement. Granite, all sandstones and all limestones, whenever fully exposed to the southwest, are generally flaked and scaled, and blocks, sometimes two and three feet thick, are cracked through and through. Marble and other limestones, where especially exposed, as in doors and window-dressings, especially if in thin slabs, have often fallen to powder. Walls of the bituminous limestone, of which there were but few, instead of melting away, as was reported, seem to have stood rather better than others; I cannot tell why. Iron railings and lamp-post, detached from buildings, are often drooping, and, in thinner parts, seem sometimes to have been fused. Iron columns and floor-beams are often bent to a half-circle. The wooden (Nicholson) asphalt-and-tar-concrete pavements remain essentially unharmed, except where red-hot material or burning liquids have lain upon them. Street rails on wood are generally in good order; on McAdam, as far as I have seen, more often badly warped.

* * * * *

"You ask whether it is in the power of man adequately to guard against such calamities—whether other great cities are as much exposed as was Chicago? All the circumstances are not established with sufficient accuracy for a final answer, and one cannot, in the present condition of affairs, make full inquiries of men who must be best informed; but to such preliminary discussion as is in order, I can offer a certain contribution.

"The prevailing drought was, I think, a less important element of the fire in Chicago—whatever may have been the case as to those other almost more terrific fires which occurred simultaneously in Wisconsin and Michigan—than is generally assumed; yet doubtless it was of some consequence

As to the degree of it, I learn that there had been no heavy rain since the 3d of July, and, during this period of three months, it is stated by Dr. Rauch, the Sanitary Superintendent, the total rain-fall had been but two and a half inches. The mean annual rain-fall at Chicago is thirty-one inches. With regard to the cause of the drought, it is to be considered that millions of acres of land hereabouts, on which trees were scarce, have been settled within thirty years by people whose habits had been formed in regions where woods abound. They have used much timber for building, for fencing, railroads, and fuel. They have grown none. They are planting none to speak of. The same is true of nearly all parts of our country in which a great destruction of forests has occurred or is occurring. If the reduction of foliage in any considerable geographical division of the world tends to make its seasons capricious, as there is much evidence, the evil both of destructive droughts and devastating floods is very likely to extend and increase until we have a government service which we dare trust with extensive remedial measures. It is not a matter which commerce can be expected to regulate.

"I can obtain no scientifically definite statement of the force of the wind. Several whom I have questioned recollect that they found it difficult, sometimes for a moment impossible, to make head against it; but I think that no year passes that some of our cities do not experience as strong a gale, and that every city in the country must expect to find equal dryness coinciding with equal force of wind as often, at least, as once in twenty years.

"The origin of the fire was probably a commonplace accident. The fire started in a wooden building and moved rapidly from one to another, close at hand, until the extended surface of quickly-burning material heated a very large volume of the atmosphere, giving rise to local currents, which, driving brands upon the heated roofs and cornices of the tall buildings to leeward, set them on fire, and through the rapid combustion of their contents, loosely piled tier upon tier, developed a degree of heat so intense that ordinary means of resistance to it proved of no avail."

Personal Experience of Hon. I. N. Arnold.

The adventures of Hon. I. N. Arnold, formerly member of Congress, on the eventful night of the fire, were very exciting, but probably not more so than those of thousands of others. His story, which he contributed to the Chicago journals, is therefore the story of many others, and will serve to illustrate some of the terrors of that fearful night:

Mr. Arnold's house was situated almost in the centre of a block, and surrounded by a garden which the owner believed afforded ample protection against the approach of the fiery foe. Accordingly no attempt was made to save any of his valuables, but the efforts of his household, consisting of him-

SECOND PRESBYTERIAN CHURCH.

SHEPHARD BLOCK, DEARBORN STREET.

self, three children, and the servants, were directed towards protecting the house, in which they were for a time successful. The narrator says: "During all this time the fire fell in torrents; there was literally a rain of fire. It caught in the dry leaves; it caught in the grass; in the barn; in the piazza; and as often as it caught it was put out, before it got any headway. When the barn first caught, the horses and cows were removed to the lawn. The fight was continued, and with success, until three o'clock in the morning. Every moment flakes of fire falling, touching dry wood, with the high wind, would kindle into a blaze, and the next instant would be extinguished. The contest after 3 o'clock grew warmer and more fierce, and those who fought the devouring element were becoming exhausted. The contest had been going on from half past one until after three, when young Arthur Arnold, a lad of thirteen, called to his father. 'The barn and hay are on fire?' 'The leaves are on fire on the east side,' said the gardener. 'The front piazza is in a blaze,' cried another, 'the front greenhouse is in flames, and the roof on fire.' '*The water has stopped!*' was the last appalling announcement. 'Now, for the first time,' said Mr. A., 'I gave up hope of saving my *home*, and considered whether we could save any of the contents. My pictures, papers and books, can I save any of them?' An effort was made to cut down some portraits, a landscape of Kensett, Otsego Lake, by Mignot—it was too late! Seizing a bundle of papers, gathering the children and servants together, and, leading forth the animals, they started. But where to go? They were surrounded by fire on three sides; to the south, west and north raged the flames, making a wall of fire and smoke from the ground to the sky; their only escape was east to the lake shore. Leading the horses and cow, they went to the beach. Here were thousands of fugitives hemmed in, and imprisoned by the raging element. The sands, from the Government pier north to Lill's pier, a distance of three-quarters of a mile, were covered with men, women, and children, some half clad, in every variety of dress, with the motley collection of things which they sought to save. Some had silver, some valuable papers, some pictures, some old carpets, beds, etc. One little child had her doll tenderly pressed in her arms, an old woman a grunting pig, a fat woman had two large pillows, as portly as herself, which she had apparently snatched from her bed when she left. There was a singular mingling of the awful, the ludicrous, and the pathetic."

Mrs. Arnold and her little daughter, Alice, had been sent away to the residence of Mrs. Scudder, and the party were accordingly separated, a circumstance which added to the anxiety of the wanderers.

After toiling along W. B. Ogden's pier, they hired a small row boat and were conveyed to the light house, where they were cordially received by the authorities, and other refugees who had preceded them. "The party remained prisoners in the light house, and the pier on which it stood for several hours. The shipping above in the river was burning; the immense grain elevators of the Illinois Central and Galena Railroads were a mass of flames, and the pier itself, some distance up the river, was slowly burning toward the light house. A large propeller fastened to the dock a short distance up the river caught fire, and the danger was that as soon as the ropes by which it was fastened burned off it would float down stream and set fire to the dock in the immediate vicinity of the light house. Several propellers moved down near the mouth of the river and took on board several hundred fugitives and steamed out into the lake. If the burning propeller came down it would set fire to the pier, the lighthouse, and vast piles of lumber, which had as yet escaped in consequence of being directly on the shore and detached from the burning mass. A fire company was organized of those on the pier, and with water dipped in pails from the river the fire kept at bay, but all felt relieved when the propeller went to the bottom. The party were still prisoners on an angle of sand, and the fire running along the north shore of the river. The river and the fire preventing an escape to the south, west and north. The fire was still raging with unabated fury. The party waited for hours, hoping the fire would subside. The day wore on, noon passed, and 1 and 2 o'clock, and still it seemed difficult, if not dangerous, to escape to the north. Mr.

Arnold, leaving his children in the light house, went north towards Lill's, and thought it was practicable to get through, but was not willing to expose the females to the great discomfort and possible danger of the experiment."

" Between 3 and 4 in the afternoon the tug-boat Clifford came down the river and tied up near the light house. Could she return—taking the party up the river—through and beyond the fire to the west side, or was it safer and better to remain at the light house; If it and the pier, the lumber and shanties around should burn during the night, as seemed not unlikely, the position would not be tenable, and might be extremely perilous; besides, Mr. A. was extremely anxious to *know* that Mrs. A. and little Alice were safe. The officer of the tug said the return passage was practicable. Rush, Clark, State and Wells street bridges had all burned and their fragments had fallen into the river The great warehouses elevators, storehouses, docks on the banks of the river, were still burning, but the fury of the fire had exhausted itself. The party resolved to go through this narrow canal or river to the south bank, outside the burning district. This was the most dangerous experience of the day. The tug might take fire herself, the wood work of which had been blistered with heat as she came down; the engine might get out of order and the boat become unmanageable after she got inside the line of fire, or she might get entangled in the floating timber and *debris* of the bridges. However, the party determined to go. A full head of steam was gotten up, the hose was attached to the engine, so that if the boat or clothes caught it could be put out. The children and ladies were placed in the pilot house, and the windows shut, and the boat started. The men crouched clear to the deck behind the butt works, and with a full head of steam the tug darted past the abutments of Rush street bridge; as they passed the State street bridge the pilot had to pick his way carefully among falling and floating timber. The extent of the danger was now obvious, but it was too late to retreat. As the boat passed State street the pump supplying cold water ceased to work, and the exposed wood in some parts was blistering. 'Snatching a handkerchief,' says Mr. Arnold, 'I dipped it in water, and covering the face and head of Arthur, whose hat the wind had blown away, I made him lie flat on the deck, as we plunged forward through the fiery furnace.' On we sped past Clark and Wells streets. 'Is not the worst over?' he asked of the Captain, as the boat dashed on and on. 'We are through sir,' answered the Captain. 'We are safe.' 'Thank God!' came from hearts and lips as the boat emerged from the smoke into the clear, cool air outside the fire lines."

The party went ashore at Lake street, and Mr. Arnold commenced a search for his wife and child, who he found had gone to Evanston. It was not until the next night that the whole family were reunited at the residence of Judge Drummond.

RELIEF MEASURES.

The greatness of the calamity was equalled by the greatness of the generosity which followed it. The world has never known such an outpouring of charity before. Scarcely had the telegraph borne the news of the disaster abroad, when in every city, town and village of the country meetings were held for the relief of Chicago. The movement was a universal and spontaneous one, city councils, corporations, railroads and steamboat interests, banks, churches, Sunday schools, theatres, men, women and children, vied with each other in generous deeds. Cash contributions and car loads of provisions of every description poured into the city until there was absolute danger, that in the plethora every thing would be wasted.

Meeting in Boston.

Among the many stirring appeals, none were more eloquent than that of Rev. Edward Everett Hale, of Boston, at Faneuil Hall, as follows:

"MR. MAYOR AND GENTLEMEN:—It is but a single word that I have to say here. I have simply to remind you that this is no mere matter of voting in which we are engaged. I have to remind you that these people, our people in Chicago, by their munificence, by their generosity, by their strength, by their public spirit, have made us debtors to them all. [Applause]. There is not a man here, the beef upon whose table yesterday was not the cheaper to him because these people laid out their world-renowned and wonderful system of stock-yards. [Applause.] There is not a man here, the bread upon whose table to-day is not cheaper because these people, in the very beginning of their national existence, invented and created that marvellous system for the delivery of grain which is the model and pattern of the world. [Applause.] And remember that they were in a position where they might have said they held a monopoly. They commanded the only harbor for the shipping of the five greatest States of America and the world, and in that position they have devoted themselves now for a generation to the steady improvement, by every method in their power, of the means by which they were going to answer the daily prayer of every child to God when praying that He will give us our daily bread, through their enterprise and their struggles. We call it their misfortune. It is our misfortune. We are all, as it has been said, linked together in a solidarity of the nation. Their loss is no more theirs than it is ours in this great campaign of peace in which we are engaged. There has fallen by this calamity one of our noblest fortresses. Its garrison is without munitions. It is for us at this instant to reconstruct that fortress, and to see that its garrison are as well placed as they were before in our service. Undoubtedly it is a great enterprise; but we can trust them for that. We are all fond of speaking of the miracle by which there in the desert there was created this great city. The rod of some prophet, you say, struck it, and this city flowed from the rock. Who was the prophet? what was the rock? It was the American people who determined that that city should be there, and that it should rightly and wisely, and in the best way, distribute the food to a world. [Applause.] The American people has that duty to discharge again. I know that these numbers are large numbers. But the providence of God has taught us to deal with larger figures than these, and when, not many years ago, it became necessary for this country in every year to spend not a hundred millions, not a thousand millions, but more than a thousand millions of dollars in a great enterprise which God gave this country in the duty of war, this country met its obligation. And now that in a single year we have to reconstruct one of the fortresses of peace, I do not fear that this country will be backward in its duty. It has been truly said that the first duty of all of us is, that the noble pioneers in the duty that God has placed in their hands, who are suffering, shall have food and clothing; that those who for forty-eight hours have felt as if they were deserted, should know that they have friends everywhere in God's world. [Applause.] Mr. President, as God is pleased to order this world there is no partial evil but from that partial evil is reached the universal good. The fires which our friends have seen sweeping over the plains in the desolate autumn, only bring forth the blossoms and richness of the next spring and summer.

"I can well believe that on that terrible night of Sunday, and all through the horrors of Monday, as those noble people, as those gallant workmen, threw upon the flames the water that their noble works—the noblest that America has seen—enabled them to hurl upon the enemy, that they must have imagined that their work was fruitless, that it was lost toil, to see those streams of water playing into the molten mass, and melt into steam and rise innocuous to the heavens. It may well have seemed that their work was wasted; but it is sure that evil shall work out its own end, and the mists that rose from the conflagration were gathered together for the magnificent tempest of last night, which, falling upon those burning streets, has made Chicago a habitable city to-day. [Applause.] See that the lesson for this community, see that the lesson for us who are here, that the horror and tears with which we read the despatches of yesterday, shall send us out to do ministries of truth and bounty and benevolence to-day. [Applause.]"

Statement of the Relief and Aid Society.

"The Executive Committee of the Chicago Relief and Aid Society are aware that the public desire to know the amount of the subscriptions to the relief fund. It is impossible at present to give a detailed account of the amounts, for the reason that purchases made in some cities—invoices of which have not yet reached us—are to be deducted from the gross amounts of the subscription. The previous report of our treasurer stated the amount actually received at that date. We are now able to give the amount received to this date, November 7th, and the probable amount of the entire subscriptions with approximate accuracy. We have actually received $2,051,023.55.

"Arrangements have been made by which the society draws 5 per cent. on all its balances in bank. So far as our present information goes, and we think we have advices of all sums subscribed, the entire fund will vary but little from three millions and a half dollars. This includes the funds in the hands of the New York Chamber of Commerce, amounting to about six hundred thousand dollars, and the balance of the Boston fund, about two hundred and forty thousand; both amounting to eight hundred and forty thousand dollars, not yet placed to the credit of this society, but which may be relied upon to meet the needs of the future.

"As to our disbursements, we can only say that we are at present aiding 60,000 people at our regular distributing points. Some of this vast number we relieve in part only, but the greater portion to the extent of their entire support. This is in addition to the work of the Special Relief Committee, for people who ought not to be sent to the general distributing points, and which is largely increasing upon our hands. It is also in addition to the expenditures of the committee on existing charitable institutions.

"The great matter pressing upon your committee is shelter for the coming winter. We may feed people during the mild weather, but where and how they are to be housed—permanently housed—we regard as the serious question. To this end we have been aiding those burned out to replace small but comfortable houses upon their own or upon leased lots, where they can live, not only this winter but next summer, and be ready to work in rebuilding the city. Of these houses (which are really very comfortable, being 16 x 20 feet, with two rooms, one 12 x 16 feet and one 8 x 16 feet, with a planed and matched floor, panel door and good windows), we have already furnished over 4,000, making permanent houses, allowing five to a family for twenty thousand people, and with the seven thousand houses which we expect to build, shall have houses for thirty-five thousand people. These houses, and some barracks, in both of which is a moderate outfit of furniture, such as stoves, mattresses, and a little crockery, will consume, say a million and a quarter dollars, leaving two million and a quarter with which to meet all the demands for food, fuel, clothing and general expenses from the 13th of October last, until the completion of the work, which cannot end with the present winter.

"The committee need hardly say that if the demand should continue as great as at present the fund would be exhausted by mid-winter; but we hope to cut this down very largely as soon as we can get people into houses, so that they can leave their families and find work. Indeed, this is being done already. Within a few days we shall arrive at the exact daily expense of food and fuel rations. But the demand is a fluctuating one. If the weather is good and men can work, it falls off; if cold and stormy, it increases at a fearful rate.

"The work has so pressed upon us night and day that we cannot present a detailed report to the public, but furnish this statement for the purpose of affording a general idea of what we have done and are trying to do, with an organization necessarily composed of unskilled forces, but the only one at hand for the emergency. We shall soon be able to give a detailed report of all sums contributed.

Ladies' Relief Society.

In connection with the Relief Society, a Ladies' Relief Society was organized on the 19th of October, at the house of Mrs. Wirt Dexter. One of its primary objects was to seek out those sufferers by the fire, who shrank from making their wants known, even to the bureau of special relief, and to relieve them as quickly and as delicately as possible.

For the supply of clothing, the society had an Employment Bureau. Rooms were opened where seamstresses were furnished with work. From thirty to fifty, under a competent forewoman, were busily engaged in making garments for the Chicago Relief and Aid Society. This work was under the careful supervision of the ladies, who allowed no waste of materials in cutting, or carelessness in sewing. Through this Employment Bureau poor, homeless girls, whose means of living were taken away by the fire, by the loss of their machines, or their places, or both, and who were rapidly coming to the extremity of poverty, found useful work, and true, kind friends. The officers are as follows:

President—Mrs. John Mason Loomis.

Vice President—Mrs. Robert Laird Collier.

Recording Secretary—Mrs. S. H. Gay.

Corresponding Secretary—Mrs. Wirt Dexter.

Treasurer—Mrs. George M. Pullman.

Assistant Treasurer—Mrs. Martin Andrews.

Employment Committee—Mrs. J. W. Foster, Mrs. G. M. Pullman, Mrs. L. Z. Leiter, Mrs. J. M. Walker, Mrs. M. Andrews, Mrs. G. C. Gore, Mrs. Wirt Dexter, Mrs. R. L. Collier, Mrs. J. C. Hilton, Mrs. S. Reeve, Mrs. A. C. Badger, Mrs. Palmer Kellogg, Mrs. N. R. Fairbank.

Distribution Committee—Mrs. Wirt Dexter, Mrs. G. M. Pullman, Mrs. Palmer Kellogg, Mrs. D. A. Gage, Mrs. F. M. Mitchell, Mrs. R. L. Collier, Mrs. L. Z. Leiter.

Visiting Committee—Mrs. C. H. McCormick, Mrs. Dr. Locke, A. C. Badger, Mrs. F. M. Mitchell, Miss N. J. Lunt, Miss N. T. Agnew, Mrs. J. M. Walker, Mrs. M. Andrews, Mrs. N. R. Fairbank.

Donations.

To give all the donations sent to Chicago in

detail would fill a large volume of itself, and we therefore content ourselves with a few of the more prominent, as follows:

St. Louis,	$200,000
Boston,	400,000
Pittsburgh,	300,000
Buffalo,	100,000
Cincinnati,	225,000
Rochester, N. Y.,	70,000
San Francisco,	100,000
Toronto,	10,000
New Orleans,	30,000
Philadelphia,	260,000
Baltimore,	200,000
A. T. Stewart, N. Y.,	50,000
Robt. Bonner,	10,000
Kansas City, Mo.,	10,000
Indianapolis,	40,000
Montreal Board of Trade,	10,000
Portland,	20,000
Leavenworth,	10,000
Quincy, Ill.,	15,000
San Francisco Stock Exchange,	8,000
Lawrence, Kansas,	10,000
Syracuse, N. Y.,	25,000
Haverhill, Mass.,	10,000
Oswego, N. Y.,	12,000
Newark, N. J.,	30,000
Trenton, N. J.,	17,000
Manchester, N. H.,	15,000
Terra Haute, Ind.,	10,000
Bloomington, Ill.,	15,000
New York Gold Exchange,	12,000
Erie, Pa.,	15 000
Detroit,	30,000
Lancaster, Pa.,	25,000
Layfayette, Ind.,	10,000

We have only given the above as indications of the immense volume of charity which flowed into Chicago. The feeling of sympathy extended to Europe, and from all the large cities of England, France and Germany, came generous contributions, which were swelled by donations from the royal purses. From the king on his throne to the poor woman in her hovel, all gave their mite. The following incident told of Mr. Edward Hudson, an Illinois Railway Superintendent, shows in a humorous way the universal sympathy, and the degree of charity to which it actuated people:

Upon hearing of the burning of Chicago, his first act was to telegraph to all agents to transport free, all provisions to Chicago, and to receive such articles to the exclusion of freight. He then purchased a number of good hams and sent them home with a request to his wife to cook them as soon as possible, so they might be sent to Chicago. He then ordered the baker to put up fifty loaves of bread. He was kept busy during the day until 5 o'clock. Just as he was starting for home the baker informed him the hundred loaves of bread were ready,

"But I only ordered fifty." said Ed.

"Mrs. Hudson also ordered fifty," said the baker.

"All right," said Ed., and he inwardly blessed his wife for the generous deed.

Arriving at home he found his little boy, dressed

in a fine cloth suit, carrying in wood. He told him that would not do; he must change his clothes.

"But mother sent all my clothes to Chicago," replied the boy.

Entering the house he found his wife, clad in a fine silk dress, superintending the cooking. A remark in regard to the matter elicited the information that she had sent her other dresses to Chicago.

The matter was getting serious. He sat down to a supper without butter, because all that could be purchased had been sent to Chicago. There were no pickles—the poor souls in Chicago would relish them so much.

A little put out, but not a bit angry or disgusted, Ed. went to the wardrobe to get his overcoat, but it was not there. An interrogatory revealed the fact it fitted in the box real well, and he needed a new overcoat anyway, although he had paid $50 for the one in question only a few days before. An examination revealed the fact that all the rest of his clothes fitted the box real nicely, for not a "dud" did he possess except those he had on.

While he admitted the generosity of his wife, he thought the matter was getting entirely too personal and turned to her with the characteristic inquiry;

"Do you think we can stand an *encore* on that Chicago fire."

LAND-OFFICE, ILLINOIS CENTRAL RAILROAD.

CROSBY'S DISTILLERY.

REPUBLIC LIFE INSURANCE COMPANY.

FIRST NATIONAL BANK.

RELIEF INCIDENTS.

A lady connected with relief operations, after the fire, says:

"Once within [the church of refuge] we found plenty to do. Beds had been hastily improvised from the seats in the lecture room for the sick. Here was a poor old grandmother, with the skin all burned from her hands. There the doctor was attending to a man whose head had been crushed. Everywhere were lost children crying pitifully, who needed comforting. One boy had gone out of town to spend the night with a friend, and when he returned, his father's house, barn, everything was gone, not so much as a fence-panel left of his splendid home. But, sadder than that, he could not find father, mother, brothers or sisters. No one could give him any information, nor any of the other poor lost children. We could only see that they had warm clothing, and urged them to eat; and, thanks to the ready forgetfulness of childhood, they all had good appetites. And didn't we give them strong coffee and tea, and all sorts of indigestible things, though? for already loads of good things were arriving from all the blessed country. There were boiled hams and tongues, roasted sirloins of beef, turkeys, chickens, cakes and genuine country dried beef, cheese and butter, and the poorest beggar in Chicago had the privilege of dining with the Mayor and his staff of assistants. 'There are no big-bugs here now,' said an old Irish woman, not, I think, without satisfaction.

"On one seat lay a beautiful babe about eight months old, that had been found on the sidewalk. It lay sucking its thumb, and gazing as contentedly up at the bright windows as if it had always lived in a church.

"In one corner was a German woman, with nine children, of all sizes. 'Where is your husband?' we inquire.

"'Ach, Gott in Himmel! I took the children and he took the feather bed, and he was so slow I think he got burned up, mit the feather bed. There was no water, and all the men on the north side drinked beer and whisky, and then they could no go fast. If I had taken the feather bed mineself, now I would have it.'

"'Yes; but you should be thankful that you have all your children,' I suggested.

"'Aber! What can I do mit the children, mitout a feather bed?' she asked in astonishment.

"Not feeling equal to a reply, we turned to another group. It is a woman who is clinging tight to her baby, and with sobs of despair telling sympathizing listeners how yesterday she had a pleasant home, a dear, kind husband and five children; now this little child is all she has left. They had slept so soundly they did not waken until their own house was burning. She had snatched her babe and escaped, she knew not how, through the flames and smoke, calling to her husband to follow with the other children. But he was too late. There was nothing left of the husband, children and home but a sickening little heap of ashes! 'Let me have the baby,' said a tearful listener: 'I will give it some warm milk, while you lie down and rest. I hope it will be a comfort to you.' So saying she undid the shawl that was wrapped around it, but quickly closed it again with a look of horror, but not soon enough to prevent the mother from seeing that her darling was dead in her arms. It had either inhaled the flame, or the mother, in falling, had killed it, and had been carrying it for miles, not knowing it was dead. The shock was too much for her. We could see from her wandering eyes that her reason had gone forever, and we could not help feeling that it was a blessing.

"In another room is a woman who has been having convulsions all day. She brings a note to the pastor, saying that her husband was cut in twain by a fire-engine.

"The next day we spend in giving out clothes. What wonderful boxes have come! What a beautiful exhibition of divine charity throughout the whole land! People were in such nervous haste they did not stop to consider what was most needed, but sent everything they could lay their hands on—ball dresses, theatrical costumes, white vests and lavender gloves, piled in with homespun jeans. Only Boston, never in her intellectual pride impulsive, telegraphed to know what was most needed; and what elegant clothing the noble citizens of the Hub sent when they received the answer 'Everything.'

"Some dear old lady has sent some brocade silks, made in the style of 1700, with immense sleeves, puffed out with eider down, and short waist with big puffs. They are really too precious to give away, say the ladies. We will have tableaux in the church this winter for the benefit of the sufferers, and use them in that way.

"And what wonderful contrasts there are in the people who come for clothes! Side by side with the miserable Irish beggars, who want something because the Poor House is burned down, come a foreign Consul, Judges of the Supreme Court, lawyers, editors, professors and merchants. An English gentleman on his bridal tour, stopping at one of the hotels, lost his trunks and money. Although he offered a man $500 to assist him, he could get no assistance. Even his wife's clothes she had on caught in the flames, and had to be torn from her back. His order called for the very best we had to give, but our very best would make a strange outfit for a wealthy young bride.

"There comes a lady in a black silk velvet suit, with diamonds to match. She put on her finest clothes to save them, and has come to ask for a calico wrapper, so that she may not be so splendid in her poverty.

"We were perfectly overwhelmed with calls for baby clothes. It seemed as though every family who was burned out was blessed with a baby—and a good many orders called for clothes for twins. They were of all ages, from two hours to two years.

"Many who had escaped from the flames with good clothes on, in wandering over the ruins fell into vaults and sewers, and lost them in that way.

"One poor Norwegian woman, who had been sitting in stony despair with her children by her cook stove, the only thing she had been able to save, on being told that she could get a bucket of hot soup every day all winter, without money and without price, burst into tears and insisted on shaking hands with everybody in the church, and then taking heart, fell to polishing her stove with such a will that it shone almost as bright as the blessed charity that had cheered her."

Rev. Robert Collyer's Boston Sermon.

On the 12th of November, Rev. Robert Collyer, the eminent Unitarian divine of Chicago, preached at Rev. E. E. Hale's Church in Boston, from the text, "A crown of life," in which he made the following allusion to the Chicago fire:

"There were men in Chicago who were wearing and had already won that coronation of life. They saw in that calamity the work of the best part of a life, as it were swept away in an instant. And what a work it was, what homes they had made for themselves! This morning they are what the world calls ruined men, all the savings of all the years melted before their eyes in fervent heat, not even the home remaining. But, thank God, there remains that which made their homes prosperous and happy. And yet I will say that I never before saw such a divine opportunity opened before these men to win this noble coronation, the crown of victory. Already we have seen dozens of them right on the way to this coronation, so clearly and completely victorious, standing among the ashes of their burnt homes and their blasted hopes, that I should not feel more sure of their divine coronation if I saw the chariots of God and His angels standing with their trumpets at their lips ready to sound the glorious consummation of their lives. And yet it is a very simple thing that I have witnessed in that city since the calamity—only the shining of clear, strong eyes, only the beating of steadfast hearts, only in the hand as clasped that of a neighbor's, only as they stood on their burnt houses ready to begin again. And I tell you if the blessed angels above knew nothing of such heart-breaking as we have had to go through there, yet I know that if they witnessed such high courage as our men have shown, and are showing, they will have anticipated God's will already done, and will have already received the crown eternal. I have a small, delicate man in my parish; I have him now in my eye; slightly dwarfed, and I know how I used to wonder how he could carry himself along the streets; when I met him he would tell me his business was not doing much for him, and that he was very poorly; all the time I had a little ache in my heart for that little man.

But he had a splendid wife, and a house full of children. God bless him for that! When the fire came it burnt him up clean. He has a rich nephew down at the East, who telegraphed at once to him, offering him a home for the winter, and to give him a new start in the spring. But that little, delicate man telegraphed back, 'I can't leave the ranks,' and he hasn't left them; he is working hard, has a nice little home, and there he lives as pleasant, comfortable and contented as ever he was." Alluding to the work which women in Chicago had done, Mr. Collyer said: "I think that in these weeks the good women of our city have already won their crown, and the angels have sung their praises. They have done such work as men never could have done; they have been as steadfast and calm through all the terrible scenes as great captains who know the whole fate of an army lies in their hands. The day of the fire was their coronation day. They not only worked hard necessarily to save their own children, sisters, brothers, mothers, fathers, but any who happened to come in their way. Through those dark days they had shown a courage and heroism far above the men; for by their example men were sustained, cheered and roused to greater effort. They could not well afford to have another such a fire, in one sense, but if such a fire would again call forth such a display of courage and devotion he would say heartily, 'God's will be done.' The only great example of hope and courage displayed anywhere during the great fire came out of the example of woman; out of the ruins of our city a crown has been gained and a coronation for every one." Mr. Collyer then referred to the many young men and young ladies, born, brought up and educated in the best manner which money could effect, who would be bettered by the experiences they had passed through, and who would now be enabled to commence life with a purpose in view, and with such an incentive as never before actuated their breasts. Speaking of his personal feeling in regard to the fire he said: "When that great calamity settled down upon us I thought I ought to try and find some view of the better meaning of it. I was fighting it for a whole week. But I couldn't find it. I said this whole thing is just as bad as it can be. The evil one, the devil, has got loose in this town, and has overcome the good God. And when I stood on the stone that had fallen from the crown of our poor church, with my poor flock around me, there was still a bitter drop in my heart, and I said, sometime we may thank God for this, but He won't expect us to do it to-day. Now I take it all back just as Job did. I said it because I couldn't say anything better; I couldn't bring myself to thank God for what he had wrought upon us; I hardly thought he could have done it; I thought the devil had overthrown God, and had wrought the destruction of our beautiful city. But I have altered my mind since then; I have begun to talk more like 'Brother Collyer.'" In conclusion, Mr. Collyer alluded to the event of a new church for himself and congregation; he couldn't ask his congregation to build it, but he would ask the Unitarians of Boston; it was their duty and their right. As long as it pleased God to give him life, no other man should stand over his congregation; it was his right until his mission was fulfilled, and he heard a voice saying: "Well done, good and faithful servant; thou hast been faithful unto me in a few things, I will make thee ruler over many. Enter thou into the joy of thy Lord."

The Feeling in England.

One of the best statements of the feeling in London produced by the details of the fire, is contained in the following letter to the Chicago *Tribune*, from its own correspondent in that city:

LONDON, *October* 28.

No event has occurred to divert the attention which the fires at Chicago attracted from the first. Money continues to pour in, and were it not for the persuasion which some of the influential are endeavoring to use, viz.: that America herself has already met the emergency, the supplies would be very much larger. People anxiously wait to learn the amount of suffering that exists; whether there is sufficient shelter; what has been saved; what are the methods of recovery. The history of the Chicago *Tribune* has been printed in every journal of the land, and the names of three or four of its staff have become familiar. For my part, I search every mail that comes in for a copy. I know it will soon be forthcoming, and that we shall have its every characteristic, freely examined and described.

The electric telegraph is freely used in connection with the Chicago intelligence. The Cunards and other steamers are boarded, and the contents of the latest papers are put on the wires without much abridgment. It was the Silesian that brought us the first long despatches. She arrived at Plymouth, from which port the news is republished, but in this instance an exception was made. The haste with which the New York press printed the early details sent from your city prevented even an ordinary discrimination from being exercised, and English readers, accustomed, I am bound to say, to more exactitude and accuracy, are puzzled to find so much that is stated contradicted a little further down. The illustrated papers were sorely tempted, and some of them "fell." We had pictures last week in two of the papers, of Chicago on fire, and this week the *Illustrated London News* supplies a cartoon of the kind. It is scarcely possible that, even at this comparatively late period, any genuine artistic reproduction can have come to hand. If the idea once gets bruited around that the cartoons in the illustrated papers are drawn from imagination, they will suffer in material fortune as well as in fame.

As soon as order is restored the authorities at Chicago will, no doubt, send some report to the people here of the mischief done and the means that have been taken to remedy it. I will suggest that this be transmitted to the Lord Mayor of London. The Lord Mayor, like the Sovereign, never dies. The present gentleman, under whose care the Chicago fund was established, retires into private life next week. But it is to the Lord Mayor the people will look, whoever that gentleman may happen to be. I may say that the despatches of acknowledgment already transmitted by the Mayor of Chicago are deemed most touching and appropriate. People shed tears on reading them, so strong are the feelings aroused. The Queen's donation was made with expressions which reveal her truly fine and sympathetic nature. The Queen reads every line from Chicago that is printed in the papers, and I am sure she will be gratified if she is made to know that the republicans of the Far West give her credit for recognizing a common human life. I am jealous of Chicago at this particular crisis of her history. I want nothing to escape her that can be laid hold of by the envious and by the misanthropic. She has been made famous alike by her prosperity and by her adversity. Let all her public acts be governed by high aims, and let the official communications with European friends be made by men who are distinguished by delicate taste as well as by good judgment. Something is thought in such circumstances even, of phrases.

Your readers would smile in the midst of their trouble could they peruse some of the curious reflections to which the peculiar calamity at Chicago has given rise. The "unco' guid" see in it a judgment by Heaven, imagining that those upon whom this "Tower of Siloam" fell were worse than the rest of the world. Others account for it by engineering defects—blunders in building—downright recklessness. Some of the philosophic class, who look at all these things through the most powerful microscope their faculties supply, propound a lazy kind of theory that Chicago was proceeding too rapidly altogether to be safe. She existed in fact, through friction! As to the future, the sort of predictions uttered and written concerning you are amazing. The general belief appears to be that you are to be rebuilt—in striking contrast to the origin of Rome—"in a day." In ruins yesterday—stately marble to-day. Jonah's gourd was nothing to it. You are credited with superhuman powers, and the English public will be sadly disappointed if they don't hear very soon that "not a trace of the late calamitous fire is to be seen."

Letter from S. H. Gay.

Mr. Sidney Howard Gay, who speaks from actual personal knowledge, and from thorough acquaintance with the workings of the Relief Society, has written a letter to the New York *Tribune*, from which we make this extract, as it shows very clearly what the society has done, and is from the pen of one in a position to know of what he writes. After alluding to the fire, and the number of people left homeless, Mr. Gay says:

"Of this 100,000 people, 20,000 probably left

the city in the course of a few days. The Transportation Committee alone has issued passes to 7,000, which the different railroads have duly honored; the railroad officers have passed many more of their own motion, and a large number have gone out of town, in various other ways than by rail, to the towns and country round about. Then 15,000 more, perhaps, found refuge with friends in the city, or could command the means to establish themselves in some sort of an abiding-place of their own. But making thus all possible deductions, there would remain from 60,000 to 70,000 persons, absolutely destitute of everything, to be fed, and clothed, and sheltered, and, indeed, now—more than a month after the fire, and when a large decrease has been made, from various causes, in the number of those who cannot take care of themselves—there stand recorded upon the books of the Relief Society 13,000 families who need to be supported wholly or in part. It is not likely that they average much less than five to a family, and that would give about 60,000 as the number who have to be looked after daily by the Relief Committee. It is a complicated business to care for an army of 60,000 men, duly mustered and in quarters, its command divided and subdivided, so that each man is under the immediate and personal supervision of a superior officer, its Commissary Department fully provided for, its whole machinery thoroughly systematized and in perfect running order, with all its traditions and regulations and checks and balances as accurately adjusted as in an eight-cylinder printing press and a first-class steam-engine. Given first this great and perfected machinery, and given then the men who are accustomed by long habit to run it, and your army of 60,000 men goes on smoothly enough, provided every man is careful and diligent in his special duty, provided no screw gets loose anywhere, and no hitch occurs anywhere from the Commissary General down to the drummer-boy's rations. But conceive of an army of 60,000 to be composed, not of marshalled, organized, and trained men, where there is a place for every man and every man knows his place, but of men and women and children, without organization or cohesion, huddled together in extremity of distress, weary, hungry, houseless, naked, cold, and in despair, and the problem is how to feed and clothe and shelter them—a problem to be solved instantly or they perish—not to be ciphered out at leisure with time enough to devise plans and appoint officers of tens and of hundreds of thousands, to provide material and places, to divide and subdivide work and duties —but the whole thing to be taken in a lump then and there, and then and there done before sundown. Conceive of this, and you have an idea of the work that was hurled at the Relief Society; of the chaos out of which they had to evolve order; of the prayer for salvation which came from those tens of thousands of pleading eyes, and those tens of thousands of outstretched hands. They did what they could; it is wonderful they did so well; none but that Power which said, 'Let there be light, and there was light,' out of such darkness could have commanded the perfect day.

"It was fortunate for Chicago that it had such an organization as this Relief and Aid Society. It has been in existence nine or ten years, has taken upon itself, during all that time, the care of such of the poor of the city as were not absolute paupers, and has been managed by picked men from among its lawyers, physicians, clergymen, and merchants. As in all such cases, the work had devolved upon a few, but those were men who, voluntarily, and from conscientious and benevolent motives, took this work of charity upon themselves, and reduced it to a system of scientific accuracy. On Monday, the 9th of October, in the first confusion of that dire disaster, and when the city was like the first resting-place of a routed and fugitive army, with no water save that dipped from the lake by hand; no gas in streets or houses; a third of the people without food, or shelter, or clothing; that pitiless south-west gale unabated in its fury, and over all that fierce glow of the smouldering fires, shedding down upon us a lurid light from a brazen sky, like a moonlight red with blood—then we turned for succor where we could. The first generous supplies of provisions, and clothing, and money, that poured in from all sections of the country were used without discrimination or judgment, and, though they relieved much suffering, where relief could hardly go amiss, there was enormous and lavish waste, as well as cruel, selfish greed. And in another sense, also, we were like a defeated army flying, with all the people round about, before a relentless enemy, for the birds of prey scented death and disaster, and gathered for the feast, and filled the air with their clamor. Here were millions of money coming, and thousands upon thousands to be dependent upon bounty, and disbursements to be made which, both as to those who made and those who received them, would be a fruitful source of power and of profit. The November election was only a month away, and to the foul brood of city politicians, it seemed that their father, the Devil, had come in just the nick of time to their assistance. A Board of Aldermen, a majority of which has aspired to be the Tamany of Chicago, and so far as it has failed, has failed for want of opportunity and ability, and not because of any fear of either God or man, counted now upon retaining place and putting their enemies under their feet, with the personal and pecuniary power which the handling of the relief fund and provisions in kind would give them. For the first three days, from Tuesday to Friday, the danger was that affairs would fall completely into the hands of this class of political bummers, and the struggle they made to retain their hold upon them was as desperate as the clutch of death.

"It was the crisis in the fate of Chicago. Whether it should ever recover from the terrible calamity that had swept over it, or whether the ruin should be utter and irrevocable, depended altogether upon

MICHIGAN SOUTHERN R. R. DEPOT.

PALMER HOUSE, STATE STREET.

the character of the men into whose hands should fall the essential government of the city at this moment. That essential government would rest with those into whose control should come the care of the needy and suffering; who should keep them in a condition for wholesome labor, and should provide it for them; should keep away from them all temptation to desperate remedies for desperate circumstances; and who should use wisely and economically the generous bounty in provisions and money which was pouring in from every quarter. Of that rich fund we should, without doubt, have seen the end ere this, had things gone on as they begun, and the laboring people of Chicago, instead of being cheerfully at work at good wages, would have been at this moment a starving, discontented, turbulent population, feeling that they were defrauded of that which an overwhelming sympathy for suffering had given for their relief, that a gang of thieving politicians might carry out their purposes in attaining or keeping political power, and grow rich upon the sustenance of the poor. But, fortunately, the Mayor of Chicago was a man of common sense, who would not give up to party what was meant for humanity. He recognized the distinction that the succor sent to Chicago was sent to the people, and not to the municipality; that it no more fell by necessity and right under the control of the Board of Aldermen or the Common Council than under that of the Board of Trade, but that it ought to go where there was the best assurance that it would be used for the purposes for which it was given, and where those who gave it would have some confidence that it would be so used. By timely proclamation, therefore, three days after the fire, but when time enough had elapsed to justify the wisdom and necessity of the step, Mayor Mason handed over the whole business of the care of the needy and the custody of everything bestowed on their behalf to the Relief and Aid Society. The 'Ring' did not submit to this decision without a desperate struggle; but fortunately the Executive Committee of the society were not only men of high standing in this community, but men of firmness and quick decision. Accepting the great trust imposed upon them, they entered instantly and vigorously upon the great work before them, heedless of partisan clamor, deaf alike to threats and offers of compromise. In three days the question was settled, and the almoners of the largest beneficence that the world, perhaps, has ever seen for a purely humane purpose, sat in perpetual session at Standard Hall, organizing and carrying out a system of relief and aid for this stricken people, so that not a dollar should be wasted or unaccounted for, and not one in this great multitude of sufferers should go hungry, or unclothed, or without shelter. There are, no doubt, here, as there would be everywhere under like circumstances, other men who, from like motives and with like ability and integrity, would have discharged the responsibilities of such a trust; but it is no more than common justice to say that every one of these men gives his invaluable services at great sacrifice of his personal affairs, and it is simply an obvious reflection to add that it was most fortunate for Chicago that such a body of men was already picked and chosen, ready and willing for so sudden and so urgent an emergency.

The Resumption of Business.

The following table will illustrate how quickly this city resumed its ordinary business, even with the want of depot facilities by many railroads. We give two days' buisness one month after the fire, and one two weeks later, compared with the business of the corresponding days of the preceding year:

Receipts and Shipments during 48 hours, Nov. 7th and 8th 1870, and Nov. 7th and 8th, 1871.

	1870.	1871.	1870.	1871.
Flour, bbls., . . .	12,826	11,443	6,596	15,088
Wheat, bushels, .	135,515	128,300	123,955	58,521
Corn, bushels, .	247,730	68,100	158,185	89,874
Oats, bushels, .	53,758	37,016	136,273	35,562
Rye, bushels, . .	28,616	5,333	18,872	
Barley, bushels, .	32,400	14,940	63,192	5,895
Grass seed, lbs., .	124,838	37,665	50,919	19,734
Flax seed, lbs., .	30,000	3,686	21,380	51,410
Broom corn, lbs.,	373,100	209,869	54,900	196,871
Cut meats, lbs., .	146,230	43,520	278,694	471,779
Beef, bbls., . . .	2,870	389	2,013	7,602
Pork, bbls., . .	16	. . .	1,285	670
Lard, tcs., . . .	74,520	. . .	287,764	280,020
Tallow, lbs., . .	16,514	48,490	. .	
Butter, lbs., . .	126,010	107,490	71,637	30,980

	1870.	1871.	1870.	1871.
Live hogs, No., .	5,275	5,182	5,182	381
Cattle, No., . .	1,971	904	904	1,467
Sheep, No., . .	625	. . .	. . .	394
Hides, lbs., . .	184,056	373,872	165,226	215,180
High wines, bbs.,	867	508	238	750
Wool, lbs., . .	268,675	56,266	38,878	144,890
Potatoes, bushels	9,397	15,460	. . .	3,012
Lumber, M., . .	14,616	15,273	3,007	4,225
Shingles, M., .	8,283	3,957	2,427	4,190
Lath, M., . . .	493	553	416	490
Salt, bbls., . .	12,135	28,865	1,718	3,625

Receipts and Shipments for the weeks ending Nov. 11*th and Nov.* 18*th*, 1871. *Compared with corresponding week in* 1870.

RECEIPTS.	Nov. 18, 1871.	Nov. 11, 1871.	Nov. 19, 1870.
Flour, bbls., . .	28,586	35,272	36,050
Wheat, bushels, .	222,345	390,538	310,570
Corn, bushels, .	846,549	817,904	291,688
Oats, bushels, .	349,382	270,367	136,559
Rye, bushels, . .	19,991	26,474	22,539
Barley bushels .	61,450	87,530	41,630
Dressed hogs, No.,	71	26	453
Live hogs, No., .	102,544	56,036	65,726
Cattle, head., . .	13,652	10,051	12,597
SHIPMENTS.			
Flour, bbls., . .	17,499	19,156	38,966
Wheat, bushels, .	146,639	413,909	549,286
Corn, bushels, .	777,953	547,634	296,388
Oats, bushels, . .	450,649	473,134	178,767
Rye, bushels, . .	42,468	37,570	51,114
Barley, bushels, .	72,980	108,726	15,750
Dressed hogs, No.,	. . .	. . .	. . .
Live hogs, No., .	27,566	26,570	20,131
Cattle, head, . .	4,728	3,498	5,207

THE NEW CHICAGO.

FROM the wreck and ruin of this great calamity, there is no one who questions the restoration and continued growth of Chicago. The first issue of each of her papers proclaimed, as its motto, RESURGAM. That was the universal sentiment. In three days after the fire there was no one selfish enough to complain of his individual losses, nor any one weak enough to doubt the reconstruction, and on a grander scale, of this great marvel of the world. Chicago has hitherto attained a world-wide fame as the greatest grain market of the world, and to thousands in the United States even, it is supposed that that is the great business which sustains her. A year or more ago the project of shipping grain to the Atlantic by means of barges on the Mississippi river, and by rail, was for a time seriously considered, and so strongly was the impression that Chicago owed all she had to that trade, and depended on that for a continuance, that a Cincinnati paper seriously propounded the question, "What, then, is the future use of Chicago?"

That this grain trade has been of immense consequence, and that it was the original means of building up the immense commerce that is done here, is true, but the grain trade itself is a consequence of the natural location of Chicago. The railroads worked a revolution in the transportation business. First the passengers and soon the freight abandoned the slower means of wagon and boat, for the speedier transit of the rail. Nevertheless, water transportation is cheaper than rail, and cost of transportation is the important item in the value of grain. Each penny added to, or taken from the cost of moving grain from the farm to New York, is a penny taken from, or added to, the value of the grain in the producer's hands. It soon became an ascertained fact, that it was as cheap to send grain to Chicago, by rail as to haul it to any town on a water course. Here it had cheap water navigation direct to New York by lake and canal. The grain came to Chicago, because Chicago was the only point where it could find a market large enough to receive all that was sent, and with facilities for shipping it to the East at comparatively small cost. The fact of this great market at the head of lake navigation has been of immense value in the filling up of the Northwest. Every man in selecting a location in the West estimates the value of his land, and of its products, by computing the distance to Chicago, and the rates of transportation. In this way the West has grown up around Chicago, and each additional mile of railway laid down towards Arkansas, Kansas, New Mexico, and the territories round to the extreme north, but brings within the circle of her tributaries, additional fields of production, additional people for whom she is to be the great market of sale and supply. The Pacific railway already constructed, and the others to follow, are but enlargements of the means by which this city is to extend her commerce. The St. Lawrence, so long neglected, will, as a route for ocean commerce, at last, fill the expectations of its early explorer, Champlain. The increase in the transportation of grain to the seaboard by rail, has given cause to many forebodings that the business will eventually pass away from the lakes, and be done by railway from local points where grain can be accumulated. So long as grain can be delivered cheaper by water than by rail, and the time is not too long, the cheaper route will be maintained. An enlargement of the Erie canal to meet the enlarged demand for transportation, the use of steam exclusively on the lake and on the canal, and a repeal of the extortionate rates of toll, will keep pace with an increase of railroad movement of grain. When, however, the St. Lawrence shall be adapted to the use of steam propellors of large capacity to and from Montreal, then Montreal, and not New York, will regulate the price, and water transportation to Montreal will approximate in time to that of rail to New York, at one-half the cost.

The position of Chicago marks it as the great centre of distribution. Hence the Northwest is supplied with all it needs. The whole range of manufactures, domestic or imported, must find their market here. The Northwest is teeming with woollen mills, but their goods must be sold here, as all those of New England are sold at Boston and New York. Chicago, as a distributing point, has the advantage over these points, that it furnishes direct to the consumers. It is in the centre of the increasing population. A thousand cities are rapidly growing up within twelve hours' travel. These are, commercially speaking, suburbs and workshops of Chicago. They manufacture; they buy material; they sell to consumers; but the seat of all this commerce is in the city of Chicago. Their growth is her growth. As they grow with the rapid settlement and increasing products of the districts around them, so Chicago grows with the increase of these numerous cities. She is the commercial agent of the West—she has States and cities for her constituencies.

The grain trade, however, has long since ceased to be the supreme or principal item in her commerce. It is, of course, immense, and is forever growing. But there are other things equally promising, and the city is not dependent upon a good crop for business. Manufactures are coming to the West. The man who pays out of his corn the cost of sending it to market, and of bringing back the exchange goods, knows the value of distance as well as time. Within reasonable distance of Chicago are inexhaustible beds of coal. The coal fields of Ohio, Indiana and Illinois have been more developed by Chicago capital and enterprise within the last five years, than they had ever been before. Large portions of this coal are specially adapted for the manufacture of iron. Upon Lake Superior are the inexhaustible deposits of iron ore, far richer in yield than any other in the land. Chicago stands midway between these coal fields and this ore, and whether the ore be carried to the coal, or the coal to the iron ore, or both be brought to Chicago, there to be converted into merchantable iron, the result is the same, that Chicago, in a very few years, will be the great distributing point from which the whole West will be supplied with its iron. Rolling mills and furnaces have already been put in operation, but when the artificial restraints upon the consumption of iron shall be removed, and each man be free to use more iron, and have it at less cost, these iron furnaces and mills, and all the forges and machine shops, steel and cutlery establishments, and all other manufactures using iron to any extent, will gather in and around this grand centre, all adding their contribution to the ever growing, ever extending volume of Chicago's trade and commerce.

With these additions to her industry of course comes the wealth and power of population. The tables of population in June, 1871 showed a total of 332,000. At first it was supposed the fire would retard the increase which had hitherto marked the history of the city; but this is a delusion; in thirty days after the fire there were as many men at work as there were before that event. A demand was created for extraordinary numbers of skilled workmen. Masons, carpenters, plumbers, painters, furniture makers, and all other mechanical trades have come hither in large numbers, but for years the supply will not equal the demand. There is not a workshop where iron and machinery is fashioned that has not been working day and night continuously since the fire, nor will they, or any of the additional ones to be put in operation at once, have any cessation of business for the next five years. By that time the old Chicago will have been forgotten in the proportions of the new. With a population in 1876 of not less than half a million of people, and possibly many thousands more, with the burnt districts all restored, but this time in solid masonry; with the buildings now standing all replaced with buildings of a new architecture, and of durable materials, she will be the great market in which twenty five millions of people will buy and sell, and from which will be distributed the supplies of exchange products. With her trunk railroads extending directly to every point of the Atlantic coast; from Portland to Galveston; with her water communication direct to Europe, retaining her character as the granary of the continent, and seated in the very heart of population, she will draw trade and commerce from all sections, and be the great heart sending forth life blood to every extremity of the American empire.

The city itself will be grand. Even in her comparative infancy precautions have been taken for the future. She has already purchased and in preparation a series of parks and boulevards, the dimensions of which have been given, which will be unequalled in their extent, beauty, and natural location, by anything of that kind on this continent. The Chicago of 1870–71 planned and bought these parks and boulevards. Their completion may be delayed a few years, by the sudden calamity of the great fire, but there are men already past middle age, who will see this grand system of improvement, so extensively carried out as to be one of the great objects of interest in the great republic.

The fire swept through the city while the people were considering the propriety of erecting a free public library. The fire settled that question and in the affirmative. Every public library, with few exceptions; every private library of any pretensions in the city, was destroyed. The next library will be a public one, and a free one, and on a scale worthy of a great city, as this is to be. Intimately connected with this plan is that of a school of practical science, which will have all the advantages of the most approved models in Europe, without their defects. Such schools, embracing the widest range of utility, are destined, under the support of an intensely practical people, to become here in Chicago the great educators of the future men of the country. The men who are to-day excavating the debris of the Chicago of 1871, are but clearing the ground, and repairing the foundations on which is to be built the great city of Chicago, the seat of commercial and manufacturing industry of the continent, the home, within this century, of a larger population than has ever been attained by an American city, and distinguished by the adornments, wealth, power, and public institutions which are incidental to a people whom no reverses can depress, to whom success is but an incentive to still greater effort.

Rebuilding Chicago.

Nature, since the memorable day of wrath on which Chicago was left half in ruins, has smiled upon the city, and the work of reconstruction has gone earnestly on, aided by the beautiful hazy weather peculiar to the Northwest, and known as the Indian Summer; but, recently a snow storm came on suddenly, and the heaps of debris and the half-built walls were covered with snow-heaps that seem to defy further progress. The snow, however, has merely impeded, not stopped the work of rebuilding; for everywhere is heard the clink of trowel and the stroke of hammer. Owners, contemplating round rents, are anxious to have their buildings up; and mechanics, in the enjoyment of wages which two months ago would have been thought fabulous, are quite superior to all meteorological inconveniences. If any one thinks that Chicago has lost her population, and with it her enterprise, he should stand upon Madison, Randolph, or Lake street bridges at dusk, and watch the myriads of laborers and mechanics that, having finished their day's work in the ruins, crowd over those structures to their homes in the West Division. So innumerable are they that they seem to rise from the brick heaps like coveys of wild fowl. It is gratifying to know that these men are toiling not only to rebuild Chicago, but, under skilful direction, and backed by shrewd capitalists, to rebuild it of marble. The foundations that they are laying are broad and deep, and the superstructures that are to rise upon them will be massive and magnificent. There is earnest promise of this in nearly all that in the way of rebuilding has already been done; and builders who propose to await the spring's coming before laying their foundations, do so that they may form their plans on the same magnificent scale.

The work of removing debris was and continues to be one of appalling proportions. Notwithstanding that the teaming facilities of the city are large, and that these are reinforced by farmers, who drive in from a circuit of 150 miles, yet the demand far exceeds the supply. Teamsters and their wagons receive about $6 a day. Potter Palmer, desirous of at once commencing work on the re-erection of the magnificent store which was occupied by Field & Leiter, sought to contract for the removal of the debris. The lowest bid he could obtain was $5,000, but, rather than pay this extraordinary sum for work which ordinarily would be performed for

$1,000 at the utmost, he set to work himself, and is rapidly accomplishing the removal. Palmer, though a millionnaire, is, when he wishes to be, an earnest worker. He watched the construction of this very building from foundation stone to turret, was prouder of it than of any of his palatial structures, and means that it shall, under his own eye, rise to greater than its old proportions.

Fortunately the basin, which is formed on the lake shore, by the outlying track and break-water of the Illinois Central Railroad, afforded a convenient dumping place for the immense quantities of rubbish taken from the ruins. If some such place were not afforded, the expense attending the removal would be increased incalculably. This rubbish, though worthless in itself, is of great value to the city, since it is making land for the city at the rate of $1,000 a day. The basin, and the adjoining land, which is known as the lake front, is nearly a mile in length, and in some places is three hundred feet in depth. Under existing laws it can be used for no other than park purposes, and, before the fire, was undergoing improvement as a park. The exigency, however, authorized the Board of Public Works to convert it, temporarily, to business purposes, and now down its entire length, rearing their pine fronts on Michigan avenue, is a row of temporary buildings, devoted mainly to the wholesale trade. Leases have been made for one year, at the expiration of which the buildings are to be removed. The rental was fixed at $500 for every twenty-five feet, but many of the merchants, on what principle of equity it is impossible to imagine, are of the opinion that the city will never enforce the collection of the rent. It is estimated by competent persons that in the course of time, with the accretions made in the manner described, the land may be sold (the needed authorization having of course been obtained) for a sum equal to the city debt, which is now, in round numbers, $13,000,000. The railway companies which had their depot at the foot of Lake street, the Illinois Central, the Michigan Central, and the Burlington and Quincy, are, and have long been desirous of extending their depot facilities, and for this purpose have sought to acquire the fee to three blocks of the lake front. The Legislature sold these blocks to the companies some years since for $800,000, which sum they were to pay the city, which was to apply it to park purposes. The payment was made, but before the companies obtained possession certain property holders who owned land abutting on Michigan avenue, and who claimed certain rights in the lake front, the most prominent of these rights being an easement, brought the matter into chancery, where it now languishes.

The Work of Rebuilding.

Wonderful as were the manifestations of the fire, the energy with which the business men of Chicago set about the work of rebuilding was even more wonderful. At first business sought a place for itself in temporary wooden shanties hastily thrown together. Once housed, merchants then commenced the permanent work. Within six weeks after the tragedy closed, many of the most enterprising and courageous were actively reconstructing two hundred and twelve permanent brick and stone buildings in the burned district of the South Division alone, covering a total street frontage of 17,715 feet, or 3½ miles. The fact seems almost incredible when it is considered what an amount of brick, stone and iron has had to be removed, also the sudden advance in price of all kinds of building material, and the coldness and general unfavorableness of the weather for out-door operations. The general appearance of the new Chicago will be greatly changed. It is the almost unanimous determination of builders to secure massiveness and solidity at the expense of ornamentation. With few exceptions the walls are of the straw colored brick, the fronts of red pressed brick, the trimmings of stone and iron, and the cornices principally of brick. It is safe to say that there will be no more eight inch walls in Chicago. Sixteen and twenty inches will be the rule; and where timber is used at all, it will be excessively heavy. The 212 buildings referred to are already commenced. Next spring Chicago will be a busy hive of labor, as the architects' books are literally crammed with orders for new and elegant buildings, some of them of the most magnificent description The buildings spoken of, are located as follows:

FIRST PRESBYTERIAN CHURCH. (SOUTH SIDE.)

ST. JAMES' CHURCH. (EPISCOPAL.)

River street,	7
South Water street,	12
Lake street,	10
Randolph street,	6
Washington street,	6
Madison street,	29
Monroe street,	26
Adams street,	2
Quincy street,	1
Jackson street,	1
Van Buren street,	1
Harrison street,	2
Polk street,	1
Michigan avenue,	8
Wabash avenue,	17
State street,	24
Dearborn street,	6
Clark street,	16
La Salle street,	4
Fifth avenue,	6
Franklin street,	9
Market street,	3
Miscellaneous,	21
Total,	212

The Future.

Said the *Missouri Republican*:—"Chicago, though stricken in purse and person as no other city recorded in history ever has been, is not crushed out and destroyed, and her complete restoration to the place and power from which she is temporarily removed is only a question of time. It would be sad, indeed, if a conflagration, though swallowing up the last house and the last dollar of a great commercial metropolis, could fix the seal of perpetual annihilation upon it, and declare that the wealth and prosperity which were once should exist no more forever. Such might be the case, perhaps, were there none other save human forces at work; but into the composition of such a city as that which the demon of fire has conquered, enter the forces and necessities of nature. Chicago did not become what she was, simply because shrewd capitalists and energetic business men so ordained it. That mighty Agent, who fashions suns and stars, and swings them aloft in the boundless ocean of space, marks out by immutable decree the channels along which population and trade must flow. When the first settlers landed at Jamestown and Plymouth, and began to hew a path for civilization through the primeval forest, it was as certain as the law of gravitation, that if this continent were destined to be a new empire, fit to receive the surplus millions of the eastern hemisphere, and contribute to the progress and enlightenment of mankind everywhere, there must and would be a few prominent centres, so to speak, around which the vast machine could revolve. Those centres were determined by geography and topography of the country; and when the advancing tide of immigration touched them they began to develop as naturally and irresistibly as the flower does beneath the genial influences of sunshine and showers. For practical purposes neither Jamestown nor Plymouth were of any special consequence;

therefore the one has ceased to exist altogether, and the other remains an insignificant town. But the inner shore of Boston harbor, the island of Manhattan, the site of Philadelphia, Baltimore, Cincinnati, New Orleans, St. Louis, and San Francisco, furnished the required facilities, and we see the result to-day. Nature declares where great cities shall be built, and man simply obeys the orders of Nature.

"The spot where Chicago river empties into Lake Michigan belongs to the same category as those we have mentioned. It was designed and intended for the location of a grand mart to supply the wants of the extreme Northwest—that portion of the central plateau lying on the line and to the north of the Union Pacific Railway, and the western part of the British possessions. The trade from these sections seeks an outlet there, and finds it better and more available than anywhere else. This fact was settled before the first brick was laid in Chicago; was settled when Chicago rose to the rank of the fifth city in the republic, and is settled just as firmly now, when, to all human appearances, her destruction is well nigh accomplished.

"Natural advantages, then, must compel the reconstruction of Chicago, even though every foot of its soil passes out of the hands of the present proprietors. And if we examine what the fire has spared, it will be found that the nucleus of a new and rapid growth is not wanting. Not more than twenty per cent. of the lumber supply has been consumed, thus affording ample material for building; the largest elevator and perhaps one or two of the smaller ones are safe; the stock yards are uninjured, and with these avenues for business open, business itself is sure to come speedily. Indeed, it is announced that several vessels received full loads of wheat from the elevators as early as Wednesday, and departed on their accustomed voyages to Eastern ports. There is also good reason to believe that at least one-half the insurance will be paid, and as this cannot be much less than $100,000,000, money will not be lacking. If we add to these resources the railway lines converging to that point, which represent an aggregate capital of $300,000,000, and remember that every railway is directly interested in the process of reconstruction, and will aid it in all possible ways, it may not be difficult for even the most incredulous to see why and how Chicago must grow again. That she is absolutely ruined or permanently disabled is a sheer impossibility which no sensible person will for a moment credit.

EMINENT CITIZENS OF CHICAGO.

As samples of the class of men who built up and gave character to the great city now in the struggle of rebuilding, after an almost total destruction of its material structure, biographical sketches of a few of the leading citizens are here inserted.

Charles Tobey

Was born in 1831, in Denis, Cape Cod, and is one of the most prominent manufacturers of the West.

In 1855 he entered Chicago without a friend there, or even a letter of introduction.

He, however, soon obtained a clerkship, and in 1856, with a $500 loan from a friend at Boston, he began business on his own account, and succeeded beyond the most sanguine expectations.

He is a man of business, promptness, efficiency, positiveness, enterprise, and indomitable perseverance, and his success in life, according to all accounts, is amply deserved.

John Van Osdel.

Among the men who have risen with Chicago, contributing to its wonderful greatness, is Mr. John Van Osdel, a native of Baltimore.

He was born in 1811, his father being a carpenter.

He was the pioneer of the famous grain elevators

of New York. Then, after engaging for a time in the iron foundry and machinery business, he returned to his early choice of architect. Recognized as the best in the city, his employment increased with the city's growth, and he accumulated a large fortune.

From his early struggles, his energy and readiness, his zeal in self-education, he well deserves the position he has attained.

Philip A. Hoyne.

Mr. Hoyne was born in New York, in 1824, and when he was thirteen he entered a book-bindery.

In 1841 he settled in Chicago, and commenced the practice of law. Becoming tired of that profession, he went to Galena, where he remained ten years. He then returned to Chicago, and is now United States Commissioner for the Northern District of Illinois. His impartiality and critical acumen have made the name of Commissioner Hoyne very popular.

Hon. Digby N. Bell.

The Hon. Digby N. Bell was born in 1804, and commenced his active life as a sailor. Soon tiring of that drudgery, he went with his young family and settled in Michigan. After farming awhile, he settled, in 1851, in Chicago, and established there the first Commercial College in Illinois. He has devoted the latter years of his life in advancing the cause of education.

Hon. Isaac N. Arnold.

This eminent merchant of Chicago was born in Hartwick, Otsego, county, New York, November 30th, 1815. His parents were natives of Rhode Island, whence they emigrated to New York in 1800. At the age of fifteen he was thrown wholly upon his own resources. He resolved to become a lawyer, and in 1836 he removed to Chicago, at that time a mere village. He has since filled the position of City Clerk, State Senator, and finally member of Congress. He was the intimate friend of President Lincoln, of whom he wrote a life.

Thomas Church.

Thomas Church was born in Onondaga, New York, November 8th, 1801.

His early life was a hard one; and one of his first experiences was earning six and a quarter cents for a day's labor in picking stones.

Become a man, his first idea was to farm, but he afterward took to commerce.

In 1834 he removed to Chicago, built a house, and opened a store. His business steadily increased, and in 1840 he took Mr. M. Salterlee into partnership, their stock consisting of groceries, paints, oils, and domestic dry goods. In 1848 he began his real estate transactions and built largely. He has been one of the busiest of men, and is president of the Chicago Firemen's Insurance Company.

Col. George B. Armstrong.

Col. Armstrong was born in Ireland, in 1822. When he was quite a child his parents emigrated to the United States, and settled at Newark, New Jersey. In 1833 the family went to Virginia, and the succeeding year settled in Baltimore. In 1854, young Armstrong went to Chicago, where, four years afterwards, he inaugurated a new system of distributing letters.

In 1864 he was authorized by the post office to test his system, and he has now made it a grand success.

James H. Bowen.

The subject of this brief sketch was born in 1822, in New York State, his father being a carpenter. In 1836 he left home to become a clerk, and in 1839 he removed to Little Falls, New York. In 1842 he was elected secretary and treasurer of a large commercial company. In 1857 he settled in Chicago, and with his two brothers started the firm of Bowen Brothers, which soon became one of the foremost even in that city of mammoth concerns.

John V. Farwell

Was born in 1827 in Steuben county, New York.

In the spring of 1855 he worked his passage, on a load of wheat, to Chicago, and set his foot in that city with three dollars and twenty-five cents capital. He obtained a situation in a dry goods house, steadily progressed therein until he became partner, and soon, by his energy, the firm was doing the vast business of ten million dollars per year.

He founded, and in a measure sustained, the Illinois Street Mission for Outcast Children, and has been an earnest friend and associate of the Young Men's Christian Association, and is still in the prime of life.

Wm. F. Coolbaugh

Is a native of Pike County, Pennsylvania, and was born in 1821.

He began business in 1842, at Burlington, Iowa.

He has long occupied a leading position in the State Legislature, and as a financier stands deservedly high.

In 1862 he removed to Chicago, and started a banking house, afterward the Union National Bank, and he soon became President of the National Bankers' Association for the West and Southwest. These positions show conclusively how Mr. Coolbaugh is regarded in the Great West.

Wm. Heath Byford.

Mr. Byford first saw the light in Eaton, Ohio, on March 20th, 1817, and at the age of twenty he placed himself under the guidance and guardianship of Doctor Joseph Maddox, of Vincennes, Indiana; commencing practice on his own account at Owensville in 1838, and obtaining a regular diploma from the Ohio College in 1845.

He has filled many important public positions, and is widely known as an author of many learned medical works.

With the burden of fifty years upon him, Doctor Byford is still stalwart, erect in person, and as vigorous as ever.

F. G. Welch.

F. G. Welch was born in Ohio, 1833. After various mercantile experiences in Colorado, San Francisco, and other towns, he emigrated, in 1863, to Chicago. His success has been great. He is the editor of the *Farmer's Friend* of that city, and has recently established the Merchants' and Commercial Travellers' Association.

Samuel Hoard.

This energetic man was born at Westminster, Mass., May 20th, 1800. Before he was six years of age both his parents died, and he then lived with relations, who gave him a good education. Commencing the study of the law, he grew dissatisfied with his progress and entered a store as clerk. In 1833 he removed to Chicago and settled as farmer, but his active mind was not satisfied with agricultural pursuits, and in 1840 he was appointed to take the State census for Cook county, Chicago, which then contained about 5,000 inhabitants. In 1842 he was elected State Senator, and was soon after appointed Clerk of the Circuit Court. In 1845 he formed a partnership with J. T. Edwards, the eminent jeweler, and the firm soon became a great success.

He was appointed by President Lincoln postmaster of Chicago, which position he retained till Andy Johnson's accession.

Julius Bauer.

Among Western business men who have achieved success with no other capital than intelligence and perseverance, few are more deserving of notice than Julius Bauer, the musical instrument maker.

Twenty-two years ago he landed in New York, a stranger in a strange land.

He started in business in New York, afterward went to Philadelphia, and in 1857 caught the Chicago fever, and started a branch house there, in the famous Crosby Opera Building.

His business progressed at the usual prodigious

Western rate, and in 1862 he became the agent of William Knabe & Co., the piano manufacturers. By his energy, attention to business, and identification with the real wants and interests of our people, Mr. Bauer is a fair type of the self-made man.

James H. Hoes.

James H. Hoes left his father's home at the age of fourteen, and started on his life-task in the year 1835.

He set out from Kinderhook, N. Y.—his native town—and went to Towanda on foot.

Having decided to go into the jewelry business, he applied to the best watchmaker in the place for a situation, and after entreating him to give him an opportunity of learning the trade, James succeeded in getting employment.

Through his industry and tact Mr. Hoes gained the good wishes and esteem of Mr. Langford, his employer. At the end of a year he offered to give him a share in the business, having already gradually promoted him to high positions.

In 1840 they both prepared to remove to New York, and enter into business there, but as sickness prevented Mr. Langford from carrying out his plans, Hoes became superintendent of a concern at Oswego and after going to Binghampton, where for two years he did business on his own account, he returned to Oswego and bought out Mr. Wilson, his former employer.

Young Mr. Hoes was thus, by his own unaided exertions, in possession of the finest establishment in that part of the country.

Having married, and removed his business to Danville, he continued in his labors at that place for eight years, at the end of which time he resolved to try his fortune in the West. He went to Milwaukee, and from there to Chicago. He bought the stock of Hoard & Avery, and began business in the Garden City. Here, after a period of unexampled success, he sold out, in 1867, to one of his former partners, and retired from active life to enjoy the fortune which he had so honorably accumulated. But absolute retirement soon proving impossible, he finally accepted the management of the Northwestern Silverware Company.

In social life Mr. Hoes has always been considered a just and charitable man.

His circle of acquaintances, which comprise the most distinguished and honored citizens of Chicago, unite alike in their praise of his private and professional character.

POEMS.

From the great number of poems inspired by the great calamity we select the following, as among the best. The number of those published was well nigh legion, but only a small proportion of them were ever worthy to appear in print.

Chicago.

BY JOHN G. WHITTIER.

Men said at vespers : All is well !
In one wild night the city fell ;
Fell shrines of prayer and marts of gain
Before the fiery hurricane.

On threescore spires had sunset shone,
Where ghastly sunrise looked on none ;
Men clasped each other's hands, and said :
The City of the West is dead !

Brave hearts who fought, in slow retreat,
The fiends of fire from street to street,
Turned, powerless, to the blinding glare,
The dumb defiance of despair.

A sudden impulse thrilled each wire
That signaled round that sea of fire ;—
Swift words of cheer, warm heart-throbs came ;
In tears of pity died the flame !

From East, from West, from South and North,
The messages of hope shot forth,
And, underneath the severing wave,
The world, full-handed, reached to save.

Fair seemed the old ; but fairer still
The new the dreary void shall fill,
With dearer homes than those o'erthrown,
For love shall lay each corner-stone.

Rise, stricken city !—from thee throw
The ashen sackcloth of thy woe ;
And build, as Thebes to Amphion's strain,
To songs of cheer thy walls again !

How shrivelled in thy hot distress
The primal sin of selfishness !
How instant rose, to take thy part,
The angel in the human heart !

Ah ! not in vain the flames that tossed
Above thy dreadful holocaust ;
The Christ again has preached through thee
The Gospel of Humanity !

Then lift once more thy towers on high,
And fret with spires the western sky,
To tell that God is yet with us,
And love is still miraculous !

NEW ENGLAND CHURCH. (CONGREGATIONAL.)

UNITY CHURCH. (DR. COLLYER.)

The Smitten City.

BY GEORGE ALFRED TOWNSEND.

I heard a parson of the school of Baalam
  Lift up the lesson of the flaming town,
And, like a pedler in the will of Heaven,
  Show how its sins invoked the Sovereign frown.

Thus the dead lion ever is insulted
  By asses' colts, whose pity is a blow,
And fallen empires find their last misfortune
  In shallow platitudes from fool and foe.

Bright, Christian capital of lakes and prairie,
  Heaven had no interest in thy scourge and scath;
Thou wert the newest shrine of our religion,
  The youngest witness of our hope and faith.

Not in thy embers do we rake for folly,
  But like a martyr's ashes gather thee,
With chastened pride and tender melancholy,—
  The miracle thou wast, and yet will be!

Not merely in the homages of churches,
  Or bells of praise tolled o'er the inland seas,—
Thou glorified our God and human nature
  With meeter works and grander melodies.

Of cheerful toil and willing enterprises,
  Of hearty faith in freedom and in man;
The hoar old capitals looked on in wonder
  To see the swift strong race this stripling ran.

How like the sun he rose above the marshes,
  And built the world beneath his airy feet,
And changed the course of immemorial rivers,
  And tapped the lakes for water cool and sweet.

How skilfully the golden grain transmuted
  To birds of sail and meteors of spark,
And, like another Noah, bade creation
  March in the teeming mazes of his ark.

Yet in his power, most frank and democratic,
  He roused no envious witness of his joy,
And in the stature of the Prince and hero,
  We saw the laughing dimples of a boy.

Still wise and apt among the oldest merchants,
  His young example steered the wary mart,
And amplest credit poured its gold around him,
  And trade imperial gave scope for art.

His architectures passed all heathen splendor,
  The immigrating Goth drew wandering near;
To see his shafts and arches tall and slender
  Branch o'er the new homes of this pioneer.

The Greek and Roman there might see rebuilded
  In vastness equal and in style as pure,
The merchants' markets like a palace gilded,
  With marble walls and deep entablature.

His two score bridges swinging on their pivots,
  The long and laden line of vessels sped,
While he, impatient, marched beneath the sluice,
  His hosts, like Cyrus, in the river's bed.

Then, when all weak predictions proved but scandal,
  And the wild marshes grew a sovereign's home,
A dozing cow o'erset an urchin's candle,—
  Once more a fool fired the Ephesian dome.

The artless winds that blow o'er plains of cattle,
  And cooled the corn through all the summer days,
Plunged like wild steeds in pastime or in battle,
  Straight in the blinding brightness of the blaze.

And down fell bridge, and parapet, and lintel,
  The blazing barques went drifting, one by one;
The mighty city wrapped its head in splendor,
  And sank into the waters like a sun!

Oh! thou, my master, champion of the people,
  TRIBUNE august, who o'er kept righteous court,
Long after fire had toppled church and steeple,
  Thou stood'st amidst the ruins like a fort.

High and serene thy cornices extended,
  Though scorched by smoke and of the flame the prey.
Above the vault where, grim and calm, and splendid,
  The sleeping lions of thy presses lay.

Till looking round on the wondrous pity,
  Thyself alone erect, intact, upreared,
Disdaining to outlive the glorious city,
  With innate heat transfigured, disappeared.

Yet, from the grave Chicago's wondrous spirit
  Comes forth all brightness, o'er the darkened town,
To say again: "Lo! I am with you, brethren;
  With all my thorns, I wear my civic crown.

"To die is sweet embalmed in your compassion;
  Your oil and wine make life in every rent.
Oh! let me lean a little while upon you,
  And walk to strength in your encouragement."

CINCINNATI, *October* 13, 1871.

Chicago.

BY BRET HARTE.

Blackened and pleading, helpless, panting, prone,
On the charred fragments of her shattered throne,
Lies she who stood but yesterday alone.

Queen of the West: by some enchanter taught,
To lift the glory of Aladdin's court,
Then lose the spell that all that wonder wrought.

Like her own prairies by some chance seed sown,
Like her own prairies in one brief day grown,
Like her own prairies in one fierce night mown.

She lifts her voice and in her pleading calls,
We hear the cry of Macedon to Paul,
The cry for help that makes her kin to all.

But happy with wan fingers may she feel,
The silver cup hid in the proffered meal,
The gifts her kinship and our loves reveal.

October 10, 1871.

Out of the Ashes.

BY HOWARD GLYNDON.

Oh ! fallen with the falling leaves,
 And level with the dust as they !
Thy beauty, City of the lake,
 Is but a thing of yesterday.

Thou wondrous blossom of the West !
 We were so passing proud of thee :
" See," said we to the elder world,
 " How cities grow when men are free."

Thy senior sisters, looking on
 With dazed, half unbelieving eyes
Saw thee, like Hercules of old,
 Swift into ripe estate arise.

And seeing thee so fair, how high
 The hearts of all thy children were !
We would not blame them if to-day
 They bowed their faces in despair ;

Or, newly risen from troubled sleep,
 Stared, with uncomprehending eyes,
On homesteads smouldering, black and bare,
 Beneath the mild October skies ;

Where, here and there, but yesterday
 Towered up such sumptuous witnesses
Of their devoted hearts and hands—
 God help them in this sore distress !

And saying this, the Nation takes
 These homeless children of the West
Into her motherly embrace,
 And hides the homeless in her breast.

Not houseless while our homes have room !
  Not homeless—all cur doors are wide !
The welcome that we send to day
  Is tinctured with exulting pride.

For who has heard one craven cry,
  Though thousands wander lorn and pale ?
Oh ! strong young city, sorest tried,
  There's bravery even in thy wail

To where thou sitt'st we bring the world,
  And show thy ruins, saying, " See !
She is not broken, only bent ;
  For hearts are strong when men are free."

Paris and Chicago.

(From the New York Evening Post.)

O bird with a crimson wing
  And a brand in thy glowing beak,
Why did'st thou flutter o'er seas to bring
  A woe that we dare not speak?

By the light of a flaming sword,
  Did the beautiful Queen of the East
Behold the awful avenging word,
  And drink the blood of the feast.

Her fires went out on the hearth,
  And the glory of Paris has fled;
Could her maddening wiles and unseemly mirth,
  Unstop the ears of the dead!

Did out of her ashes arise
  This bird with a flaming crest,
That over the ocean unhindered flies,
  With a scourge for the Queen of the West?

See homes at its bidding fall!
  At its fiery fierce attack!
While the fiends of the air hold carnival
  In the light of its lurid track.

The joys that were held so dear,
  On the glow of its breath expire;
While treasures and palaces disappear,
  Consumed by its vengeful ire.

Fly hence on thy wing of flame,
  O bird! for thy work is done;
And the queens of a different clime and name
  In their ruin and grief are one.

THE NORTHWESTERN FIRES.

THE GREAT CONFLAGRATIONS

IN THE STATES OF

MICHIGAN AND WISCONSIN.

GREAT FIRES OF THE WORLD:

ROME, MOSCOW, LONDON,

NEW YORK, PITTSBURGH, CHARLESTON, CHICAGO, PHILADELPHIA, SAN FRANCISCO, PORTLAND,

AND

OTHER GREAT FIRES.

THE NORTHWESTERN FIRES.

Wisconsin.

THE great fires which devastated the northern and northeastern portions of Wisconsin and Michigan appropriately belong to a work of this kind, for the burning of Peshtigo, Manistee, Holland and the numerous villages along the shores of Green Bay, will always be associated with the destruction of Chicago, more especially as the principal towns were destroyed on the same evening. While the loss of property may not have been so great, the loss of life was much more terrible and the areas burned over incalculably larger. The same causes in a certain degree conspired to produce this destruction. The summer had been an excessively dry one, and the usual prairie fires which occur every fall, were burning over wider tracts than usual. Had it not been for the combination of wind and fire, it is doubtful whether any material loss would have occurred. Prairie fires in these regions are so common as to attract no attention, even when they get into the woods, for green timber offers little food for combustion. The people of Peshtigo for instance, were resting in perfect security on that fatal Sabbath. The fires were about them in every direction, but they had fought them off with the appliances so familiar to frontiersmen, and dreamed of no danger. At sundown there was a lull in the wind and comparative stillness. For two hours there were no signs of danger; but at a few minutes after nine o'clock, and by a singular coincidence precisely the time at which the Chicago fire commenced, the people of the village heard a terrible roar. It was that of a tornado, crushing through the forests. Instantly the heavens were illuminated with a terrible glare. The sky which had been so dark a moment before burst into clouds of flame. A spectator of the terrible scene says the fire did not come upon them gradually from burning trees and other objects to the windward, but the first notice they had of it was a whirlwind of flame in great clouds from above the tops of the trees, which fell upon and entirely enveloped everything. The poor people inhaled it, or the intensely hot air, and fell down dead. This is verified by the appearance of many of the corpses. They were found dead in the roads and open spaces, where there were no visible marks of fire near by, with not a trace of burning upon their bodies or clothing. At the Sugar Bush, which is an extended clearing, in some places four miles in width, corpses were found in the open road, between fences only slightly burned. No mark of fire was upon them, they lay there as if asleep. This phenomena seems to explain the fact that so many were killed in compact masses. They seemed to have huddled together in what were evidently regarded at the moment as the safest places, away from buildings, trees or other inflammable material, and there to have died together. Fences around cleared fields were burned in spots of only a few rods in length, and elsewhere not touched. Fish were killed in the streams—as at Peshtigo.

Another spectator says:

"Much has been said of the intense heat of the fires which destroyed Peshtigo, Menekaune, Williamsonville, &c., but all that has been said cannot give the stranger even a faint conception of the reality. The heat has been compared to that engendered by a flame concentrated on an object by a blow-pipe, but even that would not account for some of the phenomena. For instance, we have in our possession a copper cent, taken from the pocket of a dead man in the Peshtigo Sugar Bush, which will illustrate our point. This cent has been partially fused but still retains its round form and the inscription upon it is legible. Others in the same pocket were partially melted off, and yet *the clothing and the body of the man was not even singed.* We do not know any way to account for this, unless, as is asserted by some, the tornado and fire were accompanied by electrical phenomena."

It is the universal testimony that the prevailing idea among the people was that the last day had come. Accustomed as they were to fire, nothing like this had ever been known. They could give no other interpretation to this ominous roar, this bursting of the sky with flame, and this dropping down of fire out of the very heavens, consuming instantly everything it touched.

No two give a like description of the great tornado as it smote and devoured the village. It seemed as if "the fiery fiends of hell had been loosened," says one. "It came in great sheeted flames from heaven," says another. "There was a pittiless rain of fire and sand." "The atmosphere was all afire." Some speak of "great balls of fire unrolling and shooting forth in streams." The fire leaped over roofs and trees and ignited whole streets at once. No one could stand before the blast. It was a race with death, above, behind and before them.

The appearance of Peshtigo after the fire, and the effects of the flames is well told in a letter to the Milwaukee *Wisconsin*. The writer says:

"Yesterday afternoon I rode out several miles from Menominee to the opening in the woods, where Peshtigo was. It is a level and sandy road, bordered mainly by blackened stumps and pine. We came to the Peshtigo opening. Fox river, where so many had been saved or drowned, was flowing placidly over the half-burnt dam; heaps of mortar, brick and iron, showed where the factory, dry house, mills, foundry and machine works stood,—all else was a naked waste of drifted ashes and sand. Fording the river with our team, we continued our drive for a few miles westward into the Sugar Bush settlements. The trees had been cut and pulled aside from the road. Burned culverts and small bridges filled up with logs. Outside the road on either hand, was seen the work of the tornado. Great forests of maple, oak, beach, hemlock and pine were torn as by the power of a hundred whirlwinds, and hurled length wise and cross-wise on the ground. The whole forest had been mowed down like grass; not one tree in twenty was standing. Mingled with the work of the winds, is seen the black wrath of the flames. Green maples and oaks, three feet in diameter, went down in a whirl, and were eaten up by the red flames in an hour. It was this double rage of tornado and flame that burst in upon the ill-fated village of Peshtigo. Not all the fire steamers in the world could have stayed its destruction.

"Out among the clearings of the Sugar Bush, not a trace of fence or farm buildings is seen, but a few black embers by the road side and the relics of stoves and kettles by the chimney pile.

"There were two hundred and twenty families burned out in the Sugar Bush, two hundred and fifty in Peshtigo, and full a hundred elsewhere in the track of the tornado. Nothing was saved among the farmers, except now and then a stray horse or cow and a few scanty rags that hung to their bodies. The villagers fared no better. A few attempted flight with bundles and carpet bags, but they were snatched up and devoured by the flames. No one as yet can sum up the number of the dead. One hundred and forty dead bodies have been found and identified in the lower Sugar Bush, fifty in the middle, and seventy-seven in the upper. It is thought that nearly all the farm settlers have been discovered. It is difficult to get at the number of the Peshtigo dead. There were many woodsmen, railroad men, and others, strangers in town. Up to Saturday eighty-eight bodies had been found and registered, while fully as many more were mixed with charred bones and indistinguishable remains. There were twenty-two corpses among the fifteen families at Birch Creek, and half as many up the Menominee."

Before the fire, Peshtigo was in all respects the most beautiful village between Green Bay and Marquette. A six mile railroad extended to it from the mouth of the river, where were situated the great Ogden mill and pier. It contained the works of the Peshtigo Company, including the great tub and pail factory, machine shop, foundry, saw, flour and planing mills. The pail factory alone cost over $250,000 and was the largest of its kind in the United States. The Company's property in the village was estimated at a million dollars. They employed over five hundred workmen. The village proper, on both sides of the river, covered about a mile square, and at the time of its destruction numbered about fourteen hundred people.

The whole burned district in Wisconsin takes in Brown county, at the head of the Bay, and most of the country—say fifty miles west and seventy miles north on the west, and nearly the whole peninsula

CHURCH OF THE HOLY NAME. (ROMAN CATHOLIC.)

ST. PAUL'S CHURCH. (UNIVERSALIST.)

on the east to Lake Michigan. It also took in a strip ten to twenty miles wide on the Fox river, between Lake Winnebago and Green Bay. The fire raged in this section, more or less, for two months. It is estimated that about a third of the standing timber was killed by the fire. Up to the time of the great tornado on the 8th, settlers generally had been able to save their buildings and crops, but lost heavily in fences, bridges, culverts, corduroy roads, and all wood property.

The track of the great Sunday night tornado, on the west side, commenced about six miles north of Oconto, extending fifteen miles in width, and running parallel thirty miles northward down the bay. The track on the east side, commencing in the town of Humboldt, twelve miles east from here, ranged ten miles in width, sweeping northeast forty miles to Big Sturgeon Bay. The west side district took in the village of Peshtigo, the Sugar Bush Settlements, the village of Menekaune, at the mouth of the Menominee, and the Birch Creek Settlement, eight miles beyond in the borders of Michigan. All were swept out of existence.

The Green Bay region was not so sparsely populated as is usually supposed. The census tables of 1870 show that Oconto county then contained 8,322 people; Door county, 4,869; Kewaunee county, 10,281; Brown county, 25,180. Nearly every township in the three last named counties contained settlements of people engaged in farming, and many villages clustered about the saw mills.

The people in Oconto county were generally found in villages, occupied at this season of the year in the saw mills or manufacturing establishments. The villages of Oconto, Peshtigo, Marinette and Pensaukee had, in the aggregate, over 5,000 inhabitants. Besides the counties above named, large portions of the following counties have been partially swept by the fires: Manitowoc, having 33,369 people; Calumet, 12,334; Outagamie, 18,435. All the Green Bay region has increased in the numbers of its people at least one-fifth.

Of the losses in the farming districts immediately contiguous and tributary to Peshtigo, the Peshtigo and Marinette *Eagle* of October 21st, says: "Allowing, at least, two townships of good farming land to have been entirely devastated by the fire, one-half of the same was more or less improved. Estimating the loss on improvements, stock and farm products to have been $1,000 to each forty acres of such land, the loss amounts to $576,000. Valuing the timber on the entire tract at $500 per forty acres, and we have of loss $576,000 more. We think the foregoing estimate low enough in all conscience. This makes a grand total loss of property in Peshtigo village and vicinity of $2,883,800. Add losses at Menekaune, at Menominee, and the farms up Menominee river, and the Menominee pine, the mill property in the vicinity and settlements, and the total loss will reach nearly $4,000,000 on that fatal and long-to-be-remembered Sunday night."

The roll of actual sufferers, not including those who had means to help themselves, was 3,500; the roll of the dead who perished in these terrible flames, about 1,500.

A civil engineer doing business in Peshtigo, in a letter describing his escape, says: "I went to bed about 9 o'clock, but did not go to sleep, as there was considerable noise in the house (the Peshtigo Hotel). Before long the bells rang and the whistles blew for fire, but this had happened almost every night for a fortnight. I looked out of my window, but as the sky was black, I went to bed again. Before long I looked again, and the sky was red. I then threw open the window, and the loud roar which I heard warned me of approaching danger." The writer dressed and looked out into the street, and though he saw no flames then, he had only time to assist two friends to carry out their trunks before the sparks flew in clouds and the smoke became suffocating. He immediately started for the bridge, and when he reached it the fire had not extended to the river. Before he could cross, a mill at the other end was in flames, presenting a fiery blockade. "I turned back," he says, "and for the first time the horror of the situation burst upon me. Fire on all sides; the bridge I stood on afire; the air hot and full of flame; crowds of people screeching, cattle bellowing, horses dashing through the crowds and the wind blowing a hurricane. A wooden ware factory blew in before the fire touched it." He struggled back to the other end of the bridge, though knocked down once by cattle, threw himself into the water and made the best of his way up stream, sometimes swimming and then wading, as the depth allowed, to get as far from the burning buildings as possible. "The heat increased so rapidly," he continues, "as things got well afire, that, when about 400 feet from the bridge and the nearest building, I was obliged to lie down behind a log that was aground in about two feet of water, and by going under water now and then, and holding my head close to the water behind the log, I managed to breathe. There was a dozen others behind the same log. If I had succeeded in crossing the river and gone among the buildings on the other side, probably I should have been lost, as many were. It was thought at first that the fire would not cross the river, as it is here four or five hundred feet wide; but it proved to be no obstacle at all, and those who crossed were glad enough to get back into the water. For about an hour I lay and gasped for breath, but after that the worst was over and I crawled upon the log to get out of the water, for it was very cold and I was chilled through. I lay there an hour and a half, and then was able to go ashore. It was so smoky we could not go near the burning ruins, so we built a rousing fire on the shore and tried to get dry and keep warm until morning. My watch ran through it all, and therefore I knew the length of time I was in the water. Had it not been for the watch I would have thought I was there four hours at least."

Another statement will be all that is necessary to give the reader an idea of this terrible scene. Mr. James B. Clark, of Detroit, who was at Uniontown, Wisconsin, writes: "Fires were blazing through the forests and along the prairies in every direction. At sundown there was a strong breeze, which at 9 o'clock increased to a furious gale, blowing toward the lake. The whole surface of the country to the westward, eastward and southward seemed to be one mass of flame, which almost reached to the lowering clouds, and rushed along at race-horse speed. Beyond, toward the lake, was the settlement of Williamson's Mills, comprising about fourteen families. The fire suddenly made a rush like the flash of a train of gun-powder, and swept in the shape of a crescent around the settlement. It is almost impossible to conceive the frightful rapidity of the advance of the flames. The rushing fire seemed to eat up and annihilate the trees. He says the roar of the blast was as loud as the whir of a great mill. As we stood looking on, say at about 10 o'clock, we heard another strange sound. Straining our eyes toward the fire—about seven miles distant—we could just discern something moving; now it would appear like a black mass, then it would separate into fragments, swaying to and fro, and bobbing up and down. It came toward us directly from the lurid wall of flame. So intense was the glare of light all about us that our eyes were dazed; they ran with water, and we could see only by constantly using our handkerchiefs. At last we made out by sight and sound that the moving mass was a stampede of cattle and horses thundering toward us away from the flames, bellowing, neighing and moaning as they galloped on. Finally they came rushing past with fearful speed, their eyeballs dilated and glaring with terror, and every motion betokening delirium of fright. Some had been badly burned, and must have plunged through a long space of flame in the desperate effort to escape. Following considerably behind came a solitary horse, panting and snorting and nearly exhausted. He was saddled and bridled, and, as we first thought, had a bag lashed to his back. As he came up we were startled at the sight of a young lad lying fallen over the animal's neck, the bridle wound around his hands, and the mane being clinched by the fingers. Little effort was needed to stop the jaded horse, and at once release the helpless boy. He was taken into the house, and all that we could do was done; but he had inhaled the smoke, and was seemingly dying. Some time elapsed and he revived enough to speak. He told his name—Patrick Byrnes—and said: 'Father and mother and the children got into the wagon. I don't know what became of them. Everything is burned up. I am dying. Oh, is hell any worse than this?'

"The poor fellow lay in a critical condition when I left. The next morning we drove down to the settlement. The first house we came to was that of Patrick Byrnes, father of the lad before spoken of. It was a heap of ashes. The brick chimney, the cooking stove and iron portions of farm tools were the only remnants of the place. The forest was burnt down close to the ground, the stumps only being left, smouldering and smoking. Everything was hot. Even the road was baked and cracked by the heat. About a mile further on we came to a horrible spectacle. Along side the road in a gully lay the bodies of six persons and two horses, roasted to a crisp. The iron tires of the wheels, and braces and bolts of the wagon were scattered about. Here the fire had surrounded and engulfed them. Evidently the animals in their mad struggles had reared, plunged, and fallen headlong from the road to where they died.

"We hurried on. All along the road lay the carcasses of cattle, sheep, hogs and dogs, burned to a crisp. The smaller animals were almost entirely consumed. Now we came to the village. Nothing was left but piles of ashes, smoking and smouldering. In the cellar of one house we found eight bodies. One of a man was in a stooping position over that of a child, as though he died trying to ward off the flames. This was very likely the body of Mr. Williamson, the owner of the mills, who, with his entire family, is said to have perished. In the rear of the yard of the next house were four bodies, apparently those of a mother and her children. They were scorched, not burnt crisp, and one cheek of the youngest, a girl of six, retained an expression of calmness that seemed to indicate a painless death by suffocation. But the most horrible of all was at Boorman's well. Mr. Boorman's house was the largest in the village, and in the centre of the yard, midway between the house and barn, was a large but shallow well. Several of the neighbors were supplied with water from this fountain, and it is likely that in the conflagration, when all hope was cut off, the neighbors, insane with terror thronged with one purpose to this well. The ordinary chain and wheel pump used in that place had been removed, and the wretched people had leaped into the well as the last refuge. Boards had been thrown down to prevent them being drowned; but evidently the relentless fury of the fire drove them pell mell into the pit, to struggle with each other and die—some by drowning, and others by fire and suffocation. None escaped. Thirty-two bodies were found there. They were in every imaginable position; but the contortions of their limbs and the agonizing expressions of their faces told the awful tale."

Michigan.

The destruction in Michigan was not so terrible to life as in Wisconsin and yet was very disastrous in its consequences both to property and life. The principal losses were in Huron and Sanilac counties, which contained about 24,000 inhabitants. Of these fully 10,000 were rendered homeless, and in other parts of the State nearly 5,000 more. On the west shore of Lake Huron the towns of Verona,

New River, Sand Beach, Huron City, a portion of Port Hope, Crescent, Centre Harbor, Ellen Creek, White Rock, Paris, Cracow, Meriden, Forrestville, and a Polish settlement near Forrestville were utterly destroyed. Further north and on the shore of Lake Michigan, Muskegon and Manistee in part, Glen Haven on Grand Traverse Bay, and other settlements south of Mackinaw were burned.

Of the losses, the State Relief Committee of Michigan say: "From 10,000 to 15,000 people at least in Michigan have lost their homes, food, clothing, crops, horses, and cattle. On the night of the Chicago fire 2,000 people on the east shore of Lake Michigan, and 5,000 to 6,000 on the west shore of Lake Huron were reduced to almost absolute destitution. Within two or three weeks other small villages and settlements have been blotted out. The number of individual farm houses, barns, and frontier dwellings which have been destroyed by the all prevailing fires cannot, from want of information, be accurately calculated. The fires are still burning and new ones spring up. The area of ruin and devastation is daily increasing and much suffering exists. A long, hard, and cold winter is approaching, and large numbers of people are accessible only by water, and navigation will soon be closed."

In regard to the destruction of timber the Huron county *News* thus estimates for one county alone:

"The loss to this county by the burning of pine and other valuable timber is very great. It is too soon to make anything like an accurate calculation of the total loss from this source, but from converse during the week with the supervisors and others from different parts of the country, we know we are safe in saying that it will *exceed one million dollars.* Francis Crawford, of Caseville, estimates his loss by the destruction of timber at $100,000. That of the Port Crescent Company cannot be much less. Of the Rock Falls pine, comprising many millions of feet, hardly a green tree remains. Already immense tracts of this burnt timber have been laid flat by the high winds that have since blown upon them. But not until spring will the full effect of the damage be seen; then, when the earth becomes softened by the rains and departing frost, will these forest monarchs bow before the blast, and green timber land will be the exception in the country—perhaps almost a novelty. Where the pine is scattering, it will not pay to get it out from these 'wind falls;' where it has stood thick, much of it will be got in, though at a much increased cost of lumbering. During the next two winters doubtless an extra effort will be made by all our lumbermen to rescue as much of this pine from entire destruction as possible,—as the destructive worm will be busily at work, and the chances of further burning will be largely increased."

In connection with the Michigan fires the story of Allison Weaver, who lived near Port Huron, is full of interest. A Detroit paper thus tells how the old veteran stayed to see it out:

"Weaver is a single man, about fifty years old, and served all through the war in an Ohio regiment of infantry. Up to two weeks ago he was at work for a man named Bright, ten miles from Forrestville, as fireman of a shingle mill. Two or three days before the approach of the flames, which eventually destroyed that section, Bright and his family left for Forrestville, and the next day all the men employed about the place either followed his example or made haste to reach their homes. On leaving, Bright informed his men that the fire would sweep that way, and warned them to lose no time in making their escape. Having no property to lose, or family to take care of, Weaver determined, as he says, 'to stay and see the circus out,' meaning that he intended saving the mill if possible. He has a stubborn sort of spirit, and the fact that everybody else went induced him to stay.

"As soon as the men left he set to work and buried all the provisions left in the house, and during the day buried the knives, belts and other light machinery of the mill, as well as a stove and a lot of crockery ware. There was plenty of water in the vicinity of the mill, and he filled several barrels full, besides wetting down house, mill, stock and everything that would burn, scattering several hundred pailsful of water on the ground around the buildings.

"When night came and the fire had not appeared, he began to jeer his absent comrades. But his self-conceit soon left him. About ten o'clock the heavens were so light that he could see the smallest objects around him, and there was a roaring in the forests which sounded like waves beating against rocks on the shore.

"He began to suspect that he would soon receive the visit predicted, and accordingly made preparations for it. In leveling up the ground around the shingle mill, earth had been obtained by digging here and there, and Weaver went to work and dug one of these pits deep enough for him to stand up in.

"He then filled it nearly full of water, and took care to saturate the ground around it for a distance of several rods. Going to the mill, he dragged out a four inch plank, sawed it in two, and saw that the parts tightly covered the mouth of the little well. 'I kalkerated it would be tech and go,' said he, 'but it was the best I could do.' At midnight he had everything arranged, and the roaring then was aw ful to hear. The clearing was ten to twelve acres in extent, and Weaver says that for two hours before the fire reached him there was a constant flight across the ground of small animals. As he rested a moment from giving the house another wetting down, a horse dashed into the opening at full speed and made for the house. Weaver could see him tremble and shake with excitement and terror, and felt a pity for him. After a moment the animal gave utterance to a snort of dismay, ran two or three times around the house and then shot off into the woods like a rocket.

"Not long after this the fire came. Weaver stood by his well, ready for the emergency, yet curious to see the breaking in of the flames. The roaring increased in volume, the air became oppressive, a cloud of dust and cinders came showering down, and he could see the flame through the trees. It did not run along the ground, or leap from tree to tree, but it came on like a tornado, a sheet of flame reaching from the earth to the top of the trees. As it struck the clearing he jumped into his well, and closed over the planks. He could no longer see but he could hear. He says that the flames made no halt whatever, or ceased their roaring for an instant, but he hardly got the opening closed before the house and mill were burning tinder, and both were down in five minutes. The smoke came down to him powerfully, and his den was so hot he could hardly breathe.

"He knew that the planks above him were on fire, but, remembering their thickness, he waited till the roaring of the flames had died away, and then with his head and hands turned them over and put out the fire by dashing up water with his hands. Although it was a cold night, and the water had at first chilled him, the heat gradually warmed it up until he says that he felt very comfortable. He remained in his den until daylight, frequently turning over the planks and putting out the fire, and then the worst had passed. The earth around was on fire in spots, house and mill were gone, leaves, brush and logs were swept clean away as if shaved off and swept with a broom, and nothing but soot and ashes were to be seen.

"After the fire had somewhat cooled off, Weaver made an investigation of his *caches*, and found that considerable of the property buried had been saved, although he lost all his provisions except a piece of dried beef which the fire had cooked as in an oven without spoiling it. He had no other resource than to remain around the place that day, during the night, and the greater part of the next day, when the ground had cooled enough so that he could pick his way to the site of the burned village. He was nearly twelve hours going the twelve miles, as trees were falling, logs were burning, and the fallen timber had in some places heaped up a breastwork, over which no one could climb."

To these accounts we have only to add that on or about the 8th of October, Iowa, Minnesota, Indiana and Illinois were severly devastated by prairie fires; that terrible fires raged on the Alleghanies, the Sierras, and the Rocky Mountains, and in the far away regions of the Red river of the North; that at Halifax, N. S., a fearful gale destroyed great numbers of vessels; that Montreal and Toronto were visited by a tornado which blew down numerous houses; that Galveston, Texas, experienced the ravages of a tidal wave; and that attempts were made to burn the cities of San Francisco, Louisville, Ky., Toronto and London, C. W., and Syracuse, N. Y. Add still to these, the Franco-German war, the fearful Chinese typhoon, the rapid spread of Asiatic cholera, and the unprecedented visitation of famine and plague combined in Persia,—and the year 1871 must forever be regarded as the black year of the world's history.

A Summing up of the Loss of Life and Property by the Wisconsin Fires.

A correspondent of the Milwaukee *Wisconsin*, who has travelled through the burned regions in Wisconsin, thus sums up the loss of life and property in the country through which he passed:

"After making a deduction for exaggerations, I had supposed that 500 would cover the number of dead on the west side of the bay. I now learn from reliable sources that the actual number of interments up to Monday night counted up to 504. Add another hundred for remains of ashes and charred bones at Peshtigo, and I think we have not far from the true number on the west side. Add 150 for the east side—making 750 in all—and the death-roll is nearly complete.

"It is impossible to figure the aggregate losses of pine timber and farm property with any degree of closeness. It is the interest of mill men to underrate the amount of fallen pine that must be secured this winter to save it. A medium estimate of damage to pine land in the Green Bay region is figured at $400,000. The damage on the Wolf is figured at $300,000. The loss to the fifteen saw mills burned, is put at $225,000. The loss of cord-wood, ties, hemlock bark, &c., is set at $200,000. The losses of fences, buildings, wagons, cattle, crops, among the six hundred farmers, cannot be less than $600,000—making a total aggregate of more than $3,000,000, aside from those of Peshtigo.

"The country through from Brown county north to Big Sturgeon Bay, for 400 square miles, is utterly devastated. At least 400 farms in this tornado section alone are left desolate—stripped of every improvement. Fences, barns, dwellings, implements, furniture, wagons, harness, and crops, all went up in a 'whirlwind of fire.' It will take thirty years, in that cold, hard soil for their timber to grow again. In the aggregate, their losses must foot up to $1,000 a family. Farmers here have saved half of their teams that were let loose in the woods, and a third of their stock. But they have no hay, straw, grain or feed of any sort—not even the poor chance of browse in the woods. Nearly all, with large families, have lost their last cow and pig. In a ride of six miles, on nearly a straight line, I saw but three hens and a fanning mill—the only farm implement left in town. In the Belgian settlement, on Red river, sixty-two families were burned out in a row! Not a house, not a shed, not a coop—not one fence-rail left upon another. The families had fled, almost naked, and breathless, to the few cabins on the outskirts that were saved.

"There were 300 or more, wounded sufferers remaining in hotels, boarding houses, and hospitals about the bay. Fifty of the Peshtigo sufferers were at the Dunlap House, Marinette. Half of them were able to be about. Burned ears, faces, hands and feet were common to nearly all. There

BIGELOW HOUSE.

PACIFIC HOTEL.

SAND'S BREWERY.

RUSH MEDICAL COLLEGE.

ILLINOIS AND MICHIGAN CENTRAL R. R. DEPOT, AFTER THE FIRE.

were women with great burns on the sides and limbs, with faces like kettles and hands like claws, burned to the bones. Men could fight better, and dare more than women. Most of them perished by suffocation. Little children are sadly maimed in their feet and faces. I saw one with a heel gone, and another with an eye. Nearly all will recover without loss of sight or limb. I could fill a book with stories of the hospital. Most of them suffer more from hurts of mind than body. I have a sad memory of a poor widow who lost her crippled boy, who went on crutches, and a sprightly girl, who fell between the burning logs. They were all her family. 'The screams of both,' she said, 'seemed forever sounding in my ears.' There is a future, and no doubt compensations for all these suffering ones.

"Most of these cabins that are left are crowded with two or three families each. I saw one with four men, five women, and sixteen children—two of them suckers. They had just received an outfit of clothing—warm stockings, knit hoods, thin shawls, thin gaiters, and light colored dresses for the women and girls; old fashioned hats, bursted boots, thin jackets, and summer coats and pants for men and boys. There were some occasions of laughter, but none of ridicule; all were glad and surprised at getting what they did. I saw no immediate want of provisions. Flour, pork and hard bread are distributed to all—packages of tea and coffee to most. There are nearly potatoes enough in the country, if distributed. Their stock that is left has been driven off to meadows and fields not burned over. One large-hearted old farmer was keeping eighty odd cattle belonging to his unfortunate neighbors. Without stopping to consider the ways of Providence, or the uses of philosophy, these simple-minded people seem to have understood the art of helping one another."

THE GREAT FIRES OF THE WORLD.

Rome, A. D. 64.

A HISTORY of the great Chicago conflagration would be incomplete without some allusion to the other great fires in the history of the world, by means of which comparisons in losses and extent may be made. The first which naturally occurs to the memory is the destruction of Rome, thus narrated by Tacitus:

"There followed a dreadful disaster; whether fortuitously, or by the wicked contrivance of the prince (Nero), is not determined, for both are asserted by historians—but of all calamities which ever befell this city from the rage of fire, this was the most terrible and severe. It broke out in that part of the circus which is contiguous to Mounts Palatine and Cœlius, where, by reason of shops, in which were kept such goods as minister aliment to fire, the moment it commenced it acquired strength, and being accelerated by the wind, it spread at once through the whole extent of the circus; for neither were the houses secured by enclosures, nor the temples environed with walls; nor was there any other obstacle to intercept its progress; but the flames spreading every way impetuously, invaded first the lower regions of the city, then mounted to the highest; then again, ravaging the lower, it baffled every effort to extinguish it, by the rapidity of its destructive course, and from the liability of the city to conflagration in consequence of the narrow and intricate alley, and the irregularity of the streets in ancient Rome. Add to this the wailings of terrified women, the infirm condition of the aged, and the helplessness of childhood; such as strove to provide for themselves, and those who labored to assist others; these dragging the feeble, these waiting for them; some hurrying, others lingering; altogether created a scene of universal confusion and embarrassment; and while they looked upon the danger in the rear, they often found themselves beset before and on their sides; or if they had escaped into the quarters adjoining, these, too, were already seized by the devouring flames; even the parts which they believed remote and exempt, were found to be in the same distress. At last, not knowing what to shun or even where to seek sanctuary, they crowded the streets and lay along the open fields. Some from the loss of their whole substance, even the means of their daily sustenance, others from their afflictions for their relations, whom they had not been able to snatch from the flames suffered themselves to perish in them, though they had an opportunity to flee. Neither dared any man attempt to check the fire, so repeated were the menaces of many who forbade to extinguish it, and because others openly threw fire-brands, with loud declarations, 'that they had one who authorized them;' whether they did it that they might plunder with less restraint or with orders given.

"At length, on the sixth day the conflagration was stayed at the foot of Esquilæ, by pulling down an immense quantity of buildings, so that an open space, and as it were, void air, might check the raging element by breaking the continuity. But ere the consternation had subsided the fire broke out afresh, with no little violence, but in regions more spacious, and therefore with less destruction of human life, but more extensive havoc was made of the temples and porticos dedicated to amusement. * * Nero seemed to aim at the glory of building a new city, and calling it by his own name; for of the fourteen sections into which Rome is divided, four were still standing entire, three were levelled with the ground, and in the seven others there remained only here and there a few remnants of houses, shattered and half consumed."

Moscow, 1812.

It will be remembered that on the 15th of September, 1812, the French Emperor entered the city, which the Russians had resolved to sacrifice. Allison says:

"On the night of the 14th a fire broke out in the Bourse, behind the bazaar, which soon consumed that noble edifice, and spread to a considerable part of the crowded streets in the vicinity. This, however, was but the prelude to more extended calamities. At midnight on the 15th, a bright light was seen to illuminate the northern and western parts of the city; and the sentinels on watch at the Kremlin soon discovered the splendid edifices in that quarter to be in flames. The wind changed repeatedly during the night, but to whatever quarter it veered the conflagration extended itself; fresh fires were every instant seen breaking out in all directions, and Moscow soon exhibited the spectacle of a sea of flame agitated by the wind. The soldiers, drowned in sleep or overcome by intoxication, were incapable of arresting its progress; and the burning fragments floating through the hot air, began to fall on the roofs and courts of the Kremlin. The fury of an autumnal tempest added to the horrors of the scene; it seemed as if the wrath of Heaven had combined with the vengeance of man to consume the invaders of the city they had conquered.

"But it was chiefly during the nights of the 18th and 19th that the conflagration attained its greatest violence. At that time the whole city was wrapped in flames, and volumes of fire of various colors ascended to the heavens in many places, diffusing a prodigious light on all sides, and attended by an intolerable heat. These balloons of flame were accompanied in their ascent by a frightful hissing noise and loud explosions, the effect of the vast stores of oil, resin, tar, spirits, and other combustible materials with which the greater part of the shops were filled. Large pieces of painted canvass, unrolled from the outside of the buildings by the violence of the heat, floated on fire in the atmosphere, and sent down on all sides a flaming shower, which spread the conflagration in quarters even the most removed from where it originated. The wind, naturally high, was raised by the sudden rarefaction of the air produced by the heat, to a perfect hurricane. The howling of the tempest drowned even the roar of the conflagration; the whole heavens were filled with the whirl of the volumes of smoke and flame which rose on all sides, and made midnight as bright as day; while even the bravest hearts, subdued by the sublimity of the scene, and the feeling of human impotence in the midst of such elemental strife, sank and trembled in silence.

* * * *

"Meanwhile the flames, fanned by the tempestuous gale, advanced with frightful rapidity, devouring alike in their course the palaces of the great, the temples of religion, and the cottages of the poor. For thirty-six hours, the conflagration continued at its height, and during that time above nine-tenths of the city was destroyed. The remainder abandoned to pillage and deserted by its inhabitants, offered no resources to the army. Moscow had been conquered; but the victors had gained only a heap of ruins. It is estimated that

30,800 houses were consumed, and the total value of property destroyed amounted to £30,000,000."

London, 1666.

We must go back more than a couple of centuries to find a parallel to the terrible fire which has wrapped the city of Chicago in a sea of resistless flame. On the 2d of September, 1666, the city of London was almost entirely destroyed by what has since been known as the Great Fire. This awful conflagration gained headway with the same terrible rapidity as that of Sunday night, and in five dreadful days of ruin and terror and panic laid two-thirds of the English metropolis in ashes. Like the fire at Chicago, it broke out upon a Sunday, though at a different hour—two o'clock in the morning. Nearly two-thirds of the entire city was destroyed. Thirteen thousand houses, eighty-nine churches and many public buildings were reduced to charred wood and ashes. Three hundred and seventy-three acres, within, and sixty-three acres without the walls were utterly devastated.

New York, 1835—1843.

That great event in the history of New York, the "great fire," occurred on the night of the 16th of December, 1835. At between eight and nine o'clock of the evening above stated, the fire was discovered in the store No. 25 Merchant street, a narrow street that led from Pearl into Exchange street, near where the post office then was. The flames spread rapidly, and at ten o'clock forty of the most valuable dry goods stores in the city were burned down or on fire. In all, 530 buildings were destroyed; they were of the largest and most costly description, and were filled with the most valuable goods. The total loss, estimated at about $20,000,-000, was afterwards found to be about $15,000,000. Of the buildings destroyed the most important were the Merchants' Exchange, the Post Office, the offices of the celebrated bankers, the Josephs, the Allens and the Livingstons, the Phœnix Bank, and the building owned and occupied by Arthur Tappan, then much despised for his anti-slavery sympathies.

The second great fire in New York began on the morning of the 20th of July, 1843. Altogether about 300 buildings were destroyed, among which were the costly shrines of commerce and finance and the abodes of the poverty stricken. A liberal estimate of the total loss is made at $6,000,000.

Pittsburgh, 1845.

Pittsburgh, Pa., was visited by a most destructive conflagration the 10th of April, 1845. By it a very large portion of the city was laid waste, and a greater number of houses destroyed than by all the fires that had occurred previously to it. Twenty squares, containing about 1,100 buildings, were burned over; the loss was estimated at $10,000,000.

Philadelphia, 1865.

In 1865, Philadelphia was the theatre of a terrible conflagration. The loss of property amounted to about $500,000, and fifty buildings were destroyed. On Ninth street, from Washington to Federal street, every building was burned.

San Francisco, 1851.

The most disastrous conflagration in San Francisco began on the 3d of May, 1851, and was not entirely checked until the 5th inst. The loss caused by it amounted to $3,500,000; 2,500 buildings were destroyed. Another large fire devastated a great portion of San Francisco in June, 1851. It occurred on the 22d of that month, and 500 buildings were destroyed by it. The loss was estimated at $3,000,000.

Portland, 1866.

The terrible fire which laid in ruins more than half the city of Portland, Me., commenced at five o'clock on the afternoon of the 4th of July, 1866. Beginning in a cooper's shop at the foot of High street, caused by a fire-cracker being thrown among some wood shavings, it swept through the city with frightful rapidity. Two thousand persons were rendered homeless. In all the loss was estimated at $10,000,000.

Charleston, 1838.

Charleston, S. C., was on the 27th of April, 1838, visited by one of the most destructive fires that has ever occurred in any city in this country. A territory equal to almost one-half of the entire city was made desolate. The fire broke out at a quarter past eight o'clock on the morning of the day mentioned, in a paint shop on King street, corner of Beresford, and raged until about twelve A. M. of the following day. It was then arrested by the blowing up of buildings in its path. There were 1,158 buildings destroyed, and the loss occasioned was about $3,000,000. The worst feature of the catastrophe was the loss of life which occurred while the houses were being blown up. Through the careless manner in which the gun powder was used four of the most prominent citizens of the city were killed and a number injured.

Chicago, 1857, 1859, 1866, 1868.

On the morning of the 10th of October, 1857, a fire occurred in Chicago which, though notable from the amount of property destroyed, was made awful by the loss of human life which it caused. The fire broke out in a large double store in South Water street, and spread east and west to the buildings adjoining and across an alley in the rear, to a block of new buildings. All these were completely destroyed. When the flames were threatening one of the buildings a number of persons ascended to its roof to fight against them. Wholly occupied with their work, they did not notice that the wall of the burning building tottered, and when warned of their danger they could not escape ere it fell, crushing through the house on which they were, and carrying them into its cellar. Of the number fourteen were killed and more injured. The loss in property caused by the fire amounted to over half a million of dollars.

A fire the most disastrous after that of October, 1857, took place on September 15th, 1859. It broke out in a stable, and, spreading in different directions, consumed the block bounded by Clinton, North, Canal, West Lake and Fulton streets, on which the stable was situated. From this block the fire was communicated to Blatchford's lead works and to the hydraulic mills, whence it passed to another block of buildings, all of which were destroyed. The total loss was about $500,000.

Property to the amount of $500,000 was destroyed by fire on the 10th of August, 1866. The fire originated in a wholesale tobacco establishment on South Water street, and passed to the adjoining buildings occupied by wholesale grocery and drug firms. The first two buildings and contents were utterly, while the other was but partially, destroyed.

A fire, which destroyed several large business houses on Lake and South Water streets, took place November 18th, 1866. It originated in the tobacco warehouse of Banker & Co., and the loss caused by it was about $500,000.

The fire which occurred on the 28th of January, 1868, was the most destructive by which Chicago had ever been visited. It broke out in a large boot and shoe factory on Lake street, and destroyed the entire block on which that building was situated. The sparks from those buildings set fire to others distant from them on the same street, and caused their destruction. In all the loss was about $3,000,-000.

Other Great Fires.

The other great fires of the world have been as follows:

Norfolk, Va., destroyed by fire and the cannon balls of the British. Property to the amount of $1,500,000 destroyed. January 1st, 1776.

City of New York, soon after passing into possession of the British; 500 buildings consumed. September 20th and 21st, 1776.

Theatre at Richmond, Va. The governor of the State and a large number of the leading inhabitants perished. December 26th, 1811.

City of New York; 530 buildings destroyed; loss $20,000,000. December 16th, 1835.

Washington City. General post office and patent office, with over ten thousand valuable models, drawings, &c., destroyed. December 15th, 1836.

Philadelphia; 52 buildings destroyed; loss, $500,000. October 4th, 1839.

Quebec, Canada; 1,500 buildings and many lives destroyed. May 28th, 1845.

Quebec, Canada; 1,300 buildings destroyed. June 28th, 1845.

City of New York; 300 buildings destroyed; loss $6,000,000. June 20th, 1845.

St. John's, N. F.; nearly destroyed; 6,000 people made homeless. June 12th, 1846.

Quebec, Canada; theatre royal; 47 persons burned to death. June 14th, 1846.

Nantucket; 300 buildings and other property destroyed; value, $800,000. July 13th, 1846.

At Albany; 600 buildings, steamboats, piers, &c., destroyed; loss, $3,000,000. August 17th, 1848.

Brooklyn, 300 buildings destroyed. September 9th, 1848.

At St. Louis, 15 blocks of houses and 23 steamboats; loss estimated at $3,000,000. May 17th, 1849.

Frederickton, N. B.; about 300 buildings destroyed. November 11th, 1850.

Nevada, Cal.; 200 buildings destroyed; loss $1,300,000. March 12th, 1851.

At Stockton, Cal.; loss, $1,500,000. May 11th, 1851.

Concord, N. H.; greater part of the business portion of the town destroyed. August 24th, 1850.

Congressional library, at Washington. 35,000 volumes, with works of art destroyed. December 24th, 1851.

At Montreal, Canada, 1,000 houses destroyed; loss, $5,000,000. July 8th, 1852.

Harper Brothers' establishment, in New York; loss over $1,000,000. December 10th, 1853.

Metropolitan hall and Lefarge house, in New York. January 8th, 1854.

At Jersey City, 30 factories and houses destroyed. July 30th, 1854.

More than 100 houses and factories in Troy, N. Y.; on the same day a large part of Milwaukee, Wis., destroyed. August 25th, 1854.

At Syracuse, N. Y., about 100 buildings destroyed; loss, $1,000,000. November 8th, 1856.

New York Crystal Palace destroyed. October 5th, 1858.

City of Charleston, S. C., almost destroyed. February 17th, 1856.

At Quebec, Canada, 2,500 houses destroyed; loss $2,500,000.

For comparison with these data are the following facts connected with the Chicago fire. The area of Chicago, including the recently annexed territory west of Western avenue, and also including streets, etc., is over 23,000 acres. Of this the South Division embraces 5,363, and the North Division, 2,533½. The total number of buildings in this city was about 60,000, of which about 17,000 were on the south and 10,500 on the north side of the river. On the north side there were many elegant dwelling houses, but they were nearly all east of Wells street and north of North avenue, those lying near the river being of a very inferior class. There were also large sections on the north side on which there were no houses. The district between the North Branch and the Ogden Canal on one side, and Lincoln Park and the Old Cemetery on the other, were unoccupied, and there was much vacant ground further up on the North Branch.

On the south side the fire destroyed nearly everything in the First and Second Wards, and a light portion in the northwest corner of the Third. Its southern limit on Michigan avenue was Congress street; on Clark, Harrison, and on Wells street, a point a little below Polk. The area of the burned district is 450 acres. There were destroyed 3,600

METHODIST CHURCH BLOCK.

ST. JOSEPH'S PRIORY—GERMAN CATHOLIC.

buildings, including 1,600 stores, 28 hotels, and 60 manufacturing establishments.

On the north side, 1,300 acres were burned over out of the 2,500 in that division. The total number of buildings destroyed was 10,000 including over 600 stores and 100 manufacturing establishments.

While the amount of ground burned over in the West Division was not great, not exceeding 150 acres—and while much of that was occupied by lumber yards, etc., those who did live there were very closely packed together, so that between one and two thousand people must have dwelt in the burned district. The value of the houses destroyed was comparatively small, they being nearly all frame buildings.

The whole immense area of the West Division, with its miles of dwelling houses, its stores and business blocks, is almost intact, while the south side retains the great mass of its dwelling houses of the better class, many manufactories, some of its finest churches, and the innumerable manufactories of the better class.

A city of 290,000 inhabitants is still in existence, with the energy to rebuild the burned district, and once more make it the scene of active labor and business enterprise.

Fire in the Air—A Remarkable Theory.

A writer in the *New York Evening Post* sets up a remarkable theory in regard to great fires. He says: On the night of the 27th of December, 1835, I was sitting with a literary friend, about 9 o'clock, in one of the private boxes of Hamblin's magnificent Bowery Theatre. Suddenly the big bell of the City Hall boomed loud and long over the metropolis, and "Fire!" "Fire!" echoed around and within the theatre. We were all, in an instant, rushing out of the slamming doors, and onward toward the scene of the conflagration, which was "glaring on night's startled eye" away down town.

When we reached Wall street, near Water, the Tontine Coffee House had caught, and dark smoke in huge masses, tinged with flickering flashes of bright flame, was bursting from all the upper windows. The night, as all who were out in it will remember, was intensely cold. There was but little wind, but as the fire advanced there was plainly perceptible the "food of fire" in the air, as I firmly believe there always is in all great conflagrations; something mysterious as yet, and unexplainable. It was so in our great fire, for I saw its evidences myself, and I see that reports of the same evidences are mentioned as features of the still more terrible and vastly greater conflagration in Chicago, which has "roused the world." Science, there is but little doubt, will find out, by-and-by, what this mysterious power is, and tell us how it is worked and how it may be guarded against if not conquered. Whether it is atmospheric or electric, or whatever else it may be, is yet to be determined. A word or two more concerning this a little further on.

Our great fire travelled south and west faster than a man could walk. Water froze in all the gutters; thick ice coated all the hydrants, crunched in the hose pipes that encumbered the streets, and lay in "floes" where there was a shadow from the heat and the flame. But in a little while no water was wanted. Engines were soon useless; and no energetic "Sykesy" was required to "take the butt." Clouds of smoke, like dark mountains suddenly rising into the air, were succeeded by long banners of flame, rushing to the zenith, and roaring for their prey. Street after street caught the terrible torrent, until over acre after acre there was rolling and booming an ocean of flame! "All of this I saw, and part of it I was." The printing office of the *Knickerbocker*, at first in South William street, was moved three times far beyond the prevailing fire, but was gradually followed by the raging enemy, and finally devoured.

As we were standing upon the roof of the Exchange, looking down upon the scene when in mid-progress, buildings far beyond the line of fire, and in no contact with it, burst into flames from the interior. The same thing, I observe, happened in Chicago, and was attributed to incendiaries; but there was no incendiaries suspected in our great fire. What latent power enkindled the inside of these advanced buildings, while externally they were untouched? A scientific writer at the time contended, I think in the old *Daily Advertiser*, that at a certain period there is what he called an "inflammable vacuum" in the air, which is self-igniting and irresistible. Perhaps a hundred years or so from now, some safeguard against this mysterious element, now lying latent and sleeping in nature, may be discovered. It is not so very long since the old teakettle first lifted its lid to the science of steam, and talking round the world under water is a much younger wonder.

APPENDIX.

The Origin of the Fire.

Just as our volume is about to go to press an official investigation as to the origin and progress of the fire has commenced in Chicago, and we append the most relevant portions of the testimony thus far (Nov. 27) taken, as it throws some additional light upon the commencement of the great conflagration.

The Fire-alarm Operator.

William J. Brown, the operator in the fire-alarm office, testified that he was on duty in the fire-alarm office, in the court house, on the night of the 8th of October. Mr. Schaffer, the watchman in the tower, notified him, about half-past nine o'clock, that there was a fire, and told him to strike Box No. 342. He sent that box over the wires to the engine houses, and then looked out of the office window facing south, and saw the reflection in the sky. In a short time the watchman pulled him again, and said he had been mistaken—that the fire was not so far off as he had thought when he gave him Box No. 342, which is located on the corner of Halsted street and

Canalport avenue. As the box was on the line of the fire, Brown thought the firemen would not be misled, so he did not strike a nearer box. If he did so, confusion might ensue. About ten minutes after the first alarm he struck a second, giving the same box. A few seconds afterwards several boxes were turned in, and thinking they were for the same conflagration, he did not pay any attention to them, as a second alarm had been given. Observing from the window that the fire was increasing, he sounded a third alarm, but did not cause the court house bell to be rung. He was relieved by Mr. Fuller, about quarter after twelve o'clock, and left the office. He went to the corner of Randolph and Canal streets, and, after remaining there a few moments, started down Canal to Madison street. He crossed the bridge and went south on Market street and saw that a number of shanties near the gas works were on fire. The gas works were not ignited up to that time. He saw one steamer at work near the corner of Monroe and Market streets, the pipemen having their hose lead into an alley near Farwell's warehouse and playing on some wooden buildings which were ablaze. He saw another engine, the Coventry, he thought, while he was going through the blocks to get to Madison street. He could not tell whether she was working or not. When he reached La Salle street, near Madison, he saw that the rear of the Oriental Block was all on fire. The air wa sfull of cinders and burning material, and he made his way to the court house, where he remained until the watchmen were driven out of the cupola, and the office was on fire.

The Court House Watchman.

Matthias Schaffer, watchman in the court house, corroborated the statement of Mr. Brown in regard to the alarms given. After he told Brown to strike Box No. 342, he took another look at the fire, and was satisfied that he had located it about a mile south of where it really was, and he informed the operator of it. He was relieved at eleven o'clock by Dennis Denene, but he remained in the cupola. Sparks in large numbers and burning material of different kinds were blown over the court house within half an hour after he had given the first alarm. The wind was "terribly strong." He continued watching the fire until twelve o'clock. Twice before that hour the cupola of the court house caught fire, and he got on the roof and stamped out the fire with his feet. This occurred before the fire fiend had crossed to the South Division. Some men had been fixing up the clock in the cupola and left a lot of shavings on the floor. The glass in the window had been broken, and the sparks went through the openings. There was a window on the south side of the cupola that never had any glass in it since he had been on duty in the tower, and sparks were blown into the cupola there and set fire to the woodwork. He crawled in and tried to stop the spread of the flames, but was driven out by the smoke. He had no way of putting it out, and had to let it burn. Between ten and eleven o'clock, he could not tell the exact time, but thought it was ten o'clock, he descried what appeared to be a new fire, four or five blocks north of the one he had given an alarm for; about twelve o'clock he left the court house, and went to look at the south side fire. The wind was so strong that he could hardly stand up. He returned to the court house, and helped put out two more fires in the roof. His clothes caught fire several times, and he was obliged to keep constant watch to prevent being burned up himself. He and the other men thought they could save the court house, but after the sparks went through the open window alluded to and set the under side of the roof on fire, he knew it could not be done. He halloed to Denene, who was then on watch in the tower, to come down or he would be cut off. He could not get down the stairs, but had to slide down the banisters, his whiskers being scorched, and his hands and face badly burned during his progress. Every one had to leave the building then to save their lives. When he was driven out of the building he notified the jailor in the basement that the court house was going "sure," and that he must take care of the prisoners, and not let them burn up. From seven to ten minutes after this the cupola fell in.

Mrs. O'Leary,

The owner of the cow, now so famous, which it was claimed, kicked over the lamp and started the fire, testified, that she and her family—her husband and five children—were in bed, but not asleep on that Sunday night. They knew nothing of the fire until Mr. Sullivan, drayman, who lives on the south side of DeKoven street, awoke them and said their barn was on fire. She took a look at the barn and saw that it could not be saved. She became almost crazy on account of losing all her property—a barn, wagons, harness, six cows and a horse--and was very much excited. There were three barns—two besides her own—on fire at the same time. A family named McLaughlin lived in the same house with her, and she understood they were having a "social time" on that Sunday night; that they had an oyster supper, and a Mrs. White had told her that one of the family went into the barn to milk one of the cows. She had no knowledge of it and could not say whether it was true or not. The first she saw of the fire engines was one playing on Turner's Block, on the corner of Jefferson and DeKoven streets. She thought it was a good while between the time the fire broke out and when she saw the steamer, but it might have been working some time before she saw it. She was so excited in looking after her family and property that she didn't take notice of much else.

Catharine Sullivan,

Who lives on DeKoven street, east of Jefferson, was washing dishes when she saw a bright reflection on the window panes of her dwelling. She ran into the street, and saw that O'Leary's barn and two others east of it were on fire. She had heard that the O'Leary's were asleep at the time, and that somebody awoke them. Her house caught fire several times, and citizens threw pailsful of water on it. Her son and Dennis Rogan woke the O'Leary's. She did not know of her own knowledge, whether there was a party in O'Leary's dwelling, but she had heard that there was. Pat. McLaughlin, the fiddler, lived in the front part of O'Leary's house. "'Pon her word," she could not tell how long a time elapsed after she saw the fire until the engines made their appearance.

Dennis Rogan,

Of No. 112 DeKoven street, was in O'Leary's house about half-past 8 o'clock on Sunday night. O'Leary and his wife were in bed. He asked the woman why she went to bed so early, and she said it was because she had a "sore fut." He went home, and after he had gone to bed—sometime after 9 o'clock—he heard a neighbor say that O'Leary's barn was on fire. He jumped up and ran around to the barn and tried to save a wagon that was there, but be could not. The heat drove him away. There was company at "McLaughlin, the fiddler's" and he heard music in there. He did not know who was present. It was a quarter of an hour, he thought, before the engines came. There was a high wind at the time, and the sparks were blown away some distance.

Catharine McLaughlin,

Of No. 137 DeKoven street, testified that she had lived in the front part of O'Leary's house, but did not reside there now. She knew nothing about the origin of the fire. Some one cried out "Fire," and she looked around the side of the house and saw O'Leary's barn was burning, and the rear part of Mr. Dalton's house was just igniting. There were five young men and two young women at her house that night. A "greenhorn" cousin of hers, had just arrived from Ireland and her friends and cousins came in to see him. Her husband played two tunes on his fiddle, and one of the women danced a "bout" and another a polka. That was all the dancing that was done. One of the company went out once or twice during the evening, and brought in half a gallon of beer. They didn't eat anything, and she didn't cook anything—did not start the stove. "Before God, this day," she didn't cook anything. The company was in the house at the time the fire broke out. She got along pleasantly with Mrs. O'Leary, and assisted in saving the house from being destroyed. Boys could go into the alley near the barn, as there was nothing to prevent them. She did not notice any engines when she went to look where the fire was; but a few minutes afterward there was a steamer on the corner of Jefferson and DeKoven streets. She could not tell exactly how long a time elapsed between the discovery of the fire and the arrival of the engines; but she thought about ten minutes. She did not know whether Mrs. O'Leary was in the habit of milking her cows at night. She lived in the front part of the house, and the barn could have been turned upside down and she would not have known it. Mrs. O'Leary generally did the milking about 5 o'clock. The barn was about forty feet from the house. None of the company went out to get milk for punch. She never had such a thing in the house. She did not know, of her own knowledge, that Mrs. O'Leary had saved a calf from the barn.

Patrick O'Leary, whose wife owned the alleged kicking cow, said he was in bed and didn't know anything about the start of the fire. When he saw it, only his barn was ablaze. He got on the roof of his house to protect it, but not "before his barn and the whole city was burned down." Dan Sullivan called him out of bed, and told him his barn was on fire. He put his children into the street, and then threw water on his little house until after one o'clock in the morning. He didn't see any engines for a little while. One fireman, with a stream, asked him if he was insured, and he said "No," and the water was taken away from his house. He could not tell what time the engines arrived. Water was thrown on his house by the pipemen. "They had enough to do beside that." He did not know how the fire started. He had no knowledge of it. "If he was to be hanged for it he couldn't tell. He didn't blame any man in America for it." His "woman" went to bed about eight o'clock, and he followed her half an hour afterward. He was asleep when Sullivan woke him, or he would have saved a cow. Both doors of the barn were open—the alley door and the one on the south side of the building. The latter was nailed back so that it could not be shut. On the right hand side of the barn, going north, there were some shavings and wood, and in a shed outside were some coal and more wood. He sometimes sprinkled shavings in the barn for his horse to stand on. He thought the neighbors had shavings in their dwellings. The wind was very high, and the fire spread very rapidly.

Daniel Sullivan, of No. 134 DeKoven street, was in O'Leary's house about eight o'clock in the evening, and remained there about one hour. O'Leary, and all his "young ones," except two, were in bed. He asked the "old woman" why she went to bed so early, and she said she didn't feel well. While he was there O'Leary told the two children who were up to go to bed. He left the house, and, while on the opposite side of the street, at twenty or twenty-five minutes past nine o'clock, he saw fire in O'Leary's barn. He ran across the street as fast as he could—he has a wooden leg—and cried out "Fire" as loud as he could, which was very loud, as he has strong lungs. He entered the barn, intending to cut the ropes with which the cows were tied. He cut two of them loose, but as they did not seem inclined to leave, and the fire was increasing, he thought he had better depart. As he was making for the door, his wooden leg went between two boards, and he half fell over, catching himself on his sound leg. He caught hold of the wall and pulled himself out, and just then saw a calf with a rope around its neck. The hair on its back was on fire, and when he caught hold of the rope it jumped six feet into the air. He pulled it out of the barn; and, when he reached the yard, he looked back and felt like a "whipped dog," because he hadn't saved the cows. O'Leary's house was, by this time, on fire, and a man named Ragin came along and shoved in the door, and awoke the inmates. Leary came to the door, and scratched his head as "if there was a foot of lice in it." His wife came out also, and clapped her hands for grief on account of her cows being burned up. The fire appeared to be on the right side of the barn [where O'Leary said the shavings were kept—REP.] He did not notice any one leaving McLaughlin's house. If any one had left he would have seen him. His mother kept a cow, and he frequently went to O'Leary's barn to get feed; and thus knew how the cows were tied. He had never noticed shavings on the right side of the barn. Wood and shavings were kept in the shed adjoining the barn. There was no fire in the shed when he got there. Quite a time elapsed before the engines arrived—from ten to fifteen minutes. There was any quantity of shavings in the houses of the Bohemians in the vicinity. The barn door was open. The fire did not spread very rapidly. Two barns were on fire when the engines came. There might have been more, but he was positive two were burning. The O'Leary barn was 16x20 feet and 14 feet high. There was a vacant shed, fronting on the alley, opposite O'Leary's barn, in which the boys of the neighborhood were in the habit of congregating. In front of it, facing Taylor street, was a vacant house, which, he understood, was often occupied by vagrants and loafers as a lodging place. The alley between the shed and barn was about twelve feet wide.

The above testimony is from those who lived immediately adjacent to the locality where the fire commenced, and although it does not give any very definite idea concerning the origin of the fire, it is quite evident that a drunken orgie of some description was going on, which undoubtedly had much to do with the more immediate cause of the fire. Below we append the testimony of one or two firemen, which will give the reader some idea of the fire as firemen regarded it, and of some of the difficulties under which they labored:

Michael W. Conway, the pipeman of the steamer "Chicago," testified that he worked on the Saturday night fire until half-past 4 o'clock on Sunday afternoon, and his eyes being full of cinders and his physical condition such as to render him unfit for duty, he went home and retired to rest. About 11 o'clock his wife awoke him, and said she was afraid they would be burned out. He went over to the engine house, and saw the steamer in front of the building. The fire was then near the corner of Harrison and Jefferson streets. The Chicago's house is on Jefferson street, near Van Buren. Some one told him the fire was on the south side, but he did not believe it, as he thought it was the reflection from the west side fire. The engine was short of hose, so he took the cart and went down Desplaines street to see if he could find any that had been left behind by the engines. He found two or three lengths, and went back to the house. The engine was not working. The company had had a full reel —600 feet—of hose on Sunday afternoon, but it had been lost. The Titsworth was at that time drawing water from a plug on Jefferson, south of Van Buren street. He did not know where the Chicago had been. He asked the foreman what he intended to do with the engine, and he replied that he was "played out," and he (Conway) could take charge of her. He told the foreman it was "all right," and that he would go on the south side. There was no one present to give him directions. He started and attempted to cross Madison street bridge, but could not. He crossed Randolph street bridge and went east. He saw one engine at Wells and Madison streets, another at La Salle and Madison streets, and another at Clark and Madison streets, and when he

This Page is Blank

Materials were not available when scanned.

reached the corner of Clark and Washington streets he concluded that a line was being formed on Madison street to cut off the fire, and, as there was no engine on Franklin street, he thought he would get a plug there. While passing the court house, he noticed a fire on the roof, and asked the engineer if he thought water could be thrown up there. The reply was "Yes," and he was about to attach the suction to a plug, when he noticed several men come out of the cupola with buckets and brooms. As the fire was very small, he thought they could manage it, and he continued on his way to Franklin street. He took a hydrant on Franklin street, near Washington, and led south into an alley near Barber's building. He had then about five hundred feet of hose, having procured a lead from the fire-escape hose, and worked two streams. He remained at work there until Marshal Williams ordered him to pick up and go to Schuttler's building. He led up Randolph street, and threw water on the buildings on the south side of the street. The flames came from the basements of the stores, while there was no sign of fire in any other part of the buildings. Once while going from the engine to the pipemen he saw a woman with a "duster" on her head looking out of a fourth story window. He threw up a stone or piece of wood to attract her attention, and told her if she did not leave the building at once she would be burned up. She had hardly got into the street before the flames burst out of the basement windows. The fire came from the east down Randolph street. The light of the fire in the cellars was a strange one. It looked as if whiskey or alcohol was burning. He heard a great many loud reports during the night, but thought they were caused by falling walls. He did not know of any buildings being blown up that night. The only marshal he saw until Tuesday afternoon was Williams. He went from Schuttler's to the corner of Randolph and Market streets, and remained there until the rear walls of the Washington house fell in, and the shanties on the northeast and southeast corners were burned down. He saw the Metropolitan Hall burned, and did not think it remained standing a minute after the fire took hold of it. The dome in the Briggs House caught fire. While the engine was working at Franklin and Randolph streets, he took a walk down to South Water street, and saw the Williams at work on the corner of Fifth avenue and that street. The air was oppressively warm and full of sparks, and there was a perfect gale. His eyes were in a wretched condition. While working on Barber's building the window frames of the upper floor caught fire, and, after he had kicked open the door, two policemen went up and subdued the flames. He was familiar with many of the buildings that were burned. Their roofs were generally of felt, saturated with tar and covered with pebbles. The cornices were generally of wood. Now and then there was a tin roof. Tin made the best roof if people did not walk on it. After he left the foot of Randolph street he went across the bridge and to the foot of Washington strcet. There he saw the Richard's engine throwing water on the iron works. They hadn't enough hose, so he let them have two or three lengths, by order of the chief marshal. The buildings were not on fire, but were being cooled off. He afterwards went to the foot of Franklin street, on the north side. This was about daylight on Monday morning. He went first to Ohio and Wells streets, but as he could obtain no water he went to the river. The Coventry was there when he arrived, and the Winnebago came up soon after. He threw water on the east elevator, and the pipemen of the other engines paid attention to the Galena depot, by order of Marshal Williams. The fire at that time was east of Wells street, and as far north as he could see. He was not at work on the south side over four or five hours, and did not fail to obtain plenty of water while there. The fire went diagonally from the river east, and then eat its way west. He kept a look-out to the west, so as to prevent being cut off. In case of an emergency he intended to run the engine into La Salle street tunnel. He did not see a member of the Fire Department drunk, but saw several citizens with firemen's hats on who were. The citizens got the hats from the hose carts. In a hot fire, such as that, a slouch hat was preferable to a fire hat, as the eyes and face could be shielded from the heat. A man stole his fire hat, and a policeman shoved the thief into the river, and the hat sunk. [Marshal

Williams stated that he took fire hats from two citizens who were drunk.] While Conway was at the Chicago's house, he saw no liquor. A citizen who was there was intoxicated, but he did not remain long at the house. No extra hats were carried on the hose carts. He did not know of any money being paid to firemen for special services.

Christopher Schimmels, foreman of the steamer Chicago, said the first he knew of the fire was the striking of the gong. He thought it was about 9.30. Box No. 342 was struck. This box is about a mile southwest of where the fire was. He went directly to the blaze, and took a hydrant on the corner of Forquar and Jefferson streets, and led the hose south. His was the only stream there. After working from three to five minutes, the engine was "shut down," and upon making inquiry as to why it was done, the engineer told him that a spring in the pump had broken. He told the engineer to start up again, and run the risk of breaking the pump to pieces. He did not see the marshal or the assistants, and he asked the foreman of the Illinois, which had come up, which side of the fire he would take. He replied "north," so Schimmels remained on the south line. He worked there until Assistant Marshal Benner ordered him to move and cut off the fire in the rear of some buildings. The next thing he knew, a row of buildings on Jefferson street, a little south of Taylor, were on fire. After working on them ten minutes, orders came to move and put on two streams. An order subsequently came to go further north, and try to cut off the fire. It was impossible to go up Jefferson street, so he went over to Halsted and up to Harrison, and took a plug on the corner of that street and Jefferson. He led the hose south, but was driven from his position by the heat, and nearly lost his hose in retreating. He attached another lead of hose to the engine, and kept the ground near her cool. He then started for a plug on Jefferson street, between Harrison and Van Buren, but the Titsworth was there, and he went around to Jackson and Jefferson streets. After being there three or five minutes, he saw that the fire was not coming that way, so he sent his men over to the south side. He went to his engine house, as he was completely played out, having had no sleep for thirty hours. He had worked eighteen hours on the Saturday night fire, and four of his men were nearly blind. When the alarm came in, these men, who had been at home, ran around to the engine house, but as they were useless on account of the condition of their eyes, he took three volunteers and started for the fire. None of his men were intoxicated. They all worked faithfully.

He did not know what time the fire crossed to the south side, but thought it was about 2 o'clock on Monday morning. His engine was in good order at the Saturday night fire, but they had to knock her suction from a plug to prevent her being burned up, and the "goose neck" being out of order, she could not draw water very well on Sunday. He was short of hose. Two lengths were lost on Harrison street, and there was none in reserve. There were eigteen lengths in the engine house on Saturday night, but some companies had taken it all out. His engine was also on the north side. The engineer, who had charge, came back to the house about 7 o'clock on Monday morning, and said he came near losing her three or four times. He met the Chief Marshal about 11 o'clock on Monday morning, and told him he had no hose. He was told that there was some expected at the Milwaukee depot, and went there to get it, but none had come. When he returned to the engine house, a small boy came in and said there was a Springfield steamer at the foot of Taylor street, and the men with it wanted to know where to go, as they could not see any fire. He brought them up to the house, and asked them for half of their hose—they had 1,000 feet—and the foreman said he would let him have it, if he would bring his engine out and work with him. He said "all right," and hitched the truck horses to the Springfield engine, and with his own steamer, started for the north side, crossing Division street bridge. The two engines worked on the gas works from 6 o'clock that evening until 7 o'clock on Tuesday morning, when the Springfield steamer gave out. The fire was then so as it would not spread any more, and they returned to the house, finding two strange companies in possession when they arrived. The steamer was fixed up, and he slept until noon, when orders came to go to the foot of Taylor street and throw water on some coal. He was not offered any money to play on any building, and did not think anything more could have been done to stop the fire. If there had been plenty of hose on at first it would have made a difference. Coal was scarce, and the citizens tore up the sidewalks to furnish his engine with fuel. All the hose he had had for three months previous to the fire was very poor.

Mayor Mason.

At the meeting of the Common Council of Chicago, held on the 4th of December, for the purpose of inaugurating the Mayor elect, the retiring Mayor, R. B. Mason, in his address, said:

The appalling calamity which has befallen our city made it necessary for the Mayor to assume responsibilities entirely unexpected and unprecedented. His sole object and aim was to secure means that would be the most effectual, and the soonest available, to meet the emergency, and it is believed this was done without lowering the dignity of his office or abrogating any of its powers. Our great misfortune has called forth universal sympathy and aid from almost every city and town in our own land, and to a large extent in foreign lands. And, to show our wants, it is simply necessary to state that some 15,000 families are being aided, more or less, at the present time. But all are sheltered, and their most pressing wants are being supplied.

All of the funds which have been sent here for the relief of our suffering citizens have been turned over to the Chicago Aid and Relief Society, who are operating under a charter from our State, and have had ten years' experience in aiding the poor and destitute of our city. This society is composed of some of our best and most reliable citizens, and it is confidently believed that the expenditure of this world-wide bounty will be more judiciously done, and accomplish more good, than under any other organization, and that all will be satisfactorily accounted for. Our citizens will not soon forget the great exertions made by the Aldermen and other city officers, and that is now being made by the Chicago Aid and Relief Society, to give shelter and food to the tens of thousands of sufferers by the great fire, and I tender to each and all of you my thanks for the counsel and assistance rendered to the Mayor at that trying time.

Message of Mayor Medill.

At the municipal election held since the fire, JOSEPH MEDILL, the editor and one of the leading proprietors of the *Chicago Tribune*, was elected to the office of Mayor. His inaugural message delivered on the 4th of December, contains the following statement and suggestions:

I have been called to the head of the City Government under extraordinary circumstances. A few weeks ago our fair city, reposing in fancied security, received a fearfully tragic visitation from fire, which in a few brief but awful hours reduced a large portion thereof to ashes, cinder and smoke, consuming one grand division, leaving but a fragment of another, and inflicting an ugly wound on the third. In a single night and a day 125,000 of our people were expelled from their homes and compelled to flee for their lives into the streets, commons, or lake, to avoid perishing in the flames. Many lost their lives from heat, suffocation, or falling walls—how many may never be known; and the multitudes who escaped were fain to seek shelter and food at the hand of charity. The greater part of our citizens, not burned out of their homes, lost their stores, shops, offices, stocks of goods, implements, books, accounts, papers, vouchers, business, or situations, and it is difficult to find any citizen who has not suffered directly by that fearful conflagration. Of the total property in Chicago created by labor and capital, existing on the 8th of October, more than half perished on the 9th. The money value of the property thus suddenly annihilated, it is impossible accurately to ascertain, but it can hardly fall short of $150,000,000, a comparatively small part of which will be reimbursed by the insurance companies. Such a tremendous loss cannot befall the people at large without seriously affecting their municipal affairs. The city as a corporation has lost in property and income precisely in the same proportion as have individuals in the aggregate. The municipal government has no income except what it derives from the citizens of Chicago, in the form of taxes, licenses, and rents, or obtains on their credit; and to the extent that their property and business are diminished by the terrible misfortune that has smitten them, so is the revenue of the city diminished; and, as our citizens are retrenching expenses to meet the exigencies and keep within their means, so must the municipal government do likewise.

Financial Condition of the City.

Heavy as the blow has been that has struck us, I am not discouraged. Our municipal losses, like those of the citizens, will soon be repaired, and by judicious management of our city affairs, the people will the sooner recover from their losses, and thus be able, in a short time, to bear the burdens of taxation without oppression. I shall proceed to state, in brief form, the present fiscal condition of the city, as I gather it from official sources:

Bonded debt, December 1st, 1871, . . .	$14,103,000
From this may be deducted bonds held in the sinking fund, ...	557,000
Outstanding bonds, ...	$13,546,000

This debt is composed of the following items:

Funded debt—old issues, ...	$342,000
Funded debt—new issues, ...	2,192,500
School bonds, ...	1,119,500

School construction bonds, ...	$53,000
Sewerage bonds, ...	2,680,000
River improvement bonds, ...	2,896,000
Water bonds, ...	4,820,000

In addition to the bonded debt, it is officially reported to me that there is a floating debt consisting of:

Certificates of indebtedness, ...	$138,707
Unsettled claims for deepening the canal in excess of the $3,000,000 authorized by law, ...	253,000
Current expenses for November, about, .	250,000
Tunnel balance, and other items, . . .	45,000
Total, about, ...	$686,707

The Comptroller estimates the general expenses for the remainder of the fiscal year at $1,141,000.

There stands to the credit of various special funds the following unexpended balances:

Water fund, from sale of bonds, . . .	$897,262
School building, from sale of bonds, . .	148,152
Special assessment, collected, ...	435,467
Bridewell fund, ...	45,451
Reformed School fund, ...	30,000
Total, ...	$1,556,338
From these funds the City Government has temporarily drawn for payment of current expenses, to be replaced when needed, ...	1,144,186
Balance on hand December 1st, 1871,	$412,152

The Common Council, at a late meeting, appropriated $140,000 of the water fund for repairs of the water works and extensions of mains, which, when expended will reduce the water fund to $757,262.

By the former mode of doing business with the banks, nothing was paid by them to the city on its deposits, while high rates of interest were paid by the city for temporary accommodations—the money loaned actually being the city's own funds. The interest thus absurdly paid, amounted to a very large item in the annual expenditure of the city.

Municipal Losses by the Fire.

As near as I can ascertain, the loss of city property by the fire, as estimated by the different boards, is as follows:

In Care of Board of Public Works.

City Hall, including furniture, ...	$470,000
Bridges burned, ...	171,000
Damage to street pavements, ...	270,000
Damage to sidewalks and crossings, payable out of general fund, ...	70,000
Damage to water works, ...	35,000
Damages to lamp posts, ...	15,000
Damage to fire hydrants, reservoirs, sewers, water service, etc., ...	60,000
Total, ...	$1,085,000

To this must be added $121\frac{3}{4}$ miles of sidewalks destroyed (the replacement of which should be by special assessment) valued at $941,380.

The Fire Department Loss.

Buildings worth, ...	$60,000
Furniture,.	7,500
Damage to engines, ...	8,200
Damage to hose, ...	10,000
Damage to fire-alarm telegraph, ...	45,000
Total, ...	$130,700

Police Department Loss.

Buildings worth, ...	$53,600
Furniture, fixtures, etc., ...	32,500
Total, ...	$86,100

Board of Education Lost.

Buildings, furniture, etc., worth, ...	$251,000
Board of Health lost property worth, . .	15,000
Total losses, ...	$1,567,800
Add sidewalks, ...	941,380
Grand total, ...	$2,509,180

All these burnt structures, machines, bridges, sidewalks, fixtures, and furniture, must be rebuilt and replaced at the earliest practical moment, as they are indispensable to the city and citizens.

Other Municipal Losses by the Fire.

But the destruction of this property is not the only loss suffered by the corporation. The burning of records, vouchers, books, papers, tax warrants, assessment-rolls, etc., will necessarily occasion much loss, confusion and embarrassment to the city government. But it is believed that a large part of the apparent loss of official knowledge and data can be supplied from other scources. Still, the pecuniary loss to the city will be considerable in the destruction of the evidence of delinquent taxes and special assessments.

The Records.

This list of destroyed records and papers may convey an exaggerated idea of the actual damage done. The system of keeping the city accounts was such that but little loss will be sustained by the city by reason of the destruction of the Comptroller's records. To illustrate: The appropriation for the Board of Public Works is nearly one-third of the total annual appropriation, and, including special assessments, is more than half of all the money expended on city account. The board make out a voucher for an expenditure and send it to the Comptroller's office, keeping a duplicate in their own office. The board also keep books of account, showing the expenditures of appropriations for and vouchers issued by the board. The Board of Public Works saved their books, records, vouchers, etc., and to this extent the records of the Comptroller's office can be replaced. So that it will be impossible for claimants to defraud the city by false claims.

The appropriations for the Police and Fire Departments, amounting to about $900,000, are largely made up of the pay rolls of policemen and firemen, and they were paid on Saturday preceding the fire, except a few who were on special duty.

The usual course of business in the Comptroller's office, combined with the personal recollections of the Comptroller and his clerks, will enable that office to prevent double payments, or fraudulent payments, and the danger of such will be over with when the payments for the month of November are completed.

It is in the destruction of the records, rolls and warrants of the City Collector's office that I apprehend the city will suffer the greatest loss. The City Collector, when an assessment is made, or a tax levied, receives a warrant for its collection, gives the notices required by law, and reports once in each year, generally in March, to the court, the delinquents upon all real property and special assessment accounts which come into his hands, the latter prior to the 31st of October, and of the real property warrants prior to the preceding second Sunday of December.

Combustible Character of the City.

No more important questions can engage your attention than those of the future fire limits, and a reliable supply of water for the extinguishment of fires. The first is in the nature of prevention, and the second of cure; and I shall briefly discuss them in the order of their importance. On the 9th of October more than 20,000 habitations and business places were destroyed by fire in a single day. So enormous a loss of property in so incredible short space of time, finds no parallel in the history of conflagrations. It is not difficult to explain the cause of this sudden and tremendous destruction of property. There was no other city upon the face of the earth where all the conditions for such a disaster could be found in equal perfection. To begin with, the city of Chicago is situated on the lake border of a boundless prairie, swept continually by high winds. It contained 60,000 pine-built structures, and a few thousand of brick or stone. The prevailing winds of the autumn are invariably from the west and southwest. The solidly built parts of the city, and containing the most values, lay to the eastward of the combustible portions and were completely flanked and commanded by them. Each year the wooden parts of the city have filled up thicker and thicker with the most inflammable of all building materials, viz.: pine. For miles square there was little but pine structures, pine sidewalks, pine plan-

This Page is Blank

Materials were not available when scanned.

ing mills, manufactures of pine, and pine lumber yards.

A hot, parching, southwestern gale of many days duration had absorbed every particle of moisture from the vast aggregation of pine, of which the city was mainly constructed, and reduced it to the condition of tinder. A fire broke out in the night in the heart of this combustible material; the furious wind spread it quickly and swept it onward resistlessly. When the storm of fire reached the South Branch it had acquired such strength and volume as to leap over it as though it were a tiny rivulet. It fed on the dry pine tenements on its line of march, and spreading right and left, swept everything before it with the besom of destruction, until it died out for lack of more pine to devour.

What lesson should this cruel visitation teach us? Shall we regard it as one of fortuitous occurrence, which only happens at long intervals and is beyond human foresight or control? Such a conclusion constitutes our great future danger. A blind, unreasoning infatuation in favor of pine for outside walls, and pine covered with paper and tar for roofs, has possession of many of our people, It is thought to be cheaper than any other building material, when, in point of fact, it is the dearest stuff, all things considered, that can be used. It is short-lived; rots out in a few years; rapidly becomes shabby in appearance, and of all building substances is the most incendiary. There is no economy whatever in erecting tenements of pine. The difference in first cost between it and brick is not to exceed 15 or 20 per cent., and this saving at the outset is soon lost in higher rates of insurance; larger consumption of fuel; more doctors' bills; incessant repairs, and greater discomfort. The value of real property is reduced, and its advance retarded by the presence of unsightly, decaying, and combustible wooden structures, and the owners are unable to procure loans on such property on terms satisfactory, either as to time, amount, or rates of interest.

If we rebuild the city with this dangerous material, we have a moral certainty, at no distant day, of a recurrence of the late catastrophe. The chances of future destruction increase exactly in proportion to the multiplication of combustible structures on a given space. The sirocco blast from the southwest visits us every year. We have strong winds at nearly all times from the west. All the conditions for great fires are, therefore, constantly present in the dry season. With our present mode of supplying water, there is never an adequate quantity at the point of need to combat and properly overcome a great fire. But no supply is sufficient to quench a fire with twenty minutes' start, among thousands of tinder-box structures, and propelled by an autumn gale in time of drought.

What the Future Fire-limits should be.

Can there be any doubt as to our duty in view of these conditions and considerations? it seems to me it is obvious and imperative. Those who are intrusted with the management of public affairs should take such measures as shall render the recurrence of a like calamity morally impossible. The outside walls and roof of every building, to be hereafter erected within the limits of Chicago, should be composed of materials as incombustible as brick, stone, iron, concrete or slate. Self-preservation is the first law of nature. So the preservation of the city is the highest duty of its rulers. Except for the most temporary uses, I am unalterably opposed, from this time forward, to the erection of a single wooden building within the limits of Chicago.

The fire limits, in my opinion, should be made co-extensive with the boundaries of the city, and when the latter are extended, so should be the former. There is no line that can be drawn with safety within those limits.

Any inner fire line would occasion endless discontent, and will forever be assailed and broken. Draw it anywhere inside the city limits, and it will be continually forced inward, and shrink back toward its old and useless boundaries. No satisfactory or logical reason can ever be given to interested persons why those next to and within the line should be prohibited from erecting incendiary structures, while their neighbors on the opposite side of the street or alley are permitted to indulge in that dangerous luxury. Either let us forbid the construction of those buildings which tend to jeopardize the city, or allow all citizens an equal privilege toburn down their neighbors. This is a land of equal rights and privileges, and the rule in regard to incendiary structures should also be equal and uniform. I can see no other way of securing the safety of the city, and satisfying the citizens, than by treating all alike, and extending the fire limits to the city boundaries. Special privileges are odious in a republican country.

In view of all the circumstances, I recommend that your honorable body proceed to frame and perfect a fire ordinance that will give security and permanence to the future city. The existing wooden structures will gradually disappear by the ravages of fire and decay, and the desire to replace them with permanent edifices. In a few years we can have a city solid and safe, durable and beautiful. The enactment of a fire limits ordinance, comprehending the entire city, will add tens of millions to its credit abroad, and greatly appreciate the value of its realty at home. It is the wisest financial measure that can be enacted.

An Independent Supply of Water for Fires.

The future safety of the city demands a better and more reliable supply of water for the extinguishment of fires than is afforded by the existing system. This fact was painfully demonstrated in the late calamity. When the pumping works succumbed, not a gallon of water could be procured by the Fire Department or the citizens with which to fight the fire, and hundreds, perhaps thousands, of houses perished in consequence thereof. The city should not be left wholly dependent on those machines, because they are subject to many contingencies in addition to that which disabled them. Boilers may explode and ruin the engines, or cut off the supply of steam; some of the machinery may give way while the other engines are idle, awaiting repairs; valves may fail; a main may burst from overpressure, or other cause; fire may again invade the works, or something else may happen at the critical moment, which may again leave the Fire Department helpless and the city a prey to the unpitying element.

The topography of the city forbids an elevated reservoir of capacity and pressure sufficient for the extinguishment of serious fires, such as they have in Montreal, New York, Pittsburgh, and other cities. But a simple, cheap, and reliable substitute can be found in the construction of a system of subterranean reservoirs, one at every street crossing in the densely built portions of the city, and at greater distances apart in the more sparsely built parts. These reservoirs may be connected by earthen pipes such as are used for sewerage purposes, of adequate diameter, and supplied with water by artesian wells placed at proper distances apart. The water from all the wells in each division of the city would thus be connected and made to flow into any reservoir from which the fire engines might be drawing water. A dozen artesian wells in either division of the city would supply water faster than the whole department in action could consume it. The stock of water in the reservoirs themselves would be invaluable in great emergencies.

Only one engine can draw water from a fire hydrant, and the others usually have to go long distances to find hydrants, and their delivery power is greatly diminished by distance and friction of water in the hose, while the hose itself is burst and destroyed in great quantities at every severe combat with fire. But from each of the proposed reservoirs several engines could draw water, and thus, at short range, concentrate an irresistible discharge upon the fire and quickly master it.

Artesian water is so warm that it would never freeze in the pipes, however shallow they were laid, nor in the reservoirs, because the perpetual influx of the warm water would always keep the temperature above the freezing point. The outflow of this water to the North Division and in the northern part of the West Division could be conducted into the North Branch of the Chicago river, and materially aid in its purification, without expense to the city. In other portions of the town, surplus water could be run into the street sewers, thereby saving the expense of "flushing" them, as now practiced. In the season of street sprinkling, the watering wagons could obtain water from the artesian fountains, thereby leaving a larger supply for domestic purposes. There are various other uses to which the waste water might advantageously be put, not necessary here to enumerate.

The cost of the proposed supply of auxiliary water would be insignificant when compared with its value in preserving property and adding to the safety of the city. The *annual saving of insurance*, resulting from this independent water supply, would probably exceed the first cost of procuring it. Bounteous Nature has placed under our feet, within easy reach, this fountain of water, awaiting our bidding to pour forth. Have we the enterprise and sagacity to utilize it? But I refer the further consideration of this important subject to the wisdom of your honorable body. Perhaps some better plan to accomplish the end in view—the safety of the city from destruction by fire—will be suggested by yourselves and carried into effect. But we must be admonished by the bitter and terrible experience of the past never again to depend exclusively on our pumping works for a sure and adequate supply of water for the reduction of a great conflagration.

Conclusion.

In concluding I point with pride and admiration to the gigantic efforts our whole people are putting forth to rise from the ruins and rebuild Chicago. The money value of their losses can hardly be calculated. But who can compute the aggregate of anguish, distress and suffering they have endured and must yet endure? These wounds are still sore and agonizing, though they have been greatly alleviated by the prompt, generous, and world wide charities that have been poured out for their succor and relief; and I claim in their behalf that they are showing themselves worthy the benefactions received. They have faced their calamity with noble fortitude and unflinching courage. Repining or lamentation is unheard in our midst, but hope and cheerfulness are everywhere exhibited and expressed. All are inspired with an ambition to prove to the world that they are worthy of its sympathy, confidence and assistance and to show how bravely they can encounter disaster, how quickly repair losses and restore Chicago to her high rank among the great cities of the earth.

Happily there is that left which fire cannot consume;—habits of industry and self-reliance, personal integrity, business aptitude, mechanical skill, and unconquerable will. These created what the flames devoured, and these can speedily re-create more than was swept away. Under free institutions, good government, and the blessings of Providence, all losses will soon be repaired, all misery caused by the fire assuaged, and a prosperity greater than ever dreamed of will be achieved in a period so brief, that the rise will astonish mankind even more than the fall, of Chicago.

Minor Incidents.

A ludicrous scene was witnessed in the flight of an undertaker. Finding his household goods in jeopardy from the fire, and necessity being the mother of invention, the man of coffins got his hearse ready, assited his wife to the top of the vehicle, intrusted the reins to her hands, and then rushing back with his children and his workmen to his shop, literally armed themselves with coffins, and thus bearing forth their stock-in-trade, started out in melancholy grotesque and rapid march after the hearse, thus presenting a scene which for grim suggestiveness of humor has seldom been equalled, and never excelled.

A wholesale grocer, residing on the north side, was absent from the city. His wife, a delicate woman, finding the flames suddenly upon her house, snatched up a silver cake-basket and a valuable little clock, took one of her two children in her arms and another by the hand, and fled. As she sped before the pursuing fire, she found her strength failing, and begged the driver of a passing express wagon, lightly laden, to help her in her extremity. He would for the clock. She submitted to the exaction, was carried three blocks, and then forced to get down. The cake-basket bought her another ride of about the same distance, and then she was forced to finish her flight on foot, her means of satisfying the rapacity of drivers being exhausted. Finally, more dead than alive, she reached a place of safety.

On Chicago avenue, a father rushed up-stairs to carry three children away, when he was overtaken by the flames and perished with them. The mother was afterwards seen on the street, on the northwest side, a raving maniac.

Many proprietors of the large clothing establishments, seeing that by no possibility could they save their goods, which had been moved to Dearborn Park, invited the public to help themselves—scores of persons were thus provided with winter outfits gratis.

RELIEF.

Report of the Chicago Relief Society.

Since the first edition of this work appeared, the report of the Relief Society of Chicago has been issued, which contains an extremely interesting statement of the receipts and disbursal of funds. The first thirty-two pages of the report are devoted to a general sketch of the organization and operations of the society which are already familiar to the public.

Shelter.

Concerning the work of providing the first requisite—shelter—for the houseless thousands, the Executive Committee says in its report: The Bureau of the Shelter Committee is very thoroughly organized with an efficient corps of clerks and examiners, through whom the claim of the applicant goes for a careful and thorough examination, with all possible checks to detect imposition, while all are listened to with the utmost sympathy and patience.

The houses given are of two sizes: one of 20 × 16 feet for families of more than three persons; the other of 12 × 16 feet for families of three only. The floor joists are of 2 × 6 inches timber, covered with a flooring of planed and matched boards; the studding is of 2 × 4 inches, covered with inch boards and battened on the outside; the inside walls are lined with thick felt paper; and each house has a double iron chimney, two panelled doors, three windows, and a partition to be put up where the occupant pleases. The establishment is completed in a simple but sufficient way for comfortable living by the addition of a cooking stove and utensils, several chairs, a table, bedstead, bedding, and sufficient crockery for the use of the family; the total cost of the house when thus furnished, is $125. The majority of those who receive prepared material for these houses are mechanics enough to put them together for themselves, or have the means to hire builders; but for the large class of widows, infirm or otherwise helpless persons, the house is built and put in complete readiness for the proposed tenant by the committee. There were, on Saturday, November 18th, 5,497 of these houses put up or in process of erection, most of which are completed and occupied. The applications for them, at the same date, numbered 7,246; and it is calculated that the demand for them which it will be prudent for the society to to meet, with the means at their disposal, will be about eight thousand. This will provide, at the usual estimate of five to a family, and, as the houses chosen are almost entirely of the larger size, respectable and comfortable homes for from thirty to thirty-five thousand persons. Where the committee think that the circumstances justify it, the house and its furnishings are an outright gift. In the majority of applications this is the case. But where the committee have reason to know or to believe that the applicant has means that will become available, or that he will soon be able to command, he is requested to give an obligation to repay in one year, but without interest, three-fourths of the value advanced him. So far is this from being considered a hardship, that the applicant, in most cases, prefers to accept the obligation to return the money that it may again be used to aid others who may be in need; as it frees him from being the recipient of public bounty, and allows him to retain an honorable feeling of independence. He may refund the amount before the year expires, if it shall suit his convenience; but if it shall appear at the end of that time, upon a reinvestigation of the case, that he is evidently unable to refund it, he is simply considered by the committee as belonging to that class from which no return could be expected for bounty bestowed.

The actual rental of these houses may be estimated as worth $10 per month, based upon what the society is paying, in many instances, for similar accommodations to keep people from being turned out of doors. This rental for six months would amount to $60, and as the cost of the "shelter houses," exclusive of furniture, is nearly $100, they will have paid, by the 1st of May next, 60 per cent. of their cost. It must not be understood, however, that this is a rental charged, but only a rental estimated, and which is saved to the owners of the house in six months. In no case is any rent taken from the occupants of these houses.

The stock of lumber destroyed in Chicago by the fire was not less than sixty-five millions of feet, and the supply destroyed in the lumber regions, ready for shipment to this market, was also immense. The price of lumber, consequently, has rapidly enhanced, and since the 26th of October has been $20 per thousand. By the wise forethought and activity of the Shelter Committee this rise in value was anticipated, and all their purchases have been made at an average price of $16.50 per thousand. They have used, thus far, nearly twenty-seven millions of feet with this large saving in cost.

The Barracks.

Besides the isolated houses, there are in different sections of the city four barracks, in which are lodged one thousand families. They are mainly of the class who have not hitherto lived in houses of their own, but in rooms in tenement houses. Each family in these barracks has two separate rooms to itself, and they are furnished in precisely the same way with the isolated houses. Their occupants are undoubtedly very nearly, if not quite, as comfortable as they were before the fire, and as only one thousand two hundred and fifty people are gathered together in one community, and those are under the constant and careful supervision of Medical and Police Superintendents, their moral and sanitary condition is unquestionably better than that which has heretofore obtained in that class. There has been among them but a single death up to the 25th of November.

Distribution of Supplies.

The checks upon waste or fraud in the issue of supplies of food, etc., are thus detailed: The first step was to district the city under the direction of O. C. Gibbs, who for years had been Superintendent of the Relief and Aid Society, and it was accordingly divided into five large districts, made as nearly equal as possible with regard to population. These were subdivided, at first, into thirteen smaller sub-districts, but which are now, as rearranged from time to time, and as rations are given out at longer intervals, six only. The whole are under the General Superintendent; but to each district is given a Superintendent with supervision over his whole district, and to each sub-district a Sub-Superintendent with supervision over his immediate depot of supplies. Sufficient assistance is given to each Superintendent, averaging about ninety men and women to each district, the duties of a part of whom are to administer to the wants of applicants for food and clothing. Another part of this force is made up of a corps of visitors who are constantly busy in visiting all whose names are registered in the books at the offices of the relief stations, and in searching for sufferers who need aid but do not know where to find it. It is the business of the visitor to keep himself constantly informed as to all the persons who are thus entered in his district, and to make periodical returns at the office. He is to learn by observation and inquiry the exact condition of the registered; whether they are well or ill; whether they are idle or industrious; whether they are voluntarily idle, in which case they are peremptorily cut off from aid; whether they are entitled to entire or only partial support; whether they have other means of support than public bounty; and in short any circumstances in relation to their condition, or habits, or character which will be a guide as to the care which should be given them at the stations. There a ledger account is opened with each of them, in which appear the returns of the visitors, the supplies given, with their dates, and when they were cut off, if discontinued, and the reasons why.

The Superintendents are required to keep a strict account of all their requisitions of supplies, as well as of their distribution; and as they are accountable for a judicious and energetic discharge of their duties to the General Superintendent, so they hold their own subordinates strictly accountable for all their actions. Full and careful reports are made daily from each district, and the Superintendents meet one evening in the week with the Executive Committee to make or hear suggestions, to answer criticism or complaints, to report progress and suggest improvements, if possible, in the working ma-

This Page is Blank

Materials were not available when scanned.

chinery. The districts are frequently visited by a general inspector, to examine into their condition and management; and a Committee on Complaints is always ready at headquarters to listen to any complaints of neglect or improper treatment, and to provide for their immediate correction if found, on inquiry, to be well founded.

Number of Families Aided.

The total number of families receiving aid from the society on the 11th of November was 12,765; on the 18th, 14,137; on the 25th, 15,122; total number since full reports were had, 18,478. The number increased as the cold weather came on, notwithstanding many families, having been enabled to earn their livelihood, dropped off the rolls of the society.

Rations.

Food was given at first not only indiscriminately, but in uncertain quantities, for want of conveniences in measuring and weighing. As soon as possible, however, it was reduced to fixed rations, and as the system of distribution was perfected, these were given out at intervals of two or three days, and now of a week. The following ration for a family of five persons has been found to be sufficient for one week. At first bread was given instead of flour, as the people had few conveniences for cooking, at an increased cost of forty-two cents to the ration. This is now almost wholly saved, as most the applicants are supplied with stoves, and can bake their own bread. Coffee or tea is given, as the applicant prefers, but tea, which is the cheaper, is the more usually chosen. The cost of the ordinary weekly ration given for a family of five is $1.98, as shown by the following exhibit:

Exhibit of the Amount and Costs of one Week's Rations for Two Adults and Three Children.

Three pounds pork, at 5½ cents, ...	16½
Six pounds beef, at 5 cents, ...	30
Fourteen pounds flour, at 3 cents, ...	42
One and a quarter pecks potatoes, at 20 cents, .	25
One-quarter pound tea, at 80 cents, . . .	20
One and one-half pounds sugar, at 11 cents, .	16½
One and one-half pounds of rice, at 8 cents, or 3½ pounds beans at 3¾ cents, ...	12
One and one-quarter pounds soap, at 7 cents,	09
One and one-half pounds of dried apples, at 8 cents, ...	12
Three pounds fresh beef, at 5 cents, . . .	15
Total, ...	$1.98

If bread, at 4 cents per pound, is used instead of flour, the cost is increased. . .	42
If crackers, at 7 cents per pound, ...	1 05
If 1½ pounds coffee instead of tea, ...	17

To the cost of the weekly ration of food for a family of five should be added the allowance of one ton of coal a month, or a quarter of a ton a week.

Fortunately for such an exigency as this, the supply of bituminous coal for Chicago is ample, through the Wilmington Coal Company, which owns and works extensive coal mines in Will county, Illinois, with sufficient means of transportation at their command over the Alton, St. Louis and Chicago Road. With this company the committee has made a contract for the delivery of coal by the ton or half ton, at the door, for $4.50 per ton. This brings the weekly cost of coal for the family at $1.12½ which, added to the cost of the weekly ration, brings the cost of food and fuel at $3.10½. As the demand for fuel is as constant and next in importance to that of food, a large depot of coal from other sources is kept in reserve for emergencies, as in case of interruption to railroad transportation by snow storms, or other causes during the winter.

Clothing.

The demand for clothing has been, and continues to be, incessant and immense. The larger proportion of those who were sufferers by the fire lost all their personal apparel and their household goods. Immediate and urgent need was only very partially met by the bountiful supplies which were sent forward from all quarters. Much of this supply was of second-hand summer clothing, which was all that people could lay their hands on in the first emergency. It answered a good, though only temporary purpose, and the necessity of substituting for it better and warmer garments is constant and imperative. The markets of this country cannot supply the demand for blankets alone. Where the supply of ready-made clothing has been insufficient, piece goods are given out in measured quantity to applicants to make up for themselves. In this work great assistance is rendered by associations of ladies, as the Ladies' Relief and Aid Society, the Ladies' Industrial Aid Society of St. John's Church, the Ladies' Christian Union, Ladies' Society of Park Avenue Church, and Ladies' Society of The Home of the Friendless; all of whom employ a large number of sewing women, thrown out of employment by the fire, in making up garments, bed comforters, bedticks and other articles, from piece goods supplied by the Relief Committee, and returned, thus manufactured, to the several depots for distribution.

But a comparatively small portion of those in need of warm and sufficient clothing for the winter is as yet supplied, and the labor and expenditure to meet this want must be very large for some time to come. Of the actual quantity received by gift from abroad and distributed, it is impossible to make a detailed statement, as much of that received was given out in the first calamitous days of destitution to all comers and without count. The United States Government, through the active efforts of General Sheridan, has furnished us seven thousand blankets, and has also on the way for our use five thousand each of undershirts, drawers and socks. We are promised by President Grant, through the Hon. W. W. Belknap, Secretary of War, who has recently visited Chicago, such further supplies as we may need, so far as the government may have them in store. This branch of the work, however, is being reduced to a system, like the rest, and the following table is condensed from the reports of the several districts for the week ending November 25th, giving the number distributed of several articles of prime necessity. To it is added the number previously reported since an accurate record was kept:

Distribution of Articles for the Week ending November 25.

Articles.		Previously reported.	Total.
Mattresses, . . .	2,131	8,606	10,737
Blankets, . . .	4,615	20,724	25,339
Coal tons, . . .	1,522	2,131	4,653
Stoves, ...	644	3.795	4,459
Shoes, ...	22,531		22,539
Men's wear, . . .	8,846	415,883	54,723
Women's wear, . .	8,895	57,091	65,986
Children's wear, .	8,984	35,953	44,937

The above table does not include the stoves and mattresses given out by the Select Committee, who furnished both articles to the large proportion of their houses and the barracks. Neither does it include the furniture and crockery, both large items of expenditure, the aggregate of which is not yet reached.

Pay-Rolls for the Week ending November 18.

Districts.	Persons employed.	Amount.
No. 1, ...	142	$1,549 00
No. 2, ...	116	1,190 17
No. 3, ...	106	1,347 75
No. 4, ...	50	531 82
No. 5, ...	75	855 66
Special bureau, ...	9	118 50
Superintendents' salaries, . .		225 50
Warehousemen, receiving, storing, and delivering supplies,	111	1,259 87
Transportation, ...		2,148 87
Total for distribution, . .		$9,226 64
Employment bureau, ...	2	36 00
Clerks in offices of Treasurer, Auditor, Transportation Committee, Purchasing Committee, and Executive Committee, ...	32	496 34
Total general business, . .		$9,758 98

Charitable Institutions.

The Committee on Charitable Institutions, N. S. Bouton, Chairman, have extended aid to the following institutions: The Home for the Friendless, the Protestant Orphan Home, the St. Joseph Asylum for Orphans, the Old Ladies' Home, the House of the Good Shepherd, the Foundlings' House, the Half-Orphans' Home. To all of these institutions a monthly allowance in money is given, and those which have been burned out have been supplied, in addition, with food, clothing, bedding, and stores sufficient for their immediate necessities. Still further aid will be extended to them all, if it should be found requisite to carry them through the winter. There were other institutions of a similar character which were destroyed and their inmates dispersed. These have not yet provided themselves with permanent residences, and the committee do not feel justified, by the means at their disposal, to advance the large sums that would be required for their re-establishment. They can only undertake to supplement, in some measure, to those whose responsibilities are still existent, the resources of which they are deprived by the general disaster. The Sailors' Home only was made an exception to this rule. Though that institution lost its house by the fire, the inmates were kept together, and the Shelter Committee has offered to put up a temporary building for them, at a cost not to exceed $5,000.

Employment Bureau.

There has been no lack of employment, particularly of unskilled labor, since the fire, but as that could not be foreseen it was thought prudent to establish an employment bureau in connection with the general work. An employment committee, N. K. Fairbank, Chairman, was, therefore, appointed, with headquarters in a temporary building in the

Court House yard. This has been a sort of labor exchange in the very heart of the burnt district, where those wanting mechanics or laborers could find them, and where those in need of work were provided with it. The Superintendents at all the points of distribution are instructed to send every able-bodied man or boy who applies to them for aid to the bureau of the Employment Committee, and the ticket he takes becomes a certificate of character. If labor is found for him—as is almost invariably the case—he surrenders the ticket and it is returned to the Superintendent who issued it. If the ticket is not presented at the Employment Bureau, and not returned, therefore, to the Superintendent, it is presumptive evidence that the bearer prefers to eat the bread of idleness rather than work for his own subsistence, and if he again presents himself at the distributing station, his claim for relief is rejected. If, having obtained work—of which the returned ticket is evidence—he asks again for relief, the proper inquiry decides whether his labor is not sufficient to sustain himself and his family, if he has one, or whether he has asked for bounty of which he is not in need.

Most of the mechanics who apply at the Employment Bureau for work are in want of tools, without which they can do nothing at their trades. This want the committee has supplied, and by giving the applicant from ten to twenty dollar's worth of tools he is at once made self-supporting, and ceases to be dependent upon the Relief Society. A large number of carpenters have thus been effectively and permanently helped, as the demand for their labor is greater than for that of any other class. Brick layers, gas fitters, shoemakers and other mechanics have also been aided in the same way. The bureau has not undertaken to find employment for women, but has turned that class over to the organizations who have hitherto made its care their special business. Excepting seamstresses—who are received and cared for by the Bureau of Special Relief—women seeking employment have been left under the direction of such societies, and especially of the Ladies' Christian Union, which, in this part of the work, has been a valuable coadjutor of the Relief and Aid Society.

Nationalities of Beneficiaries.

The following table is an accurate return from the books kept at all the distributing stations:

Nationality.	No. families.	Nationality.	No. families.
American,	1,724	Russian,	2
English,	599	Jewish,	43
Scotch,	195	Hungarian,	4
Irish,	5,512	Bohemian,	208
German,	7,280	Welsh,	10
French,	185	Belgian,	23
Italian,	112	Holland,	5
Canadians,	94	Greek,	1
Swiss,	30	Scandinavian,	2,104
Danish,	14	African,	241
Spanish,	2		
Polish,	90	Total,	18,478

Future Expenses.

The committee makes the following estimate of expenditures for six months, from October 9th, 1871, to April 9th, 1872:

Food and fuel rations for 15,122 families of 5 persons each, at \$3.10½ per week,	\$46,953 81	\$1,220,790 06
Shelter Committee, 8,000 furnished houses, at \$125 each,	1,000,000 00	
Barracks and furniture for 2,000 families, at \$80 each,	160,000 00	
Hospital and store houses,	83,000 00	
		1,243,000 00
Stoves, in addition to those used in new houses and barracks,		75,000 00
Special Bureau,		250,000 00
Charitable institutions,		25,000 00
Deducting contributions of clothing and mattresses and furniture furnished by the Shelter Committee, already charged, it is estimated that 10,081 of the 15,122 families must be supplied with clothing, shoes, furniture, bed and bedding, at a cost of		866,966 00
Current expenses, at \$9,758.98 per week, 26 weeks,	253,733 48	
General expenses Shelter Committee,	42,000 00	
		295,733 48
		\$3,976,498 54
Total of contributions,		3,418,188 20
Deficit		\$558,310 34

How Certain Articles Were Got.

If, say the committee, the fund at our disposal were sufficient to buy all needed things, it is simply impossible to purchase in so short a time any considerable portion of the necessary articles that were to be found in the houses of a hundred thousand people. Take as an illustration the article of stoves. No stoves were saved from the fire. To replace them a medium sized soft coal cook stove was needed. No other would answer. To some extent wood stoves were sent, but we had no wood. Under the active direction of A. B. Meeker, the society has managed to buy, between the Atlantic and the Missouri river, eight thousand five hundred stoves of the kind demanded, and here and elsewhere have obtained pipe and furniture for them. But with the stoves purchased, our difficulties were by no means surmounted. We have been subjected to delays in railway transportation, and movement of goods about the city in common with our merchants, many of whom had merchandise lying three weeks within a few miles of Chicago, which could neither be received nor stored. Every possible facility and courtesy has been extended to this society by railway and express companies connected with Chicago, and also by the Western Union Telegraph Company, and the Atlantic Cable Company in transmitting free our answers to despatches and orders for goods. Yet with all these advantages, we have been able to actually deliver, up to November 25th, but six thousand six hundred stoves. There is precisely the same difficulty in the delivery of mattresses, blankets, and many articles furnished by the society which have been drawn from Buffalo, Detroit, Montreal, St. Louis, Indianapolis, Louisville, Cincinnati, and other points. With this delay in the arrival of goods, the best we could do was to give applicants orders to be filled in turn, informing them at the same time of the situation. Some of these orders, we regret to say, were many times presented at our depot without being filled; but this was not the result of any defect in our system, but simply because a supply of the article was not to be had. Nor was there any delay in contracting for these things. Within three days from the time the society assumed the work of relief, large engagements were made both in the United States and Canada for supplies which it was plain would be needed. We refer to these facts in order that applicants as well as the public at large may form some idea, if possible, of the difficulties surrounding the transaction of all business in Chicago during the last few weeks. Yet we may be allowed to call attention to the fact that we have just passed through two weeks of unusually severe winter weather, accompanied by snow, but that the needy are provided for and the sick and infirm attended to.

Treasurer's Report of Donations.

George M. Pullman, Treasurer, submits the following report to date, embracing the receipts and expenditures of the society passing through his books since the 14th of October, when the duty of Treasurer devolved upon him. The donations for convenience of reference are placed under the proper States and cities contributing them.

New York.

New York City,	$237,314 79
Astoria,	2,000 00
Syracuse,	27,350 00
Oneida,	100 00
Baldinsville,	100 00
Rome,	2,061 50
Cohoes,	2,500 00
Coxsakie,	35 00
Watton,	35 00
Buffalo,	2,540 00
Seneca Falls,	2,656 75
Long Island City,	225 00
Utica,	911 00
Troy,	10,880 40
Brooklyn, L. I.,	9,059 01
Jamaica,	638 00
Canandagua,	3,965 00
Oswego,	8,796 61
Kingston,	3,635 25
Port Jervis,	839 55
Havana,	50 00
Poughkeepsie,	5,010 00
Greene,	69 00

New Rochelle, ...	$1 00
Jamestown, ...	1,350 00
Albany, ...	21,616 65
New Hamburgh, ...	10 00
Catskill, ...	1,370 90
Clifton Park, ...	8 00
Morrisania, ...	999 68
Watkins, ...	1,000 00
Rural Grove, ...	34 50
Palmyra, ...	378 60
Stanley Corners, ...	152 00
Elmira, ...	8,700 00
Saugertus, ...	2,000 00
Cazenovia, ...	400 00
Kinderhook, ...	350 90
Newburg, ...	5,012 50
Nyack, ...	140 00
Pike Road, ...	727 00
Clyde, ...	931 00
Sauquoit, ...	30 00
Ogdensburgh, ...	869 00
Carmansville, ...	24 62
Unadilla, ...	25
Clifton Springs, ...	618 65
West Troy, ...	1,000 00
Saratoga Spring, ...	1,800 00
Wellsville, ...	50 00
Williamsburgh, L. I., ...	626 75
Hudson, ...	6,000 50
Rochester, ...	670 50
Niagara Falls, ...	1,800 00
Brockport, ...	51 00
Norwich, ...	200 00
Ithica, ...	5 00
Pawling, ...	2 00
Williamson, ...	1 00
Elyria, ...	50 00

Fort Edward, ...	$50 00
Amsterdam, ...	859 00
Binghampton, ...	5,291 00
Livonia, ...	10 00
Watertown, ...	30 75
Weisseic, Duchess county, ...	50 00
Hamilton, ...	6 00
Deerfield, Oneida county, ...	153 00
Hastings, ...	57 07
Hoosic Falls, ...	53 28
Lansingburg, ...	1,262 34
Waverly, ...	5 00
Port Morris, ...	200 00
Sag Harbor, ...	50 00
Sandy Hill, ...	100 00
West Point, ...	203 50
Glenn's Falls, ...	1,000 00
Sing Sing, ...	1,500 00
Rondout, ...	2,000 00
Port Byron, ...	250 00
Gloversville, ...	1,675 00
Suspension Bridge, ...	450 00
Wappingore Falls, ...	611 46
Geneva, ...	1,124 45
Vatervleit, ...	10 00
Peterboro, ...	500 00
White Plains, ...	129 50
Lima, ...	155 60
Amenia, ...	100 00
Peekskill, ...	259 25
Caragoharie, ...	2 00
Champlain, ...	155 00
Lockport, ...	3,000 00
Waterford, ...	125 00
Total, N. Y., ...	$401,556 96

Massachusetts.

Boston,	$133,557 26
Fitchburg,	1,000 00
Salem,	15,950 00
Chelsea,	1 00
Holyoke,	2,767 00
Newburyport,	2,163 00
Pittsfield,	5,500 00
Lowell,	9,233 77
Clinton,	30 00
Fall River,	20,242 68
New Bedford,	4,100 00
Middlebro,	2 00
Florence,	718 00
Haverhill,	10,000 00
Chicopee,	630 79
Greenfield,	1,000 25
Charleston,	12,276 16
Lawrence,	13,300 00
Housatonic,	373 50
Springfield,	14,861 00
Dalton,	350 00
Leicester,	1,388 00
Westbro,	1,110 00
Hadley,	46 27
Taunton,	123 25
Marlbro,	21 00
Jamaica Plains,	15 00
Baldwinsville,	27 87
East Longmeadow,	20 00
Ware,	5 00
Andover,	5,443 10
Lynn,	10,117 70
Waltham,	4,176 00
North Chelmsford,	160 00

This
Page
is
Blank

Materials were not available when scanned.

This Page is Blank

Materials were not available when scanned.

Rockport, ...	$15 00
East Hampton, ...	320 00
Beverly, ...	3,000 00
Fairhaven, ...	488 00
Westfield, ...	3,074 33
Lexington, ...	478 05
Worcester, ...	10,000 00
Cambridge, ...	8,000 00
Marblehead, ...	1,000 00
Peru, ...	27 10
Peabody, ...	25 00
Northampton, ...	205 00
Athol Depot, ...	173 04
Total, ...	$297,305 12

Pennsylvania.

Philadelphia, ...	$104,788 00
" Drexel & Co., Treas., in bank,	157,690 86
Titusville, ...	11,573 50
Washington, ...	1,306 85
St. Mary's, ...	223 85
Pittsburgh, ...	51,100 00
Tidioute, ...	1,172 75
Towanda, ...	50 00
Birmingham, ...	107 00
Kittaning, ...	1,372 00
Easton, ...	2,121 57
Wilkesbarre, ...	900 22
Chambersburg, ...	600 00
Thorndale, ...	66 25
Minersville, ...	27 00
Reading, ...	106 07
Comly, ...	1 00
York, ...	1,900 00
Pottsville, ...	1,055 00

Glenden,	$350 00
Allentown,	3,000 00
Bristol,	50 00
Mifflinburg,	40 62
Johnstown,	46 00
Leighton,	13 75
Mauch Chunk,	341 26
Mountjoy,	171 85
Cornwall,	1,250 00
Lykens,	202 00
Susquehanna shops,	626 20
West Fairview,	14 00
Canonsburgh,	16 00
Warrington,	72 85
New Brighton,	70 00
Euphrata,	3 00
Palo Alto,	154 00
Burnsville,	1,000 00
Meadville,	2,000 00
Phillipsburgh,	209 25
Parnassus,	127 00
Millersville,	170 00
Statington,	50 00
Shamburgh,	343 00
Erie,	15,000 00
Scranton,	4,598 00
Harrisburgh,	4,400 00
Harris Township,	385 01
Bellefonte,	1,000 00
Baldinsville,	229 75
Marietta,	5 00
Oil City,	20 00
Sharon,	639 24
Sharpsburg,	400 00
Susquehanna depots,	621 70
Montrose,	20 00
McKeesport,	797 75

Lancaster, ...	$50 00
Pine Grove Centre, ...	78 00
Mount Holly Springs, ...	28 25
Westchester, ...	500 00
Chester, ...	3,000 00
Morristown, ...	742 68
Catasauqua,.	415 60
Huntington, ...	500 00
Total, ...	$228,363 37

New Jersey.

Jersey City, ...	$37,010 62
Madison, ...	401 00
Newark, ...	42,936 25
Elizabethtown, ...	132 00
Trenton, ...	18,550 00
Rahway, ...	238 00
New Brunswick, ...	5,099 00
Paterson, ...	8,650 00
Elizabeth, ...	857 75
Nawayanda, ...	10 00
Belvidere, ...	111 00
Franklin Furnace, ...	5 00
Freehold, ...	34 00
Lambertsville, ...	1,103 22
Red Bank, ...	372 00
Hammontown, ...	350 00
Crawford, ...	275 00
Bayonne, ...	1,000 00
Sommerville, ...	500 00
Morristown, ...	3,000 00
Highstown, ...	100 00
Samptown, ...	25 50
Pemberton, ...	123 77
Tricksburgh, ...	16 50

Ocean Grove,	$5 00
Long Branch,	107 00
West Hoboken,	204 34
Burlington,	2,333 00
Branchville,	64 50
Bloomfield,	779 60
Tom's River,	100 00
Salem,	285 27
Total,	$124,464 32

Connecticut.

New Haven,	$5,135 00
Wallingford,	55 00
Hartford,	29,392 00
Bridgeport,	10,252 00
Fairhaven,	121 56
Seymour,	57 00
Westminster,	12 50
Portland,	500 00
New London,	2,100 00
West Haven,	137 00
Stamford,	2,050 00
Stratford,	239 00
Norwich,	10,000 00
West Cornwall,	60 00
South Woodstock,	31 00
New Britain,	4,659 73
Willimantic,	5 00
Windham,	33 55
Windsor Locks,	560 00
Liberty Hall,	21 00
Stonington,	10 00
Deep River,	100 00
Putnam,	161 00
Hampton,	70 84

Naugatuck,	$25 00
Middletown,	100 00
South Norwalk,	100 00
Total,	$65,968 68

Ohio.

Toledo,	$4,000 00
Kelley's Island,	130 00
Bellaire,	106 25
Miamisburg,	19 00
Lancaster,	5 00
Larue,	40 00
Chagrin Falls,	255 92
Belmont County,	39 00
Morristown,	29 05
Leesburg,	118 25
Bucyrus,	180 00
Delaware,	650 00
Niles,	500 00
Clarksville,	17 00
Canton,	203 35
Cleveland,	4,568 75
Circleville,	2 00
Columbus,	10,000 00
Harrison County,	610 00
Chillicothe,	3,000 00
St. Clairsville,	5 00
Oxford,	27 20
Wooster,	1,000 00
Steubenville,	2,769 74
Middletown,	40 00
Mount Union,	31 75
Gallipolis,	1,250 00
Bellevue,	1,100 00
Norwalk,	1,000 00

Ironton,	$2,874 75
Tiffin,	2,325 00
Oberon,	559 25
Cardington,	217 00
Marion,	246 25
Barnesville,	500 00
Zanesville,	3,202 50
Eaton,	317 25
Ripley,	159 25
Marietta,	500 00
Ravenna,	20
Crestline,	50 00
Elyria,	51 25
Versailles,	100 00
Akron,	1,838 25
Youngstown,	5,000 00
Hanging Rock,	1,098 50
Jefferson,	16 00
Homer,	1 00
Portsmouth,	30 00
Wauseon,	100 00
Total,	$50,714 71

California.

Sacramento,	$21,117 50
Petaluma,	46 90
Oakland,	11,215 00
Cadwell,	64 00
Mokelumne,	17 63
Benicia,	22 72
San Francisco,	110,718 26
Stockton,	1,111 75
San José,	2,500 00
Salinas,	151 40

Haywood,	$35 00
Chico,	556 25
Nevada County,	720 19
Total,	$148,281 60

Missouri.

Tipton,	$25 09
St. Louis,	723 35
Kirksville,	36 35
Moberly,	213 00
St. James,	30 00
Palmyra,	154 00
Harrisonville,	112 75
Hannibal,	1,000 00
Clinton,	916 25
Cameron,	20 00
Liberty,	193 20
Springfield,	440 00
Kansas City,	13,110 00
Total,	$16,174 70

Iowa.

Muscatine,	$1,501 00
Keokuk,	702 25
Oskaloosa,	374 80
Ledar,	113 00
Buckingham,	117 85
Charlton,	265 00
Manchester,	500 00
Stuart,	32 00
Nora Springs,	72 00
Wilson,	10 00

Mount Vernon,	$149 50
Winterset,	40 00
Blairstown,	11 00
Lyons,	170 00
Victor,	26 00
Fredericksburg,	5 00
Bonaparte,	58 25
Fort Madison,	17 00
Burlington,	180 70
Toledo,	11 45
New Sharon,	59 70
Casey,	11 00
Sioux City,	2 00
Onowa,	116 50
Illyria,	10 25
Tipton,	40 00
Total,	$4,596 25

Illinois.

Chicago,	$4,075 00
Batavia,	61 00
Pittsfield,	20 75
Mt. Carroll,	300 00
Florence Station,	5 00
Good Hope,	23 50
Mason City,	261 00
Springfield,	2,220 55
Mound City,	314 25
Danville,	1,753 00
Durant,	114 35
Grand Tower,	79 50
Nashville,	250 00
Minier,	71 10
Loundale,	61 75
Toulon,	100 00

Whitehall, ...	$557 00
Knoxville, ...	831 65
Virden, ...	911 05
Peoria, ...	4,750 00
Irvington, ...	70 50
Utah, Warren Co., ...	5 00
Farmington, ...	523 80
Kankakee, ...	373 32
Hillsboro, ...	10 00
Mendon, ...	47 50
Decatur, ...	71 00
Shawneetown, ...	1,000 00
Olney, ...	505 65
Bloomington, ...	13,820 77
Jacksonville, ...	4,690 00
Litchfield, ...	271 35
Petersburg, ...	584 00
Lena, ...	300 00
Sheffield, ...	25 50
Momene, ...	45 00
Bunker Hill, ...	10 00
Ashley, ...	33 25
Albany, ...	10 00
Lebanon, ...	300 00
Buser, ...	7 50
Delavan, ...	181 00
Warsaw, ...	44 75
Charleston, ...	30 00
Cairo, ...	659 50
Savanna, ...	104 77
Marshall, ...	20 00
Joilet, ...	319 00
Mound City, ...	319 25
Galena, ...	1 00
Freeport, ...	168 00
Enfield, ...	39 50
Greenfield, ...	200 00

Pekin, ...	$193 03
Edwardsville, ...	775 00
Morgan County, ...	377 20
Port Byron, ...	40 10
Canton, ...	268 63
Mt. Vernon, ...	225 00
Carrollton, ...	1,018 25
Mattoon, ...	87 41
Franklin Grove, ...	5 00
Carlyle, ...	500 00
Sparta, ...	381 40
Peru, ...	391 18
Dwight, ...	159 40
Total, ...	$45,950 96

Indiana.

Connersville, ...	$89 25
Peru, ...	10 00
South Bend, ...	8 84
Goshen, ...	250 00
Rolling Prairie, ...	30 00
Logansport, ...	178 15
Attica, ...	60 00
Kokomo, ...	94 15
Ligonier, ...	30 00
Derby, ...	12 00
North Vernon, ...	94 25
Green Castle, ...	600 00
Terre Haute, ...	5,730 55
Jeffersonville, ...	3,190 65
Crawfordsville, ...	500 00
Vevay, ...	10 00
Tipton, ...	5 00
Indianapolis, ...	10,000 00

York Township,	$21 00
Washington,	360 00
Danville,	285 00
Shelbyville,	1,000 00
Covington,	235 00
Williamsport,	75 00
Evansville,	2,000 00
Brookville,	10 00
Harmony,	72 00
Total,	$24,750 84

New Hampshire.

Rindge,	$2 00
New Ipswick,	110 50
New London,	122 15
South Newmarket,	84 00
North Conway,	28 00
South Newbury,	9 50
Portsmouth,	5,796 00
Keene,	100 00
Manchester,	15,000 10
Epping,	50 00
Hampstead,	189 75
Concord,	150 00
Warner,	106 00
Dover,	86 00
Total,	$21,834 75

New Mexico.

Santa Fe,	$424 00
Albuquerque,	65 00
Fort Union,	311 00

Los Vegas, ...	$400 00
Moreno Mines, ...	555 00
Grand Army of the Republic, . . .	40 00
Total.	$1,495 00

Rhode Island.

Providence, ...	$40,101 63
Middletown, ...	30 00
Newport, ...	3,205 00
Portsmouth, ...	30 00
Bristol, ...	424 79
Carolina Mills, ...	122 50
Pawtucket, ...	143 91
Warner, ...	571 87
Woonsocket, ...	550 00
Total, ...	$45,179 70

Kentucky.

Cynthiana, ...	$136 50
Paris, ...	500 00
Glasgow, ...	82 00
Paducah, ...	868 19
Maysville, ...	1,003 50
Owensboro, ...	400, 00
Lexington, ...	1,000 00
Caseyville, ...	110 40
Uniontown, ...	9 05
Louisville, ...	1,044 20
Mount Sterling, ...	55 15
Total, ...	$5,108 90

Virginia.

Charlemagne,	$2 50
Leesburg,	35 81
Richmond,	848 41
Danville,	5 00
Petersburg,	37 19
Hampton,	10 50
Norfolk,	231 00
Alexandria,	50 00
Warm Spring,	15 00
Total,	$11,238 41

Colorado.

Denver,	$3,713 73
Greeley,	294 50
Golden City,	341 00
Central City,	2,100 00
Georgetown,	1,203 80
Total,	$12,653 03

Vermont.

Bennington,	$160 00
Middlebury,	410 00
Burlington,	3,000 00
Proctorsville,	2 00
Bethel,	20
Woodstock,	120 00
Total,	$3,692 20

Maine.

Portland, ...	$10,300 00
Eastport, ...	50 00
Auburn, ...	5 00
Biddeford, ...	1,000 00
Rumford, ...	1 00
Bucksport, ...	155 00
Winthrop, ...	15 26
Castine, ...	50 00
York, ...	40 00
Total, ...	$11,616 26

Kansas.

Topeka, ...	$5,400 00
Leavenworth, ...	10,185 90
Oswego, ...	34 00
Paola, ...	5 00
White Cloud, ...	100 00
Lawrence, ...	5,000 00
Wyandotte,.	437 50
Fairtown, ...	5 10
Hopkinston, ...	90 35
Total, ...	$21,257 00

Minnesota.

St. Paul, ...	$20,516 00
Winona, ...	3,000 00
Stillwater, ...	500 00
Leroy, ...	7 00
Chatfield, ...	80 00
Cannon Falls, ...	5 40
Total, ...	$24,108 40

Georgia.

Cartersville,	$25 50
Atlanta,	25 00
Sparta,	25
Augusta,	1,000 00
Savannah,	1,005 00
Cockspur Island,	5 00
Americus,	6 00
Total,	$2,065 75

Tennessee.

Springfield,	$100 00
Winchester,	1 25
Memphis,	20,521 05
Flintville,	7 00
Chattanooga,	321 55
Knoxville,	263 25
Nashville,	2,441 10
Total,	$23,655 20

Maryland.

Baltimore,	$176,625 24
Lonawing,	170 00
Cumberland,	1,612 85
Annapolis,	538 28
Hagerstown,	81 47
Mount Savage,	300 00
Total,	$179,327 84

Michigan.

Detroit, ...	$16 00
Cassopolis, ...	173 00
Quincy, ...	141 25
Chelsea, ...	264 00
Hudson, ...	38 00
Paw Paw, ...	100 00
Total, ...	$632 25

Nebraska.

Omaha, ...	$12,000 00
Plattsmouth, ...	569 00
Fremont, ...	25 00
Lincoln, ...	100 00
Total, ...	$12,689 00

South Carolina.

Charleston, ...	$821 50
Orangeburg, ...	50 00
Columbia, ...	70 00
Beaufort, ...	60 00
Total, ...	$1,001 50

North Carolina.

Wilmington, ...	$100 00
Newburn, ...	54 00
Charlotte, ...	10 00
Total, ...	$164 00

This Page is Blank

Materials were not available when scanned.

Wisconsin.

Viroqua, ...	$300 00
Arena, ...	1 00
Kenosha, ...	55 00
Total, ...	$356 00

Mississippi.

Vicksburg, ...	$28 50
Yazoo City, ...	20 00
Total, ...	$48 50

West Virginia.

Wheeling, ...	$12,508 10
Parkersburg, ...	3,018 30
Total, ...	$15,526 04

Nevada.

Virginia City, ...	$1,308 83
Mountain City, ...	197 80
Total, ...	$1,506 63

Washington Territory.

Vancouver, ...	$500 00
Olympia, ...	100 00
Total, ...	$600 00

29

Delaware.

Wilmington, ...	$7,945 70
Middletown, ...	125 00
Total, ...	$8,070 70

Louisiana.

New Orleans, ...	$11,604 80

Arkansas.

Little Rock, ...	$2,536 55

Florida.

Pensacola, ...	$1,049 23

Alabama.

Selma, ...	$5 00

Oregon.

Portland, ...	$10,000 00

District of Columbia.

Washington, ...	$34,065 65

FOREIGN.

Canada.

Keswick, ...	$1,000 00
Simcoe, ...	5 00
Barrie, ...	25 00
Guelph, ...	67 17
Toronto, ...	10,698 65
Collingwood, ...	555 00
Aurora, ...	41 00
Stayner, ...	74 30
St. Armand, ...	48 65
Montreal, ...	60,000 00
Sherbrooke, ...	1,803 89
Hamilton, ...	2,000 00
Madoc, ...	500 00
Kingston, ...	2,145 88
Goderich, ...	500 00
St. Catharines, ...	2,000 00
Belleville, ...	500 00
Clifton, ...	468 73
Lynedoch, ...	100 00
Quebec, ...	112 30
Halifax, ...	50 00
Total, ...	$82,695 57

England.

London, ...	$312,764 02
Cheshire, ...	500 00
Newcastle on Tyne, ...	5,444 10
Bradford, ...	31,582 38
Birmingham, ...	8,320 20
Total, ...	$358,410 72

Germany.

Berlin,	$25,020 00
Burmen and Elberfeld,	4,821 70
Dresden,	1,315 00
Sonneburg,	1,200 00
Mannheim,	4,000 00
Total,	$30,356 70

Ireland.

Dublin,	$8,126 10
Limerick,	1,620 55
Belfast,	27,201 53
Total,	$36,948 18

Scotland.

Glasgow,	$26,000 00
Aberdeen,	5,000 00
Total,	$31,000 00

Cuba.

Havana,	$10,000 00

Austria.

Vienna,	$12,500 00

France.

Paris,	$42,200 00

Holland.

Rotterdam,	$112 00

Italy.

Genoa,	$271 38

Miscellaneous.

From various sources,	$327 20

Recapitulation.

New York,	$401,556 96
Massachusetts,	297,305 12
Pennsylvania,	228,363 37
California,	148,281 60
Maryland,	179,327 84
New Jersey,	124,464 32
Connecticut,	65,968 68
Ohio,	50,714 71
Rhode Island,	45,179 70
Illinois,	45,950 96
Maine,	11,616 26
Louisiana,	11,604 80
Virginia,	11,238 41
Oregon,	10,000 00
Delaware,	8,070 70
Kentucky,	5,108 90
Iowa,	4,596 25
Arkansas,	2,536 55
Georgia,	2,065 75
Vermont,	3,692 29
Nevada,	1,505 83
District Columbia,	34,065 65
Indiana,	24,750 84
Minnesota,	24,108 40
Tennessee,	23,655 20
New Hampshire,	21,834 85
Kansas,	21,257 85

Missouri, ...	$16,974 70
West Virginia, ...	15,526 40
Nebraska, ...	12,689 00
Colorado, ...	12,653 03
New Mexico, ...	1,495 50
Florida, ...	1,049 23
South Carolina, ...	1,001 90
Michigan, ...	632 25
Washington Territory, ...	600 00
Wisconsin, ...	356 00
North Carolina, ...	105 00
Mississippi, ...	48 50
Alabama, ...	5 00
Total, ...	$1,875,062 80

Foreign.

England, ...	$358,410 72
Canada, ...	82,695 57
France, ...	42,200 00
Ireland, ...	36,948 18
Germany, ...	36,356 70
Scotland, ...	31,000 00
Austria, ...	12,500 00
Cuba, ...	10,000 00
Italy, ...	271 38
Holland, ...	112 00
Miscellaneous, ...	327 20
Total, ...	$610,821 75
United States, ...	1,875,062 80
Grand total, ...	$2,485,884 55

Ledger Statement.

The following is the ledger. statement to November 18th, inclusive:

Donation fund, ...		$2,485,884 55
Cash on hand, ...	$189,864 93	
Pay rolls, ...	34,009 20	
Insurance, ...	697 50	
Expense, ...	809 22	
Office furniture, ...	1,503 31	
Postage, ...	261 15	
Transportation (city teaming), ...	2,927 34	
Freight, ...	800 91	
Stationery, printing and advertising, ...	2,557 22	
Supplies—of clothing, food, stoves, bedding, etc., etc., .	130,870 71	
Shelter—Lumber and building materials, ...	311,162 46	
Hospital expenses, ...	1,984 80	
Rents—of supply depots and offices, ...	2,174 83	
Buildings, ...	85 64	
Cash advances, ...	3,033 00	
Employment Committee, ...	5 80	
Bureau of special relief, ...	2,555 27	
Passenger fares, ...	22 00	
Deposits in banks, ...	1,800,559 26	
Total, ...		$2,485,884 55

Bank Balances.

Chicago—	
Third National Bank,	$103,087 25
Union National Bank,	103,060 24
Northwestern National Bank,	33,017 15
First National Bank,	87,667 92
Merchants' National Bank,	58,340 97
Mechanics' National Bank,	33,100 00
German National Bank,	33,257 74
Second National Bank,	19,394 33
Fifth National Bank,	46,752 31
Manufacturers' National Bank,	6,285 12
Total,	$523,963 03
New York—	
National City Bank,	$275,109 78
Bank of Commerce,	209,000 00
Drexel, Morgan & Co.,	493,982 22
Total,	$969,092 00
Boston—	
Kidder, Peabody & Co.,	$128,461 84
Second National Bank,	82,239 30
Total,	$210,701 14
Montreal—	
Bank of Montreal,	$68,803 09
Providence, R. I.,	28,000 00
Total,	$1,800,559 26

All the above bank balances are drawing 5 per cent. interest.

THE BURNING OF CHICAGO:

A POEM.

BY WILL M. CARLETON.

[*The following Poem, from " Our Fireside Journal," of Chicago, Ill., is transferred to our pages by permission of the Publishers of that Journal.*]

THE BURNING OF CHICAGO.

By Will M. Carleton.

I.

'Twas night in the beautiful city,
The famous and wonderful city,
The proud and magnificent city,
The Queen of the North and the West.
The riches of nations were gathered in wondrous and plentiful store;
The swift speeding bearers of commerce were waiting on river and shore;
The great staring walls towered skyward, with visage undaunted and bold,
And said, "We are ready, O Winter! come on with your hunger and cold!
Sweep down with your storms from the Northward! come out from your ice-guarded lair!
Our larders have food for a nation! our wardrobes have clothing to spare!
For off from the corn-bladed prairies, and out from the valleys and hills,
The farmer has swept us his harvest, the miller has emptied his mills;
And here, in the lap of our city, the treasures of Autumn shall rest,
In golden crowned, glorious Chicago, the Queen of the North and the West!"

II.

'Twas night in the church-guarded city,
The templed and altar-decked city,
The sacred and spire-dawned city,
The Queen of the North and the West.
And out from the beautiful temples that Wealth in its fulness had made,
And out from the haunts that were humble, where Poverty peacefully prayed,
Where praises and thanks had been offered to Him where they rightly belonged,
In peacefulness quietly homeward the worshipping multitude thronged.
The Pharisee, laden with riches, and jewelry costly and rare,
Who proudly deigned thanks to Jehovah he was not as other men are;
The penitent, crushed in his weakness, and laden with pain and with sin;
The outcast, who yearningly waited to hear the glad bidding, "Come in;"
And thus went they quietly homeward, with sins and omissions confessed,
In spire-adorned templed Chicago, the Queen of the North and the West.

III.

'Twas night in the sin-burdened city,
The turbulent, vice-laden city,
The sin-compassed, rogue-haunted city,
Though Queen of the North and the West
And low in their caves of pollution great beasts of humanity growled,
And over his money-strewn table the gambler bent fiercely, and scowled;
And men with no seeming of manhood, with countenance flaming and fell,
Drank deep from the fire-laden fountains that spring from the rivers of hell;
And men with no seeming of manhood, who dreaded the coming of day,
Prowled, cat-like, for blood-purchased plunder from men who were better than they;
And men with no seeming of manhood, whose dearest-craved glory was shame,
Whose joys were the sorrows of others, whose harvests were acres of flame,
Slunk, whispering and low, in their corners, with bowie and pistol tight-pressed,
In rogue-haunted, sin-cursed Chicago, though Queen of the North and the West.

IV.

'Twas night in the elegant city,
The rich and voluptuous city,
The beauty-thronged, mansion-decked city,
Gay Queen of the North and the West.
And childhood was placidly resting in slumber untroubled and deep;
And softly the mother was fondling her innocent baby to sleep;
And maidens were dreaming of pleasures and triumphs the future should show,
And scanning the brightness and glory of joys they were never to know;
And firesides were cheerful and happy, and Comfort smiled sweetly around;
But grim Desolation and Ruin looked into the window and frowned.
And pitying angels looked downward, and gazed on their loved ones below,
And longed to reach forth a deliverance, and yearned to beat backward the foe;
But Pleasure and Comfort were reigning, nor danger was spoken or guessed,
In beautiful, golden Chicago, gay Queen of the North and the West.

V.

Then up in the streets of the city,
The careless and negligent city,
The soon-to-be sacrificed city,
Doomed Queen of the North and the West,
Crept, softly, and slyly, so tiny it hardly was worthy the name,
Crept, slowly and soft through the rubbish, a radiant serpent of flame,
The South-wind and West-wind came shrieking, "Rouse up in your strength and your ire!
For many a year they have chained you, and crushed you, O demon of fire!
For many a year they have bound you, and made you their servant and slave!
Now, rouse you, and dig for this city a fiery and desolate grave!
Freight heavy with grief and with wailing her world-scattered pride and renown!
Charge staight on her mansions of splendor, and battle her battlements down!
And we, the strong South-wind and West-wind with thrice-doubled fury possessed,
Will sweep with you over this city, this Queen of the North and the West!"

VI.

Then straight at the great quiet city,
The strong and o'er-confident city,
The well-nigh-invincible city,
Doomed Queen of the North and the West,
The Fire-devil rallied his legions, and speeded them forth on the wind,
With tinder and treasures before him, with ruins and tempests behind.
The tenement crushed 'neath his footstep, the mansion oped wide at his knock;
And walls that had frowned him defiance, they trembled and fell with a shock;
And down on the hot, smoking house-tops, came raining a deluge of fire;
And serpents of flame writhed and clambered, and twisted on steeple and spire;
And beautiful, glorious Chicago, the city of riches and fame,
Was swept by a storm of destruction, was flooded by billows of flame.
The Fire-king loomed high in his glory, with crimson and flame-streaming crest,
And grinned his fierce scorn on Chicago, doomed Queen of the North and the West.

VII.

Then swiftly the quick-breathing city,
The fearful and panic-struck city,
The startled and fire-deluged city,
Rushed back from the South and the West.
And loudly the fire-bells were clanging, and ringing their funeral notes;
And loudly wild accents of terror came pealing from thousands of throats;
And loud was the wagon's deep rumbling, and loud the wheel's clatter and creak,
And loud was the calling for succor from those who were sightless and weak;
And loud were the hoofs of the horses, and loud was the tramping of feet,
And loud was the gale's ceaseless howling through fire-lighted alley and street;
But louder, yet louder, the crashing of roofs and of walls as they fell;
And louder, yet louder, the roaring that told of the coming of hell.
The Fire-king threw back his black mantle from off his great blood-dappled breast,
And sneered in the face of Chicago, the Queen of the North and the West.

VIII.

And there, in the terrible city,
The panic-struck, terror-crazed city,
The flying and flame-pursued city,
The torch of the North and the West,
A beautiful maiden lay moaning, as many a day she had lain,
In fetters of wearisome weakness, and throbbings of pitiful pain.
The amorous Fire-king came to her—he breathed his hot breath on her cheek,
She fled from his touch, but he caught her, and held her, all pulseless and weak ;
The Fire-king he caught her and held her, in warm and unyielding embrace ;
He wrapped her about in his vestments, he pressed his hot lips to her face ;
Then, sated and palled with his triumph, he scornfully flung her away,
And blackened and crushed in the ruins, unknown and uncoffined she lay,
Lay, blackened and crushed by the Fire-king in ruined and desolate rest,
Like ravished and ruined Chicago, the Queen of the North and the West.

IX.

And there, in the desolate city,
The treasure-strewn, fire-beaten city,
The savage and desperate city,
The torch of the North and the West.
A ruffian crept stealthily prowling, with mean and unholy desire,
And bore, in dark alleys and corners, his torch of destruction and fire.
The multitude caught him and held him—they gazed in his villanous eyes—
They dragged him about on the pavement—they stifled his cowardly cries.
And one rose and said, "When our city comes thus to the torch of a knave,
Each man is a judge and a jury—each gutter a criminal's grave!
The best line of action to follow for yonder unprincipled scamp,
Is simply a line of stout cordage—one end on the post of a lamp!"
And high in the hot air they hung him—unpitied, unwept, and unblest,
For laying foul hands on Chicago—the Queen of the North and the West.

X.

'Twas morn in the desolate city,
The ragged and ruin-heaped city,
The homeless and hot-smoking city,
The grief of the North and the West.
But down from the West came the bidding, "O Queen, lift in courage thy head!
Thy friends and thy neighbors awaken, and hasten, with raiment and bread!"
And up from the South came the bidding, "Cheer up, fairest Queen of the Lakes!
For comfort and aid shall be coming from out our savannahs and brakes!"
And down from the North came the bidding, "O City, be hopeful of cheer!
We've somewhat to spare for thy sufferers, for all of our suffering here!"
And up from the East came the bidding, "O City, be dauntless and bold!
Look hither for food and for raiment—look hither for credit and gold!"
And all through the world went the bidding, "Bring hither your choicest and best,
For weary and hungry Chicago—sad Queen of the North and the West!"

BAKER & Co ENG
BEALE Del.

XI.

O crushed, but invincible city!
O broken, but fast-rising city!
O glorious, but unconquered city,
Still Queen of the North and the West!
The long, golden years of the future, with treasures increasing and rare,
Shall glisten upon thy rich garments—shall twine in the folds of thy hair!
From out the black heaps of thy ruins new columns of beauty shall rise,
And glittering domes shall fling grandly our nation's proud flag to the skies!
From off the wide prairies of splendor the treasures of Autumn shall pour,
The breezes shall sweep from the Northward, and hurry the ships to thy shore!
For Heaven will look downward in mercy on those who've passed under the rod,
And happ'ly again they will prosper, and bask in the blessings of God.
Once more thou shalt stand mid the cities, by prosperous breezes caressed,
O, grand and unconquered Chicago, still Queen of the North and the West!

www.ingramcontent.com/pod-product-compliance
Lightning Source LLC
LaVergne TN
LVHW021305110826
845150LV00003B/486

* 9 7 8 1 4 2 5 5 5 9 3 7 3 *